Health Psychology

Karen Rodham

PALGRAVE INSIGHTS IN **PSYCHOLOGY**

SERIES EDITORS:
NIGEL HOLT & ROB LEWIS

palgrave
macmillan

First published 2010 by
PALGRAVE MACMILLAN

Palgrave Macmillan in the UK is an imprint of Macmillan Publishers Limited, registered in England, company number 785998, of Houndmills, Basingstoke, Hampshire RG21 6XS.

Palgrave Macmillan in the US is a division of St Martin's Press LLC, 175 Fifth Avenue, New York, NY 10010.

Palgrave Macmillan is the global academic imprint of the above companies and has companies and representatives throughout the world.

Palgrave® and Macmillan® are registered trademarks in the United States, the United Kingdom, Europe and other countries.

ISBN: 978–0–230–24945–5

This book is printed on paper suitable for recycling and made from fully managed and sustained forest sources. Logging, pulping and manufacturing processes are expected to conform to the environmental regulations of the country of origin.

A catalogue record for this book is available from the British Library.

A catalog record for this book is available from the Library of Congress.

10 9 8 7 6 5 4 3 2 1
19 18 17 16 15 14 13 12 11 10

Printed and bound in Great Britain by
CPI Antony Rowe, Chippenham and Eastbourne

For David John Gadd, my lovely Dad

Contents

List of figures

Note from series editors

Health psychology has its origins in a number of different areas including sociology, medicine and the politics of policy-making. Karen Rodham draws all these areas into a single book with style.

Karen was chosen to write this book in the series because of the special demands that this title makes. We needed a writer who would be able to produce a book that would be relevant to a wide range of readers. She has not disappointed. Karen is blessed with a personality that is easy-going while remaining focused and this comes through in her book. She has managed to maintain a levity and energy throughout and we found her book extremely informative as well as surprising in places (watch out for the Zombies).

- *If you are reading this book as a preparation for university study* you will find material you will be studying here. Karen works, researches and publishes in health psychology and is well placed to translate the material into a form you'll find useful. Existing books can feel dry and disjointed but Karen has managed to produce a coherent and satisfying read.
- *If reading this book while at university* you are probably on one of the many courses that touch upon health psychology, and are in training within nursing, psychology, sociology, midwifery, or medicine to name but a few degree routes. Karen is aware of how her subject finds a home on many courses and has had this in mind when writing the book.
- *If you are reading the book as part of a pre-university course such as an A-level* you may well have found some of the material in this book

in your A-level textbook. This book includes the material you need and more and we hope it whets your appetite for further study. The Reading Guide at the end of the book tells you where different A-level specifications appear.

The range of areas in which health psychology finds a home are numerous and can include nursing, medicine, midwifery, social policy and social work as well as psychology and other related disciplines. Karen has managed to pull together material from a range of sources that will make the book an indispensable addition to many bookshelves. Whether reading the book as support for other books you read on your course, or whether reading this as the main text, we are confident that it will be useful and informative. We are very pleased to add it to our series.

NIGEL HOLT AND ROB LEWIS
Series Editors

Preface

This book is not a comprehensive description of the whole of health psychology but is an overview of some of the key issues within the discipline. In writing this book I have attempted to take on the role of 'tour guide'. What I mean by this is that usually when you take a 'package' holiday, on arrival there is a welcome meeting. At this event, it is the task of the chirpy holiday representative to give an overview of the different excursions available to you in the hope that they will whet your appetite enough for you to want to visit these places. My role is rather similar, in that I have a short amount of space in which to provide you with information so that you gain insight into the profession and discipline of health psychology. I hope that in sharing my enthusiasm for this discipline you will be tempted to delve deeper and read more about each of the topics highlighted.

Health psychology is concerned with the study of psychological processes in health, illness and healthcare (Kaptein and Weinman, 2004). Health psychologists study the behavioural factors that are associated with staying healthy, as well as exploring how people who are ill can be helped to adapt to, or recover from, their illness. The focus of the health psychologist is very much in the realm of physical disorders, for example chronic illness, cancer, pain, stress, smoking cessation and weight loss.

Many people confuse health psychology with clinical psychology, and it is perhaps useful to briefly highlight the differences between the two disciplines. Whilst clinical psychologists focus on mental health problems, for example phobias, anxiety disorders and depression, the focus of health psychology is on physical disorders. Specifically, health psychologists apply psychological research and methods to four key areas: the prevention and management of illness; the identification of psychological factors contributing to physical illness; the promotion and maintenance of health; and the improvement of the healthcare system and the formulation of health policy.

The prevention and management of illness

The prevention and management of illness focuses on those who have been identified as being potentially at risk of disease and aims to detect symptoms at a stage early enough that the development of illness can be eliminated or slowed down through the implementation of psychological interventions.

The identification of psychological and behavioural factors contributing to physical illness

Health psychologists regard the relationship between psychology and health as direct and indirect. In other words, it is recognized that the way in which a person might experience their life can have a direct impact on their body, which in turn can have an effect on their health. Thus, feeling stressed can impact directly on the body's physiological processes. In contrast, an indirect relationship is represented by the way in which a person's behaviour can be influenced by the way they think; it is engaging in this behaviour, for example drinking/eating too much, which then impacts on their health. Health psychologists have researched many different illnesses and in so doing have identified the psychological factors that might contribute to the development or maintenance of illness. For example, coronary heart disease has been related to behaviours such as smoking, food intake and lack of exercise, whilst some cancers are linked to diet, smoking, alcohol and failure to attend for screening or check-ups (Ogden, 2007: 5).

The promotion and maintenance of health

The promotion and maintenance of health is directed towards healthy individuals in order to raise awareness of the ways in which health can be protected and maintained. This focus is usually on understanding and changing health behaviours.

The improvement of the healthcare system and the formulation of health policy

Health psychologists are also concerned with understanding the impact of the healthcare system and health policy on our behaviour. Although research in this area is not so abundant as in the other three, it is nevertheless an important aspect of the role of health psychologists. As such, the UK Division of Health Psychology of the British Psychological Society coordinates a database of expert health psychologists who are able to respond to government initiatives to ensure that the profession's concerns are addressed and included in new health-related policies.

Overview

Throughout the book, you will find that key terms have been emboldened to indicate that you will find them in the Glossary at the back of the book, which gives definitions of some of the more technical terms I have used.

This book is intended to provide you with an insight into health psychology. It is structured into three sections. The first section, Health Behaviour, contains three chapters. Chapter 1 considers what it means to be healthy and presents an overview of what health behaviours are and how they can be measured. Chapter 2 explores the variety of factors which are thought to influence our health behaviours, and Chapter 3 describes the different models that have been developed and explains how these might be used to predict behaviour change.

The second section, Health Promotion, consists of two chapters. Health promotion is one of the means by which health psychologists attempt to encourage behaviour change. Chapter 4 focuses on defining health promotion and explaining the different approaches that have been taken when implementing health promotion interventions. Chapter 5 explores the ways in which health promotion interventions are planned and evaluated. In particular, the factors which can influence the success (or otherwise) of interventions are discussed, along with a description of how we can know whether or not a health promotion intervention has had the desired effect.

The third and final section, Examples of Health Issues, consists of four chapters which cover two major topics in health psychology: stress and eating behaviour. Chapter 6 explains what stress is and outlines the physiological systems through which stress is thought to operate. We also explore how stress can be measured and what its impact on us might be. Chapter 7 examines how we might best cope when we are stressed. A variety of coping styles and strategies are covered and the different variables that influence the relationship between stress and our response to it are explored. Chapter 8 considers eating behaviour. What we eat and how we eat plays an important role in our long-term health and in addition to a focus on dieting, this chapter explores biological, evolutionary and psychological explanations for eating behaviour. Lastly, Chapter 9 explores specific eating disorders, including anorexia nervosa, bulimia nervosa and the problem of obesity.

Lots of people have helped me to produce this book. Having already thanked them in person, I would like to take this opportunity to formally thank them in writing – you know who you are. Thank you.

Karen Rodham
December 2009

Every effort has been made to trace copyright holders and obtain permission to reproduce figures and tables. Any omissions brought to the attention of the publishers will be remedied in future editions.

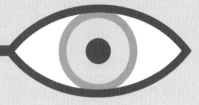

Section One

Health
Behaviour

Chapter 1

What is health behaviour?

👁 Introduction

Health behaviours are usually thought of as being actions we engage in with the intention of maintaining, attaining or regaining good health. However, they can also refer to actions we take in order to prevent illness. Health behaviours are extremely important because it is through encouraging them that we can enhance our opportunity to experience good health.

In this chapter, we will examine:
- What it means to be healthy
- What health behaviour is
- How we can measure health behaviour

👁 What does it mean to be healthy?

In order to answer the question 'What does it mean to be healthy', it is necessary to first consider how 'health' is defined. The concept of health is extremely broad and embodies many different meanings. As noted by Naidoo and Wills (2003), there are commonsense views of health which are otherwise known as 'lay' or non-professional concepts of health. These are often 'passed down through generations as part of a common cultural heritage' (Naidoo and Wills, 2003: 6). Popular definitions of health were identified by Blaxter (1995) and include the following:

- *Health as not ill* – a person considers themselves to be healthy if they are not experiencing physical symptoms and rarely visit the doctor
- *Health, despite disease* – a person considers themselves to be healthy if they feel well, in spite of being diagnosed with a disease
- *Health as physical fitness* – a person considers themselves to be healthy if they are physically fit
- *Health as psychosocial wellbeing* – a person considers themselves to be healthy if they feel they are able to 'live life to the full' or if they 'feel happy'
- *Health as function* – a person considers themselves to be healthy if they are able to do the things they normally engage in.

The way in which people explain and understand health can have important ramifications for their subsequent behaviour. Thus, a person who perceives health as being the absence of symptoms may be more likely to seek health advice if they begin to experience symptoms, whereas an individual who perceives health in terms of function may not seek health advice until their symptoms begin to impact upon their ability to engage in their usual activities.

Furthermore, the way in which we interpret health will be influenced by our cultural heritage. For example, Greenhalgh and colleagues (1998) explored the experience of diabetes in British Bangladeshis. In their paper, they note that 'successful treatment of diabetes requires that we understand the lifestyle, beliefs, attitudes, and family and social networks of the patients being treated'. They reported that a commonly cited cause of diabetes among the 18 participants was 'absence of sweating due to the cold British climate', along with a belief that the diabetes would resolve if they were to return to a hot country. Greenhalgh and colleagues (1998) highlight the importance for health professionals to be aware of lay explanations for health (and illness) and suggest that treatment and education should be tailored to incorporate and build on the beliefs held. This is because health advice may be ignored if it runs counter to lay beliefs.

In terms of professional explanations of health, the definition which is most often used is that from the World Health Organization (1946):

> Health is a state of complete physical, mental and social well-being and not merely the absence of disease or infirmity.

Curtis (2000) suggests that such a definition takes both a positive view of health, suggesting that health is concerned with the presence of a positive quality, 'well-being', as well as a negative view, suggesting that health is also defined by the 'absence of disease and infirmity'. Other authors take this a step further and view health in more holistic terms. As such, Aggleton and Homans (1987) and Ewles and Simnet (1995) suggest that the state of health involves a number of different dimensions, each of which needs to be considered. In addition to physical, mental, emotional, social, spiritual and sexual health, holistic definitions also include societal influences which are concerned with the way in which society is structured as well as environmental influences.

Summary

There are many definitions of health that are utilized by lay and professional people alike. It is clear therefore that, when working as a psychologist in the field of health, it is of paramount importance to find out what view of health is held by the people you are working with. Clarifying how you as a professional understand and define health, as well as being aware of what the people you are working with understand health to mean, is an essential first step towards ensuring clear communication. Having described the difficulties of defining 'health', we turn to 'health behaviour'. The topic of health behaviour is similarly characterized by numerous professional and lay definitions.

What is health behaviour?

When we think of health behaviour, we often associate it with negative actions, such as drinking heavily, smoking, (ab)using drugs, eating poorly and so on. However, health behaviours can also be actions we engage in with the intention of maintaining, attaining or regaining good health as well as actions we take in order to prevent illness. Positive actions therefore include not just the reverse of negative actions, for example giving up smoking or drug use, reduction of alcohol intake, improving diet and engaging in regular exercise, but also implementing preventive behaviours such as accepting health screening invitations or simply engaging in protective behaviours such as teeth cleaning and hand washing.

Health behaviour is therefore an action taken which has an impact (positive or negative) on a person's health. Much of the focus of health psychology concerns health behaviour or, more specifically, finding ways to encourage the adoption of positive health behaviours. As noted by Mark Forshaw (2002: 1), health psychologists try to find out

> why people behave in the ways that they do which endanger their health. They work on finding ways in which information can be provided to promote health so that people understand it, remember it, and act on it.

A first step in this process is to find a way of measuring health behaviours, because once we have a method of quantifying health behaviours, we are in a position to assess the impact our interventions have had on the behaviour concerned.

How can we measure health behaviour?

Traditionally in Western societies, the dominant view of health has been represented by the **medical model**. This model assumes that health is a function of biology and is not something which is influenced by the culture, thoughts and beliefs of a person (Forshaw, 2002). However, in the same way that definitions of health have become more encompassing, this traditional model has been rejected in favour of a more holistic model known as the **biopsychosocial model**. This model accepts that people are biological organisms and that therefore their biology can influence a proportion of behaviour. However, the model also takes into account the potential impact that thoughts, feelings, culture and environment can have upon a person's behaviour. The biopsychosocial model is therefore used as a framework which emphasizes the need to 'understand the person in the context of their life' (Forshaw, 2002: 5). This model is discussed in more detail in the next chapter. Whether the more traditional medical model or the more holistic model is adhered to, the way in which we measure health behaviour relies upon the discipline of epidemiology.

Epidemiology

Epidemiology is the study of the distribution and determinants of health and illness in populations (Rugulies et al., 2004). Epidemiological studies enable the observation of the magnitude and distribution of particular illnesses in populations. Epidemiology also provides evidence for the potential causes of health and illness. Early studies were concerned with the causes of communicable diseases and this work remains essential because it can lead to the identification of preventive methods. More recently, epidemiology has been used to study the influence of behaviour, lifestyle and preventive intervention through health promotion. It is also used as a means to describe the health status of different population groups. This knowledge is essential for health authorities that try to use limited resources in the most efficient manner by identifying priority health programmes for prevention and care. Epidemiologists have also been involved in evaluating the effectiveness and efficiency of health services, for example by working out the appropriate length of stay in hospital for specific conditions. In short, the epidemiological perspective is a key component in identifying health needs, examining the pattern of disease problems within and between populations, searching for the causes of disease, formulating health promotion and disease prevention strategies, studying the natural history of disease and planning and evaluating health services.

Very early epidemiological research was focused on identifying factors associated with infectious disease. For example, Sir Percivall Pott (1714–88) was a doctor who made several important contributions to medicine in the 18th century, which included work on wounds and bone injuries as well as tuberculosis of the spine. He was one of the first physicians to find a correlation between a particular cancer and an occupational or environmental cause. In what represents one of the earliest epidemiological studies, Pott observed that chimney sweeps in England had higher rates of scrotal cancer than the rest of the population. In doing their jobs, the chimney sweeps often had to climb naked into chimneys and suffered prolonged exposure to soot containing what are known today as 'carcinogens'. By proposing that chimney sweeps bathe more frequently, Pott implemented a preventive tactic even before the advent of public health practice and preventive medicine. As a result of increased bathing and improved hygiene, the observed rate of scrotal cancers in this particular group of workers declined dramatically (Kipling and Waldron, 1975).

However, it was John Snow (1813–58) who became known as the 'father of epidemiology'. He was able to demonstrate that cholera was transmitted by impure water, with his now famous investigations involving the London cholera epidemic of 1854. In 19th-century London, water distribution was done by private companies, one of which was the Southwark and Vauxhall Company. Snow worked out that cholera mortality rates were 5–10 times higher in households served by this water company compared with households served by other companies. Further work showed that the Southwark and Vauxhall Company took its water from waters polluted with infected human waste, which he concluded were the ultimate source of the cholera. Snow took a very methodical approach to studying the outbreak of cholera. He engaged in 'disease mapping', whereby he marked the deaths, house by house on a street plan, and noticed a pattern emerging. It was through this process of mapping that he was able to narrow down the source of the outbreak to the water pump on Broad Street. However, he also went further and explored 'mysteries that on the face of it seemed to undermine his theory' (Hempel, 2006: 216). For example, he noticed that the workhouse was located in the middle of the 'danger zone', yet only 5 of the 535 people who lived there died. Similarly, the Lion Brewery was located close to the pump, yet none of the workers died. Snow discovered that the workhouse and brewery workers used a different pump for their water and that, in addition, the brewery workers were paid in part with alcohol, which they drank largely instead of water and, in so doing, avoided infection. This amazing account is detailed in an excellent book by Hempel (2006), which draws inspiration for its title from the idea that epidemiologists work to solve the mystery of who gets sick and why – *The Medical Detective*.

Summary

In short, the epidemiological perspective is a key component in identifying health needs, examining the pattern of disease problems within and between populations, searching for the causes of disease, formulating health promotion and disease prevention strategies, studying the natural history of disease and planning and evaluating health services. Health promoters use epidemiological evidence to identify health problems, at-risk groups and the effectiveness of interventions. The next section focuses on briefly outlining the ways in which epidemiological studies can be implemented.

How are epidemiological studies implemented?

Epidemiological studies can be classified as either observational or experimental. This section briefly outlines the most commonly used methods of study.

Observational studies

Observational studies essentially allow nature to take its course. The investigator measures, but does not intervene. Typically, there are three types of observational epidemiological study: the descriptive, the case-control and the cohort study.

Observational: descriptive

A simple description of the health status of a community, based on routinely available data, is often the first step in an epidemiological investigation. In many countries this type of study is undertaken by a national centre for health statistics. **Descriptive studies** make no attempt to analyse the links between exposure to the illness under study and the impact of exposure, they simply record the **mortality** (death) or **morbidity** (illness) **rates**. Although such studies can provide us with a picture of the health (or perhaps more accurately, the illness) status of a population, they do not give the whole picture, and, in particular, cannot provide an understanding of the illness experience. For example, Naidoo and Wills (2003: 53) highlight that conditions such as 'arthritis or schizophrenia cause considerable suffering and pain, but do not lead to premature death, and so are not reflected in mortality rates'. Thus, the figures require interpretation, a process whereby the social context can perhaps be taken into account as a means of explaining the figures obtained.

Observational: case control

Case-control studies are relatively simple and economical to carry out and are increasingly used to explore the causes of diseases, especially rare diseases. They include people with a disease (or other outcome variable) of interest and a suitable control group of people who are not affected by the disease or outcome variable. The occurrence of the possible cause is then compared between cases and controls. Researchers look back in time for associated events to try to explain the occurrence of the disease/event of interest. Data is collected from more than one point in time – this means that case-control studies are also longitudinal. They are sometimes called 'retrospective', because the investigator is looking backwards from the onset of the disease to search for a possible cause. A classic example of a case-control study was the discovery of a link between the drug thalidomide and unusual limb defects in babies born in the Federal Republic of Germany in 1959 and 1960. The study, which was conducted in 1961, compared affected children with non-affected children (Mellin and Katzenstein, 1962). Of 46 mothers whose babies had typical malformations, 41 had taken thalidomide between the fourth and ninth weeks of pregnancy, whereas none of the 300 control mothers, whose children did not have limb defects, had taken the drug at these stages.

Observational: cohort

Cohort studies, also called 'follow-up' or 'incidence studies', begin with a well-defined group of people (a cohort) who are free of disease, who are classified in subgroups according to exposure to a potential cause of disease or outcome. Thus, variables of interest are specified and meas-ured from the start of the study and the whole cohort is followed up to see how the subsequent development of any new cases of the disease differs between the groups with and without exposure. Cohort studies are thought to provide the best information about the causation of disease and the most direct measurement of the risk of developing disease. Although simple, they are major undertakings and may need long periods of follow-up because disease may happen a long time after exposure. One example is that of the catastrophic poisoning of residents around a pesti-cide factory in Bhopal, India in 1984, where a chemical leak killed more than 3,800 people and poisoned 200,000 others. The acute (more imme-diate and short-term) effects were easily studied with a **cross-sectional design**, but the more subtle chronic (longer term) effects and effects developing only after a long latency period are still being studied using cohort designs (e.g. Cullinan et al., 1997; Sharma, 2005; Sriramachari, 2004, 2005).

Experimental studies

Experimental studies take place when a researcher wishes to manipu-late a condition in order to identify whether changing that condition has an impact on a particular outcome of interest. By way of example, researchers might be interested in comparing a new treatment with a **placebo** as a way of working out how effective the new treatment is. The 'gold standard' experimental study is the randomized controlled trial.

Randomized controlled trial

A **randomized controlled trial** is an epidemiological experiment to study a new preventive or therapeutic programme. Subjects in a popul-ation are randomly allocated to groups, usually called **intervention/**

treatment and **control groups** and the results are assessed by comparing the outcome in the two or more groups.

For example, Sniehotta (2009) explored the impact of three different types of communication style on participants' knowledge of local sports and recreation facilities and subsequent engagement in physical activity. He randomly assigned participants to treatment (those receiving a physical activity message in a specific communication style) and control (those not receiving a physical activity message) groups. Although he showed that, overall, small changes in cognitions (level of knowledge) did not lead to behaviour change, he did find that one specific type of communication style (that which focused on influencing participants' feelings that they had some control over whether or not they performed the behaviour – **perceived behavioural control**) did have a small significant effect, which resulted in increased attendance at the local sports and recreational facilities. Sniehotta (2009) concluded that current interventions aiming to increase participation in physical activity are excellent at increasing intention to engage in this behaviour, but that more research is needed to explore how people translate their intentions into action.

Summary

Epidemiological research tends to take either an observational or an experimental approach. Health psychologists use epidemiological data to help plan health promotion campaigns, interventions and health education messages. A light-hearted article which delivers a serious message about the application of epidemiological data was written by Munz and colleagues (2009). Rather than focusing on a current epidemic (such as swine flu), the authors chose to focus on the rather less likely, but perhaps more memorable potential epidemic of 'zombie attack'. In their paper, published in *Infectious Diseases Modelling Research Progress*, they explore different scenarios for dealing with the potential rapid spread of zombie infection and conclude that 'a zombie outbreak is likely to lead to the collapse of civilisation, unless it is dealt with quickly' (Munz et al., 2009: 146). Their article highlights the processes through which epidemics are modelled as a means of identifying the potential impact of different treatments or cures. Should we ever find ourselves in the horrifying position of facing such an epidemic, health psychologists would do well to refer to this article when planning related health interventions.

◉ Conclusion

This chapter has explored what we mean when we use the terms 'health' and 'health behaviour'. The ways in which health behaviours are measured have been outlined and the importance of the field of epidemiology emphasized. Epidemiology is concerned with the incidence and determinants of illnesses. Epidemiologists provide useful information about possible causes of illnesses, which psychologists can then draw from and incorporate into health promotion and health educational messages aimed at preventing ill health and maintaining good health. In the next chapter, we explore in more depth the way in which our health has been shown by epidemiological work to be affected by a variety of personal, social, cultural and environmental factors.

◉ Further reading

Greenhalgh, T., Helman, C. and Chowdury, A.M. (1998). Health beliefs and folk models of diabetes in British Bangladeshis: A qualitative study. *British Medical Journal*, 316, 978–83.
Hempel, S. (2006) *The Medical Detective: John Snow, Cholera and the Mystery of the Broad Street Pump.* London: Granta.

◉ Key search terms

Epidemiology, health behaviour, health, incidence

Chapter 2

Influences on health behaviour

👁 Introduction

In the previous chapter, we explored what it means to be healthy and identified how 'health behaviour' has been defined. We also established that the more traditional medical model has been replaced by the biopsychosocial model; a model which recognizes that many factors influence health and our health behaviours. Indeed, as Forshaw (2002: 2) noted:

> People are influenced by their upbringing, by their peers, by their financial status, by whims, by ambition, by culture, by society, by law, by random events which occur, by plans they have which may or may not be foiled, and sometimes, seemingly, by nothing at all. When a psychologist undertakes to discover why someone does something, they take on the world in all its complexity.

In this chapter, we explore the complexity described by Forshaw in the above quote, and look more closely at what the biopsychosocial model is before we identify the different factors which are believed to influence health-related behaviours.

In this chapter, we will:
- Describe the biopsychosocial model
- Identify the factors which are thought to influence health behaviours

◉ What is the biopsychosocial model?

The biopsychosocial model puts forward the idea that biological, psychological and social factors interact. This process of interaction is what determines the onset, progression and recovery from illness. The biopsychosocial model was first developed by Engel (1980) and challenged the dualist notion underpinning the medical model. The dualist philosophy considers that the mind cannot influence physical systems and vice versa, and therefore suggests that psychological processes are completely independent from any illness or disease process (Albery and Munafo, 2008). The more holistic emphasis of the biopsychosocial model acknowledges that 'people are biological organisms, and that their biology can determine a lot of their behaviours, but also recognizes that thoughts and feelings can have a significant influence on what people do' (Forshaw, 2002: 5). Ghaemi (2009: 3) suggests that 'no single illness, patient or condition can be reduced to any one aspect' and claims that the three influences – biological, psychological and social – are all 'more or less equally relevant, in all cases at all times'.

Miro and colleagues (2009) explored the impact of biopsychosocial factors on chronic pain by surveying almost 300 people who had a form of muscular dystrophy. Muscular dystrophy is a genetic (inherited) condition where slow, progressive muscle wasting leads to increasing weakness and disability. They concluded that their findings provided support for the use of a biopsychosocial model for understanding chronic pain in this patient group. They also suggested that all the different elements of the biopsychosocial model contributed to the experience of chronic pain. In particular, they highlighted the importance of identifying psychosocial factors that might play a significant role in helping patients adjust and respond to pain. Similarly, Jull and Sterling (2009) advocate that future research addresses biological (physical), psychological and social features concurrently in order to be in a position to understand how these features interact.

Summary

The biopsychosocial model is a useful framework which can be used to understand health behaviours by taking into account the person concerned within the context of their life, *as well as* acknowledging the potential influence of biology. The rest of this chapter focuses on identifying and exploring some of the myriad factors which have been shown to influence our health behaviour.

What are the factors which influence health behaviour?

As we have noted above, there are a great many factors which can potentially influence our health-related behaviours. Indeed, there are too many to cover in detail in this chapter. Therefore, those factors which have a greater evidence base, in other words those that have been researched more comprehensively, are focused upon.

Age

Our age plays a significant role in terms of influencing our health behaviours. As we get older our body naturally undergoes physical changes. These changes can impact on our ability to engage in health behaviours we previously took for granted. In addition, with greater age and therefore experience, our attitudes, beliefs and opinions are likely to alter. Finally, Forshaw (2002: 45) points out that 'older people are often poorer people and that as a result, they may eat less healthily ... in order to save money'.

At the other end of the age spectrum, the period of adolescence is one of great change: physically, psychologically and emotionally. Adolescence is also a time when we may take risks with our health, perhaps due to the desire to experiment, or as a consequence of peer pressure and the desire to 'fit in'. Adolescents might also take risks without fully understanding the longer term consequences for their health. Brewer and colleagues (2006) explored adolescents' perceptions of risk and challenge. For example, one teenage girl, who was aware of some of the evidence which suggests that taking the contraceptive pill increases the risk of developing particular forms of cancer, weighed up the risks of developing cancer if she were to remain on the contraceptive pill versus the risk of pregnancy if she were to stop taking the pill. She did not consider alternative forms of contraception, neither did she acknowledge the need to use barrier methods of contraception to protect her from sexually transmitted diseases. Therefore, although the adolescents in Brewer and colleagues' (2006) study demonstrated that they were aware of the types of risks and complexities involved in arriving at a decision about whether or not to engage in a particular behaviour and were confident in their ability to make appropriate decisions having weighed up the advantages and disadvantages, there was some evidence to suggest that their lack of life experience and knowledge could lead to errors in judgement when decisions about risk behaviour were made. These studies show clearly that whatever stage of the life span is focused upon, age can play an important role in influencing our health behaviours.

Gender

Men and women are different. At a most basic level, we are biologically different, but the social and cultural environments we inhabit also exert an influence over the way in which gender can affect health behaviour. For example, Forshaw (2002: 44) notes that factors such as the nature of the hormones circulating in our bodies, the way in which we are socialized and the way in which men and women are treated in society can mean that 'men and women have their own specific health problems'. Similarly, Charles and Walters (2008) explored gender differences in health talk, how such talk is informed by discourses at a societal level and the extent to which talking about health is a way of 'doing gender'. They conducted in-depth interviews with 48 women and men in their twenties and thirties and showed that gender influenced both the way people spoke about health and their willingness to engage in health talk. Furthermore, in a study which explored the extent to which men and women differed in their health beliefs, Courtenay and colleagues (2002) found consistent gender differences. Men reported engaging in riskier behaviours and holding riskier beliefs than women. The researchers concluded that if men are to live longer, healthier lives, they will need to change both their beliefs and their behaviours. But the researchers also sounded a note of caution in that they recognize there are still complex questions which need answers. For example, it is only when we understand why it is that, with regards to their health, men behave more destructively than women that health professionals will be able to develop effective interventions for improving men's health.

Curtis (2000) notes that evidence concerning gender differences in the use of healthcare services suggests that women are, on average, twice as likely as men to visit their GP. This finding was replicated in 2009 by Gerritson and Deville. In addition, Pennebaker and Skelton (1978) showed that women report more symptoms to their GP than men.

However, Macintyre and colleagues (1996) reviewed the literature and indicated that the findings were not as clear-cut as researchers had been suggesting. For example, they highlight that

> one frequently cited explanation for apparently higher rates of morbidity among females is that they are more sensitive than men to bodily discomforts and more willing to report symptoms of distress and illness. Yet the evidence, though limited, is conflicting.
>
> (Macintyre et al., 1996: 622)

They conclude by arguing that summarizing the morbidity experiences of men and women is 'exceedingly difficult'.

Han and colleagues (2007) highlight the difficulty of explaining the fact that the prevalence of chronic obstructive pulmonary disease (COPD) in women is increasing and also that the number of women dying of COPD in the USA now surpasses men. In their paper, the authors present current knowledge regarding how gender might influence the epidemiology, diagnosis and presentation of COPD, whilst also taking into account physiological and psychological issues. Curtis (2000) calls for caution and suggests that many gender differences could be almost exclusively due to social factors, with the suggestion that men are socialized into being 'strong' and so refuse to admit that their illness is serious enough to warrant medical attention. It is also likely, however, that socioeconomic factors also play a role.

Socioeconomic factors

Those who belong to higher socioeconomic groups tend to experience fewer symptoms and report a higher level of health than those in lower **socioeconomic status** (SES) groups (Pennebaker and Skelton, 1978). The Black Report (Townsend and Davidson, 1982) published findings on social inequalities in health outcomes in the UK. A key finding was that people in lower social groups (unskilled and skilled manual workers) were more likely to die than those in higher occupational groups (professional and managerial workers). This may be because people in low SES groups have been shown to wait longer before seeking healthcare. Waiting longer means that treatment might be more difficult because the condition is more advanced. This in turn makes hospitalization more likely (Brannon and Feist, 1997). Kramer and colleagues (2000) reviewed the evidence concerning socioeconomic disparities in pregnancy outcome and asked the question: 'Why do the poor fare so badly?' They concluded that socioeconomic status was an important influencing factor, both for the birth of premature babies, and for full-term babies born underweight. In Germany, Reime and colleagues (2006) showed that being unemployed, a single mother and older than 39 years was associated with an increased risk of low birth weight babies. Similarly, in Denmark, a study exploring the risk of preterm birth concluded that the level of educational achievement attained by mothers was the strongest socioeconomic predictor of preterm birth (Morgen et al., 2008).

Albery and Munafo (2008) suggest that although various explanations have been offered for the impact of SES, the one to which many contemporary researchers adhere is that social inequalities in health such as those reported above are not a result of a direct relationship between health and SES, rather the relationship is indirect and is mediated by behavioural or psychosocial factors. What this means is that researchers have come to believe that the reason people in different social groups may experience certain health outcomes is not solely a consequence of their SES, but because of the differing ways in which they behave in their social settings.

Type A, B, C and D personality

Much research has been conducted that explores whether or not people with different types of personality are more or less likely to engage in particular kinds of health behaviours. Two types of personality (Types A and B) were linked to coronary heart disease. More recently, Type C, linked to cancer, and Type D, linked to coronary heart disease, have been identified.

Type A and B personality

The **Type A personality** has been associated with an increased risk for coronary heart disease, whilst conversely the **Type B personality** has been associated with a lower risk. Type A and B personalities were first put forward by cardiologists Friedman and Rosenman (1959, 1974). Typical Type A behaviour includes impatience, intolerance, competitiveness, attempts to achieve too much in too little time, vigorous speech pattern and hostility, whereas Type B behaviour is characterized by a more relaxed, easy-going, cooperative style. Research into Type A and B personalities has produced mixed results and, as a consequence, researchers have tried to separate out the Type A characteristics in order to identify the one which appears to have the most influence. More recent work has focused on hostility (e.g. Dembrowski et al., 1989; Miller et al., 1996) and concludes that there is a good relationship between hostility and coronary heart disease.

Type C personality

Albery and Munafo (2008) note that researchers have identified a personality profile that is associated with increased cancer risk. This has been labelled the **Type C personality** (Temoshok, 1987). A person considered to be Type C would typically be cooperative, appeasing, passive, non-assertive, self-sacrificing as well as being someone who inhibited their emotions. Shaffer and colleagues (1987) showed that people who inhibited their emotional expression were more likely to develop cancer. More recently, Temoshok and colleagues (2008) explored the impact of Type C personality on disease progression in HIV and concluded that Type C coping was associated with poorer immune functioning.

Type D personality

A person who experiences but inhibits the expression of negative emotions, and who at the same time actively avoids social interaction for fear of encountering feelings of disapproval is said to have a **Type D personality** (Denollet, 1998). The possession of a Type D personality has been shown to be predictive of physiological indicators of coronary heart disease (Habra et al., 2003). The relationship between Type D and cardiovascular reactivity to experimentally induced stress was investigated by Williams and colleagues (2009). They invited 84 healthy young adults (50% males) to complete measures of Type D personality, stress arousal and a stress-inducing procedure involving a taxing mental arithmetic task. Cardiovascular measures were recorded throughout the experiment. They found that whilst Type D males exhibited significantly higher cardiac output during the stressor phase compared to non-Type D males, there was no relationship between Type D and cardiovascular reactivity in females. They conclude that their findings provide new evidence as to how Type D mechanisms might affect health through increased cardiac output and higher subjective feelings of stress following acute stress.

Hardiness

Hardiness is a personality type which has been characterized by three factors (Albery and Munafo, 2008):

- commitment – a sense of purpose in life events and activities
- control – the belief of personal influence over situations
- challenge – seeing adaptation and change as a normal and positive experience.

The possession of hardiness has been shown to protect or 'buffer' individuals against the likelihood that situations of high stress will lead to the development of illness. For example, Kobasa and colleagues (1982) showed that 'high hardiness' people who were exposed to high levels of stress not only reported lower illness scores when compared to 'low hardiness' individuals, but also their illness scores were shown to be no different to those who had experienced only low levels of stress. Similarly, Farber and colleagues (2000) examined the hardiness dimensions of commitment, challenge and control to see whether they acted as resilience factors for 200 persons with symptomatic HIV disease and AIDS. Commitment was the hardiness factor that most frequently made a unique contribution to predicting adaptation to HIV/AIDS. In addition, the relationship between hardiness and stress in the lives of college students has received a significant amount of empirical attention (e.g. Banks and Gannon, 1988; Harris, 2004; Pengilly and Dowd, 2000; Soderstrom et al., 2000). More recently, the concept of hardiness has been explored in the military context. Dolan and Adler (2006) surveyed 629 US soldiers and found that military hardiness, defined as the context-specific adaptation of psychological hardiness, was shown to moderate the effects of deployment stressors on soldiers' health.

Health beliefs

Health beliefs, or the way in which we think about health, have a huge impact on our subsequent engagement in health behaviour. Our beliefs about health can be informed by many different factors, including our lay understanding of what it means to be healthy. This was discussed in detail in Chapter 1, and so will only be briefly mentioned here. In addition, our health behaviour can be influenced by our locus of control, cultural identity and our level of knowledge. We describe each of these factors below and conclude with the presentation of Leventhal's

Self-regulatory Model, which proposes a means of mapping out the processes we experience when we encounter ill health.

Lay beliefs and adherence to medical regimes

As mentioned in Chapter 1, lay concepts of health are often 'passed down through generations as part of a common cultural heritage' (Naidoo and Wills, 2003: 6). The way in which people explain and understand health can have important ramifications for their subsequent behaviour. Our understanding of illness, disease and health is dynamic and changes in response to personal experience and circumstance. Most of us develop our health beliefs from what are known as 'folk models', which encapsulate health-related information, often in short phrases. Such phrases in common usage in the UK include 'feed a cold, starve a fever', 'carrots help you to see in the dark', and 'cracking your knuckles causes arthritis'. We also develop our beliefs from exposure to the mass media as well as from beliefs held within our family and friendship groups.

Our health beliefs can be used to justify engaging in positive or negative types of health behaviour. For example, Benson and Britten (2002) explored the perceptions held by patients diagnosed as having hypertension (high blood pressure) about taking antihypertensive drugs. They interviewed 38 patients and found that three-quarters of them had reservations about drugs generally. These reservations tended to revolve around the idea that taking drugs was something which should be avoided where possible. Some of them explained that their beliefs had come from personal experience, others that they felt that their body would become resistant or, worse, addicted to the drugs in question. Still others saw drugs as signifying ill health or felt that their doctors prescribed drugs too readily. However, there were also a number of more positive viewpoints which patients balanced against their more negative views. Those patients who willingly took antihypertensives tended to say that they did so because it made them feel better. The authors of the study note that such a perception is at odds with conventional medical opinion in the UK, which holds that raised blood pressure is usually without symptoms. Benson and Britten (2002) conclude that patients may decide to take or not take antihypertensive drugs depending on how the risk of doing so is presented to them. However, presenting the risks alone is not enough, they also highlight that a patient's perceptions of risk *as well as* the way in which they balance their perceptions needs to be appreciated, because different patients 'balance similar perceptions differently' (Benson and Britten, 2002: 877).

A more light-hearted example of how we justify engaging in behaviour we know is considered unhealthy can be found on the website of Victor Saunders, the respected mountaineer. Victor was leading an expedition to climb Cho Oyu (a very big mountain in the Himalayas), and as is often the case on such trips, there was a period of enforced inactivity; this time as a consequence of monsoon flash floods. This particular delay led to the team devoting their time developing a complex theory about how to reduce the risk of developing acute mountain sickness (AMS). In short, the expedition members noted that super-fit marathon runners do poorly at high altitude and they suffer more than most from AMS. This, the climbers suggested, is possibly caused by being strong and fit enough to climb high faster than their body will acclimatize, whereas in comparison, those they described as 'less fit' climbers will be too weak to climb fast enough to get themselves into trouble. Having identified this potential relationship between fitness and AMS, Saunders and colleagues (2009) developed a formula which grew ever more complex as different factors such as IQ and alcohol consumption were accounted for. They argued that the resultant theory and accompanying formula justified the consumption of alcohol during the expedition (something not recommended at altitude) as a means of warding off AMS. What is not known is what level of altitude the team had reached when they composed their theory – it is entirely possible that they were at an elevation sufficiently high to be experiencing the beginnings of AMS themselves, which may have affected their calculations. Nevertheless, their nascent and untested, but strangely compelling theory can be found in full on the website (Saunders et al., 2009) and is a clear illustration of how lay beliefs might translate into health behaviour.

Health beliefs and speed of recovery from illness

Our health beliefs can also influence our speed of recovery from illness. McCarthy and colleagues (2003) investigated whether patients' expectations (or beliefs) influenced their recovery from a relatively minor operation. Surgery is often associated with the expectation of stressful and painful medical procedures and is characterized by the anticipation that pain and disability will be experienced during the recovery period (McCarthy et al., 2003; Newman, 1984). Work conducted prior to the McCarthy and colleagues' (2003) study had found that preoperative expectations of pain, swelling and interference with daily activities were linked to the level of postoperative pain experienced, number of pain tablets taken, and length of healing time (George et al., 1980; Gidron et al., 1995). However, this work did not control for anxiety. McCarthy and colleagues (2003) therefore took into account the variable 'anxiety' when measuring expectations and outcomes. They found that preoperative expectations were far more predictive of recovery measures than were medical factors. They therefore demonstrated the importance of taking into account patients' beliefs about their outcomes during the planning stages of the surgical intervention. They conclude by suggesting that perhaps interventions aimed at specifically addressing preoperative expectations could be designed, with the aim of improving speed of recovery.

Locus of control

How much control a person perceives that they have in determining whether or not they engage in a particular behaviour will have an influence on whether or not that person decides to implement (or not) particular health behaviours. The term **locus of control** was coined by Rotter (1966) to encapsulate the idea of perceived control. The notion underlying the term is that over time individuals come to expect that things that happen to them are determined either by factors internal to themselves – in other words, their own actions or beliefs; or by factors external to themselves – in other words, as a result of chance or luck. Thus, it was suggested that people who feel that they have control over their lives have an 'internal locus of control', whereas those who tend to feel that their lives are governed by chance have an 'external locus of control'. The implication is that if you have an external locus of control, and therefore see your life as being governed by factors outside your influence, you are less likely to engage in health protective behaviours or to adhere to medical regimes, because you are less likely to believe that you can make a difference to your health status than someone who has an internal locus of control (Ozolins and Stenstrom, 2003; van de Putte et al., 2005). For example, it has been argued that individuals with high internal locus of control are more likely to abstain from smoking and drinking and to follow recommendations related to preventive medicine (e.g. Booth-Butterfield et al., 2000; Burkhart and Rayens, 2005; Tokuda et al., 2007). It is important to highlight that the findings published on locus of control have not been homogeneous. Forshaw (2002: 47) sounds a note of caution when he flags up this issue and notes that research into the locus of control construct has yielded mixed and in some cases contradictory results. It is important to be aware of this when interpreting studies publishing data on locus of control.

Nevertheless, whether locus of control impacts on self-management behaviour among patients who have been diagnosed with chronic illness is an area which has been commonly focused upon by researchers. For example, Trento and colleagues (2008) note that the process of adapting to diabetes is not a straightforward process. It requires patients to recognize the seriousness of their disease and to be aware that they can potentially improve their health outcomes by actively engaging in health protective behaviours. In order to do so, they need to internalize the disease.

Type 1 diabetes occurs when the body does not make any insulin, insulin being the hormone that controls levels of sugar in the blood. The onset of Type 1 diabetes is usually before the age of 40. Type 1 diabetes requires a strict regimen that typically combines changes in health behaviours concerning a carefully calculated diet and planned physical activity, with more medical interventions including home blood glucose testing several times a day, and multiple daily insulin injections.

In contrast, Type 2 diabetes occurs when the body doesn't make enough insulin or cannot use insulin properly. This type of diabetes can happen at any age, is linked to being overweight, and accounts for 90% of cases of diabetes (NHS, 2009). Treatment for Type 2 diabetes typically requires the individual concerned to make changes to their diet and exercise routine. It is less likely that a person with Type 2 diabetes will require insulin injections.

Trento and colleagues (2008) suggested that people with Type 1 and Type 2 diabetes might differ in the way they adapt to their disease, which could reflect differences in their locus of control. They explored the locus of control of groups of Type 1 and Type 2 patients whom they had been following over a period of five years and reported that individuals with Type 1 diabetes had lower levels of internal control than those diagnosed with Type 2 diabetes. This difference could possibly be explained by the fact that whilst there is nothing you can do to avoid the onset of Type 1 diabetes, a healthy lifestyle can help you to avoid the onset of Type 2 diabetes. The way in which diabetes can start might impact on a person's locus of control; essentially, Type 1 diabetes can happen to you regardless of your lifestyle, so the fact that there is nothing you can do to stop its onset might lead to a lowering of individuals' locus of control. Furthermore, given that patients with Type 1 diabetes are typically younger than those with Type 2, Trento and colleagues (2008) speculate that these patients' perceptions of the future may be modified because, through the treatment and need for constant monitoring of their condition, they are being constantly reminded of the finiteness of life. One of the important implications of their findings was that patients with Type 1 and Type 2 diabetes might benefit from different versions of group care specifically designed to take into account the typical style of locus of control exhibited by the two groups.

In another study of chronic disease, van de Putte and colleagues (2005) explored whether locus of control differed between adolescents with chronic fatigue syndrome (CFS) and healthy adolescents and their respective parents. CFS is characterized by chronic and disabling fatigue. Many explanations have been offered, but as yet none has been shown to be the cause of CFS. The fact that at present no clear understanding of its cause exists means that treatment is limited to addressing symptoms and behaviours associated with CFS. If treatment relies on individuals engaging in health behaviours, understanding the locus of control of a patient group will have implications for treatment strategies, for, as we have noted above, those with an external locus of control are less likely to believe they can make a difference to their health by engaging in specific health behaviours.

Van de Putte and colleagues (2005) reported that families with an adolescent with CFS had reduced levels of locus of control when compared to 'healthy' families. Families with CFS held a stronger belief that chance or physicians could influence their illness. People with CFS tended to feel that their symptoms could not be influenced and that control over CFS was therefore impossible. This is an important finding, because research by Newman and colleagues (2004) showed that the outcome in chronic illness is improved by increasing patients' control over their illness. Thus, van de Putte and colleagues' (2005) finding that both adolescents with CFS and their parents had reduced internal locus of control, something which is linked to poorer health outcomes, requires that attention be paid to patients' health beliefs within any treatment strategies.

Cultural factors

Many studies have been conducted exploring the influence of culture on health meanings, practices and values. Cultural differences can account for differences in the way we respond to threats to our health, as well as in the way in which we engage in health protective behaviours. One of the earliest reports on differences in health behaviour was provided by Zola (1966), who noticed that when visiting their doctors, Italian Americans tended to report a larger number of symptoms compared to Irish Americans. Irish Americans, in contrast, were more likely to present with ear, nose and throat problems than were Italian Americans. Since then, much work has been conducted in the field which clearly demonstrates the impact of cultural differences on health behaviour. For example, in Sweden, Hjelm and colleagues (2005) explored the health and illness beliefs of men with diabetes from different cultural backgrounds. They conducted focus groups with 35 men, 14 who had been born in Arabic countries, 10 in the former Yugoslavia and 11 in Sweden. They found that Swedish participants were more likely to focus on heredity, lifestyle and management of diabetes, whereas non–Swedes claimed that the influence of supernatural factors (such as the will of God or evil spirits) as well as emotional stress caused by their experience of being an immigrant were viewed as factors that led to the development of diabetes. Hjelm and colleagues (2005) also showed that while general knowledge about diabetes among all the men was limited, Arabs took a more active role in seeking information compared to the Swedes and Eastern Europeans. The Arabic participants in particular had sought care from healthcare professionals, whereas the Swedes were more likely to use self-care measures. Hjelm and colleagues (2005) showed that there were differences in beliefs about health and diabetes between the three cultural groups studied. These differences in beliefs accounted for differences in adherence to medical regimes and in health behaviours, and highlight the need for men's cultural backgrounds and spiritual beliefs to be considered in the context of diabetes healthcare.

In a study exploring dietary beliefs, McEwen and colleagues (2009) examined the dietary beliefs and self-reported eating behaviours of a Somali population in London. The study was implemented in response to the realization that although Somalis comprise one of the largest asylum-seeking populations in the UK, little was known about how their migration to the UK has affected their traditional attitudes towards food. The results of the study showed that fruit and vegetable consumption was an insignificant component of the Somali UK diet. Meat, on the other hand, was seen as a important part of the diet. Meat was linked to wealth and social status: 'Most Somalis believe that if they do not have meat and rice, they haven't had lunch.' Another theme to emerge from the study concerned the participants' cultural identity as nomadic herders. McEwen and colleagues (2009: 119) note that due to civil unrest in Somalia, it was unlikely that participants had been engaged in camel herding before coming to the UK, nevertheless, there was a strong identification with this traditional nomadic background. They suggest that eating behaviour amongst this group may therefore have been linked to notions of Somali identity. The diet of meat with rice was seen very much as the Somali diet and, in being seen in this way, was more than just a personal choice about food. Indeed, McEwen and colleagues (2009: 119) note that the cultural association held by the Somali people, which links fruit and vegetables to poverty and red meat with affluence, goes some way to explaining the less than optimum consumption of fruit and vegetables among this population.

Van Cleemput and colleagues (2007) explored the health-related beliefs and experiences of Gypsies and Travellers in the UK. They found that the cultural beliefs and attitudes of this population clearly underpinned their health-related behaviour. In particular, the experience of poor health and daily encounters of ill health among extended family members were normalized and accepted. Typically, the participants had low expectations of health, relied on themselves, had a strong need to retain control, and a reluctance to seek professional help. In addition, participants expressed a strong sense of fatalism in conjunction with a fear of death. The greater understanding of the Gypsy and Traveller experience of health enables the development of informed, culturally appropriate and sensitive services that might improve the health experience of this population.

Our level of knowledge and expectations

The health beliefs that we hold depend upon the level of knowledge we have, which in turn can impact upon our ability to recognize or even interpret correctly the symptoms we are experiencing. In the study of Gypsies and Travellers conducted by van Cleemput and colleagues (2007: 208), the participants had low expectations of health. A couple of quotes from their study illustrate this issue well:

> I suffers with asthma and I had, must be getting on two years ago, I had about like, four or five mini strokes. Well I just took me tablets now for it [frozen shoulder] and that so I got tablets really to control that ... arthritis, I got that and ... so I still got this stuff when I starts walking and I finds I'm getting a little pain or a bit breathless,

I just takes that. So I'm very happy. (woman with angina, frozen shoulder, arthritis, asthma and several 'mini-strokes')

My health is perfect, lovely … I only have a bad back all the time … that's since I was 15. (woman with chronic back complaint, a history of severe allergies and skin complaint)

As a consequence, symptoms that perhaps people from different cultural backgrounds would act upon were 'normalized' by the Gypsies and Travellers. Similarly, both Ruston and colleagues (1998) and Horne and colleagues (2000) found that the way in which symptoms were interpreted reflected patients' beliefs and therefore impacted on their help-seeking behaviour and their willingness to adhere to medical regimes. In the case of the participants in both of these studies (people experiencing a cardiac event), any delay in seeking help can be catastrophic in its consequences. Both papers conclude that the experience and interpretation of symptoms are of paramount importance for ensuring help is received in a timely manner. Ruston and colleagues (1998) found that of those who had delayed seeking help for more than 12 hours following onset of their cardiac symptoms, most had thought that a heart attack was something dramatic and sudden. They associated heart attacks with collapse and death:

Mine wasn't excruciating pain like you hear, you know, heart attacks are excruciating and you never forget it … and falling down with crushing pain, nothing like you've ever had before – in reality it's not like that. (Ruston et al., 1998: 1063)

On the other hand, those who sought help relatively quickly, within four hours of experiencing the symptoms, were more likely to have previously seen themselves as being potentially at risk, and knew that there was a wider range of symptoms than chest or arm pain. Similarly, Horne and colleagues (2000) found that patients reached hospital sooner when they experienced stereotypical symptoms of a heart attack (chest pain), when their symptoms were of a rapid onset and matched their prior expectations of what a heart attack would be like.

A more recent study reported by Seale and colleagues (2009) explored Australian healthcare workers' attitudes towards a proposed response to a potential influenza pandemic. They found two potentially worrying issues (both concerning health beliefs) that could undermine the best of pandemic plans. First, there was a low level of confidence in antivirals as an effective medical measure to combat flu, and second, non-clinical workers were an overlooked group, whose lack of knowledge and awareness could seriously undermine pandemic plans. They propose education for clinical and non-clinical workers to ensure that inaccurate health beliefs are addressed and, if necessary, corrected. These studies show dramatically how our health beliefs can have important ramifications for our health behaviour and subsequently our health outcomes.

Leventhal's Self-regulatory Model

The way in which our understanding of health or our beliefs about illness (otherwise known as **illness representations**) guide our response to illness has been encapsulated in the **Self-regulatory Model** (SRM) put forward by Leventhal and colleagues (1980). This model takes a problem-solving approach, which suggests that we deal with illness and illness symptoms in the same way that we deal with other problems. It assumes that we as individuals have a need to maintain our equilibrium, so that when we encounter a problem which threatens our psychological or physical being, we are motivated to engage in activities that will work towards reinstating the status quo. Illness is regarded as an unstable state that counters the 'normal' state of being healthy. The assumption is that when our state of health is threatened, we will work towards re-establishing our balanced state of health.

Leventhal and colleagues (1980) defined illness representations as being a person's own commonsense beliefs about their illness. They argued that illness representations provide us with a framework consisting of five dimensions for coping with and understanding illness:

- *Identity* – the label given to the illness, either by a doctor offering a diagnosis of your symptoms, or via self-diagnosis. By way of example, Albery and Munafo (2008: 126) suggest that when we think of the last time we woke up to find we had a headache, a sore throat, a stiff neck and a lack of energy, depending on our prior experience, we might label these symptoms as hangover, cold or the start of flu.
- *Perceived cause* – this refers to our beliefs about what may have caused the illness, such as exposure to another ill person (an external attribution) or having engaged in negative health behaviour, perhaps drinking too much the night before. Our understanding of the cause can similarly be derived from our own

experience and assumptions or from those of a health professional offering an opinion.

- *Time line* – this is how long we think our illness will last, which can also be based on our own assumptions, or on information offered by health professionals.

- *Consequences* – this concerns how individuals think the illness might impact on their life – will there be pain, disability or emotional consequences, or indeed a combination of these factors?

- *Curability and controllability* – this is a twofold belief and concerns whether an individual perceives that their illness can be cured and treated, as well as whether they feel that the outcome of their illness is controllable (either by themselves or healthcare professionals).

The SRM is divided into three stages: interpretation, coping and appraisal. The process of assessing each of the five dimensions detailed above takes place during the first phase of 'interpretation'. Moving through these five dimensions is what creates a person's illness representation. As noted by Forshaw (2002: 35), 'you cannot begin to do something about being ill, unless you get to grips with the illness itself and what it seems to involve'. Another dimension to the interpretation stage involves our emotional response; being ill can create anxiety and fear about the outcomes and also about the implications of being ill – perhaps taking time off work when you have deadlines looming – which may add to the anxiety and emotional response. This is also the stage where our beliefs influence the way in which we understand and interpret our symptoms.

The second stage is 'coping', where we begin to act on our interpretation. We may, for example, seek advice from friends and family, we may decide to take the day off work and make an appointment with our GP and, in more extreme circumstances, we may decide we need to call an ambulance. Therefore, once a person is exposed to an illness-related stimulus, illness representations (health beliefs) are activated and are characterized by each of the five dimensions outlined above. Activating an illness representation allows us to compare our current experiences with those we have had in the past and enables us to assess our ability to cope with the illness we have encountered.

The third and final stage of the SRM is 'appraisal'. This is the point at which individuals assess the coping strategies they have chosen and, depending on the results of their assessment, may choose to continue with their chosen strategy, or adopt a new strategy. Forshaw (2002: 37) notes that some research seems to suggest that not everyone reaches the appraisal stage and that this might be because they tend to take avoidant action or, indeed, perhaps because they are only open to one type of coping, and therefore are not aware of the need to assess the effectiveness of their chosen strategy. Nevertheless, the SRM has been influential in the study of how people identify and respond to the threat or onset of illness. The model is useful in that it acknowledges the dynamic interaction between the way in which we think about illness and the way in which we experience illness and the impact of that interaction on our ability to cope with illness. It provides us with a useful framework that can help us to understand individuals' reactions to health threats and has been widely applied to studies of recovery from actual life-threatening and/or chronic health conditions (e.g. Griva et al., 2000; Moss-Morris et al., 1996; Petrie et al., 1995, 2002; Steed et al., 1999).

◉ Conclusion

In this chapter, we have explored the application of the biopsychosocial model, identified the different factors which are believed to influence health-related behaviours and we have introduced Leventhal's Self-regulatory Model. In the next chapter we turn our attention to the models which have been developed as a means of assessing and evaluating health behaviours.

◉ Further reading

Radley, A. (1994) *Making Sense of Illness: The Social Psychology of Health and Disease.* Sage: London.

◉ Key search terms

Health belief, illness belief, biopsychosocial model, Self-regulatory Model

Chapter 3

Explaining health behaviour

⊙ Introduction

Models of behaviour change have been described by Curtis (2000) as simply descriptions of 'how something *might* work, rather than being an explanation of how something actually *does* work' (Curtis, 2000: 11). As such, they do not provide us with a clear explanation of what is happening, but offer an opportunity to identify the factors that are likely to be operating. Such models can therefore be used to predict behaviour change or indeed to design successful health intervention strategies (a process we focus on in Chapters 5 and 6).

In this chapter, we turn our attention to the key models of behaviour change which have been developed as a means of identifying, evaluating and changing health behaviours. We focus on the three most commonly referred to health psychology models that have been used to try and understand how people move from engaging in a poor health behaviour towards a self-protective health behaviour. Specifically, this chapter focuses on the Health Belief Model, the Theory of Planned Behaviour and the Stages of Change Model. All three models are categorized as **social cognitive approaches**. Social cognitive approaches emphasize that we as individuals are information processors. This means that we are considered to play an active role in interpreting the information around us. The social cognitive models therefore focus on the **social context** of behaviour change as well as the cognitive processes we engage in to make sense of the social context. The idea is that it is the interaction between the social context and our cognitive processing which determines whether or not we engage in behaviour change.

In this chapter, we will:
- Consider why we need social cognitive models of health behaviour
- Outline three key social cognitive models of health behaviour
- Provide examples of the application of these three models
- Discuss the utility of the existing models

◉ Why do we need social cognitive models of health behaviour?

Changes in causes of death throughout the 20th century can in part be explained in terms of changes in behaviour-related illnesses. As our understanding of the causes and treatment of disease has progressed, and in parallel our understanding of the importance of hygiene has improved, many previously life-threatening conditions are now treatable. This means that mortality rates are now more commonly linked to conditions that are associated with health-impairing behaviours. These illnesses include coronary heart disease, cancers and HIV, all of which are associated with health-impairing behaviours like smoking, not practising safe sex, drinking too much, poor nutrition and lack of physical exercise.

As we discussed in Chapter 2, health behaviour has traditionally been defined as behaviour undertaken by individuals to enhance or to maintain their health. However, lots of behaviour that has implications for our health is engaged in for other reasons, for example dieting because we equate slimness with looking good, or drinking to feel more confident in social situations. It has therefore been argued that health behaviours also need to be defined in terms of their impact on health. As a result, health behaviours are now talked about in terms of **health-impairing behaviours** (smoking, unprotected sex), which have a negative impact on health, and **health protective behaviours** (exercising, eating healthily), which have a positive effect. Researchers hope that by understanding the factors underlying these behaviours they will be able to develop effective health promotion/disease prevention strategies.

One way in which psychologists have attempted to understand these factors is through the development of social cognitive models. It is important to be aware that there are many models and new theories continue to be put forward (whilst the old ones do not disappear or change). As a result, it can become a little confusing as to which theories are most valued, which constructs are the most important and which theories are the most appropriate to form the basis for interventions. The remainder of this chapter focuses on three of the most commonly applied social cognitive models: the Health Belief Model, the Theory of Planned Behaviour and the Stages of Change Model.

Health Belief Model

In an attempt to understand why many individuals did not practise preventive health behaviours, and in particular to look at why they did not use available health services (like screening tests), a group of social psychologists in the USA in the 1970s developed the **Health Belief Model** (Figure 3.1). Researchers often refer to this model as the 'grandparent' of all models. A key assumption underpinning this model is that whether or not a person engages in a health protective behaviour depends on a number of health beliefs.

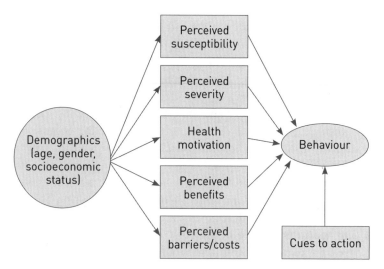

Figure 3.1 The Health Belief Model
Source: Conner, M. and Norman, P. (2005). *Predicting Health Behaviour: Research and Practice with Social Cognition Models* (2nd edn). © Reproduced with kind permission of Open University Press. All rights reserved.

The Health Belief Model (HBM) suggests that the likelihood an individual will engage in a particular health behaviour is determined jointly by their perception of the health threat posed by the current situation they are in and their evaluation of the recommended course of action. The core elements of the model are:

- **Perceived susceptibility**: Does the individual think that they are likely to succumb to the particular illness or disability in question?
- **Perceived severity**: How bad would it be for them if they were to succumb?
- **Perceived benefits**: If they adopt the healthy behaviour in question, what are the benefits that will accrue?
- **Perceived barriers/costs**: What are the things that get in the way of them adopting a particular behaviour? If they adopt/do not adopt the behaviour, what are the likely costs? The example of condom use is often offered: what are the perceived benefits of condom use (protection against sexually transmitted diseases) and what are the disadvantages (embarrassment of negotiating condom use)?
- **Health motivation**: Health motivation is what accounts for the fact that individuals may differ in terms of the value they attach to their health, as well as in their willingness to take part in health-promoting activities.
- **Cues to action**: These are prompts that trigger the behaviour. These might be internal cues (like perceived symptoms) as well as external cues (like health education campaigns, or perhaps the illness or death of a close friend).

It is suggested that these core elements act together in determining how likely we are to engage in a particular behaviour. Of particular importance in these elements is the word 'perceived'. This highlights that it is our perceptions which play a central role in this process and therefore that our behaviour may not be based on objectivity, but on perception.

What is the evidence for the Health Belief Model?

How can you measure the different facets of the HBM? Although Sheeran and Abraham (1996) have given detailed information as to how to construct a questionnaire to measure the different elements of the HBM, de Wit and Stroebe (2005) highlight that there is currently no standard HBM questionnaire. This is problematic, in that different researchers may be measuring the constituent elements of the HBM in slightly different ways, which has implications for our ability to compare reported findings. Nevertheless, the HBM has been used successfully for a number of different health behaviours. For example, it has been shown to predict regular screening for cervical cancer (Gorin and Heck, 2005). If an individual perceives that she is highly susceptible to cancer of the cervix, that cervical cancer is a severe health threat, that the benefits of regular screening are high and that the costs of such actions are relatively low, she is more likely to attend screening. Similarly, researchers have demonstrated that dietary compliance (Sharifirad et al., 2009), safe sex (Lau et al., 2007), having vaccinations (Reiter et al., 2009) and dental care (Renz and Newton, 2009) are related to the individual's perceived susceptibility to the related health problem, their belief that the problem is severe and their perception that the benefits of preventive action outweigh the costs.

Researchers have also looked at different components of the model and have found that perceived barriers are the best predictors of clinic attendance (Wringe et al., 2009). Others have looked at the role of cues to action in predicting health behaviours, especially external cues. For example, Schofield and colleagues (2007) explored the smoking-related beliefs of older people with chronic obstructive pulmonary disease (a condition caused by smoking that obstructs airflow within the lungs). They found that cues to take action came from either the increasing severity of their participants' condition or events that were external to the individual such as advice from a doctor. Such work is of particular relevance to health promotion interventions which typically rely on external cues to change beliefs and thereby promote future healthy behaviour.

Applying the Health Belief Model

In order to understand more clearly how the HBM has been applied, it is helpful to consider one study in detail. Norman and Brain (2005) examined the behaviour of breast self-examination (BSE). In their paper, they report a study which explored the application of the HBM to predicting BSE among women with a family history of breast cancer. BSE is a simple, low-cost method of detecting lumps which might indicate the presence of breast cancer. However, in spite of the ease with which this behaviour can be implemented, many women (even those who have a family history of breast cancer) do not perform BSE on a regular basis.

Norman and Brain (2005) were particularly interested in trying to understand the psychosocial predictors of BSE among women with an elevated risk of breast cancer. They recruited 833 women aged between 17 and 77 years (mean age 41 years) who completed two questionnaires.

One questionnaire was completed prior to attending a clinic, the second was completed nine months after attending the clinic. Included in the questionnaire was a breast cancer worries scale which assessed anxiety specific to breast cancer. Women were also asked to report how often they performed BSE and finally completed a questionnaire which measured different elements of the HBM (including a measure of **self-efficacy**) as they related to breast cancer. These are some examples:

- *Perceived susceptibility:* What level of risk do you personally think you have? What would you say the chances of getting breast cancer are?
- *Perceived severity:* If I had breast cancer, my whole life would change; if I got breast cancer, it would be more serious than other diseases.
- *Perceived benefits:* Means that breast cancer can be found early on, gives me peace of mind.
- *Perceived emotional barriers:* Finding BSE emotionally distressing/ embarrassing.
- *Perceived self-efficacy barriers:* I am confident I can examine my breasts; I prefer to let the doctor examine my breasts.

On the basis of their responses to the questions, the women were then categorized as 'infrequent', 'appropriate' or 'excessive breast self-examiners'. Infrequent was equivalent to completing the behaviour up to three or four times a year, appropriate was classified as monthly or fortnightly BSE, and excessive as weekly or daily BSE.

The study found that there were differences in terms of the HBM dimensions that distinguished infrequent, appropriate and excessive BSEs. Women who performed BSE infrequently reported more self-efficacy and emotional barriers and saw fewer benefits to engaging in BSE compared to women who performed appropriate or excessive BSE. It was also found that high levels of perceived severity and breast cancer worries could lead to hypervigilant BSE, which can mean that breast cancer is not detected early. This is because although women who engage in excessive BSE carry out more frequent examinations, they tend to be less thorough, which might result in missed lumps. Norman and Brain (2005) concluded that perceived barriers were the strongest predictor of BSE. On the basis of these findings, they were able to highlight practical implications arising from their study, not least the need to emphasize the positive benefits of performing monthly BSE as well as developing ways to address the barriers that were reported by women in this study, especially self-efficacy barriers, in terms of increasing women's confidence to perform BSE effectively.

Summary

The HBM is a useful framework for investigating health behaviours, although some studies have produced conflicting findings. In addition, the model has been criticized for a reliance on the notion that individuals are rational processors of information and its emphasis on the individual (at the expense of the social and economic environment). The model also does not overtly take into account the role of emotions and their potential influence (e.g. fear). It is important to highlight that the model was originally developed to predict whether people would, for example, obtain immunizations and it continues to be useful at predicting one-time health behaviours, rather than at predicting habitual behaviours.

◉ The Theory of Planned Behaviour

The **Theory of Planned Behaviour** (TPB) built on the **Theory of Reasoned Action** which was developed by Ajzen and Fishbein (1970, 1980). This original model proposed that behaviour could be predicted by looking at a person's intention to engage in a particular behaviour, and that this intention is in turn predicted by the individual's attitude towards the behaviour and the perceived social norm. The TPB built upon this and introduced the notion of perceived behavioural control into the equation and suggested that how much a person believed they had control over a particular behaviour was important (Figure 3.2).

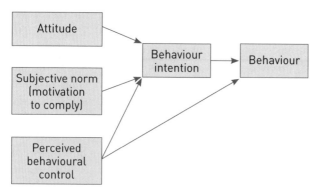

Figure 3.2 Theory of Planned Behaviour
Source: Adapted from Ajzen, I. (1991). The theory of planned behaviour. *Organizational Behavior and Human Decision Processes*, 50, 179–211. With permission from Elsevier.

The TPB consists of three core elements:

- *Attitudes:* positive or negative feelings about engaging in a particular behaviour. It is important to remember that your attitudes are also a function of your beliefs.
- **Subjective norms**: these are an individual's beliefs about whether or not other people would support them in their engaging in a new behaviour and whether they are motivated to follow the beliefs of these important others, who may be family, friends, or perhaps partners.
- *Perceived behavioural control:* the extent to which a person believes they can successfully engage in a particular behaviour. It is a combination of that person's past experience with the behaviour as well as their beliefs about their ability to engage in the behaviour. For example, if you are trying to lose weight, but have failed in the past to resist a particular brand of ice cream, and you doubt whether your willpower is strong enough to resist eating it now, your perceived behavioural control will be low. Perceived behavioural control is also thought to have a direct link to behaviour, as well as having a causal link to intentions.

By way of example, if an individual believed that reducing their alcohol intake would make their life more productive and be beneficial to their health (attitude to behaviour) and, at the same time, believed that the important people in their life wanted them to cut down (subjective norm), and finally, also believed that they were capable of drinking less alcohol, this would predict high intentions to reduce their level of alcohol intake (behavioural intention).

What is the evidence for the Theory of Planned Behaviour?

There has been some discussion as to whether other factors also need to be considered. These include moral norms and self-identity (e.g. Connor and Armitage, 1998; Sheeran, 2002). Another factor which has more recently been mentioned is that of anticipated regret. This means that the perception that in the future we will regret undertaking a particular behaviour may influence our intention to act. In addition, there has been discussion about whether or not intentions are actually translated into practice – this is known as the **intention–behaviour gap**. Some researchers (e.g. Sniehotta et al., 2005) have suggested that participants should be encouraged to engage in **action planning** – making a detailed plan about how, when and where the behaviour in question can be implemented – because the process of doing so increases the likelihood that intentions will be translated into behaviour.

Nevertheless, the TPB argues that the key factor which precedes our actual engagement in health behaviours is our behavioural intention. In other words, if we intend to engage in a particular behaviour, research has shown that there is an increased likelihood that we will do so. Whether or not we have an intention to behave in a particular way will depend on the three factors described above: attitudes, subjective norms and perceived behavioural control. The TPB has been successfully applied to many different types of behaviour including smoking (Rise et al., 2008), alcohol consumption (Abraham et al., 2007), sexual behaviours (Gredig et al., 2006), health screening attendance (Cooke and French, 2008), exercise (Boudreau and Godin, 2009), food choice (Wong and Mullen, 2009) and testicular self-examination (McLenahan et al., 2007).

Applying the Theory of Planned Behaviour

Cardiac rehabilitation is proven to benefit people who have had a cardiac event, but uptake of rehabilitation services can be low. Some studies show that only 21% of patients attend a programme. Some studies have suggested that psychological factors, such as the way in which a patient understands their illness, might influence attendance. In order to explore whether uptake of cardiac rehabilitation services could be improved, Wyer and colleagues (2001) applied the TPB to the process of inviting patients to attend rehabilitation programmes.

Eighty-seven patients took part in the study and were assigned to either a control group, which received treatment as normal, or an experimental group, which received two letters designed using the principles of the TPB. The first letter was sent out three days after the cardiac event, in which they were told about the cardiac rehabilitation programme and were invited to attend. The second letter was sent out three weeks after the cardiac event to those who had accepted the invite to attend the rehabilitation programme:

- *Letter: introduction* – 'Like many other patients who have had a heart attack, you will shortly be offered a place on a cardiac rehabilitation programme.'

- *Letter: perceived control* – 'During this programme you will be offered advice and information on how best to recover after a heart attack. It will be up to you to follow these if you want to recover as well and as quickly as possible. Experience has shown that the more effort you put in, the more quickly results will be achieved.' This paragraph is phrased in such a way as to encourage the perception of patients that they will have some control over their progress.
- *Letter: subjective norm* – 'The medical and nursing professions recommend that people who have had an MI should attend a cardiac rehabilitation programme.' Here the letter is phrased in such a way that patients will perceive that it is normal to attend cardiac rehabilitation after a cardiac event.
- *Letter: attitude* – 'This is because those who attend such a programme are more likely to recover sooner and better than those who do not attend. In addition, research has shown that attendance can reduce the chances of dying from another heart attack.' This last part of the letter is phrased in such a way as to positively influence patients' attitude towards the programme.

The researchers found that uptake of cardiac rehabilitation programmes increased and that those in the experimental group were not only significantly more likely to accept the invite to the cardiac rehabilitation programme, they were also more likely to attend the programme. They concluded that the TPB acted as a guide to persuading patients to accept the offer of cardiac rehabilitation and to encourage them to attend after they had accepted. Wyer and colleagues (2001) argued that it enhanced motivation in those who had not yet decided to attend and increased the likelihood of the implementation of action in those who had decided to attend.

Summary

Reviews tend to support the TPB. It has been widely tested and success-fully applied to a range of health behaviours. It incorporates important cognitive variables and acknowledges the potential role of social pressure. The TPB has identified a number of factors that might be important for understanding how and why we make decisions about which health behaviours to engage in. It has been less successful at explaining the intention–behaviour gap.

👁 Stages of Change Model

The **Stages of Change Model** is also known as the Transtheoretical Model (TTM) of behaviour change. The TTM was originally developed by Prochaska and DiClemente (1983) as a way of synthesizing 18 therapies that described the processes involved in generating and maintaining change. This model recognizes that behaviour change is a complex process and that individuals make changes in a gradual fashion, and not necessarily in a neat and logical order. A key part of the TTM suggests that people move from one stage to another in a spiral fashion, sometimes missing out stages and at other times slipping back to earlier stages before moving forward again. The model is often represented as a spiral (Figure 3.3).

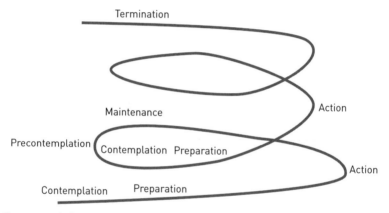

Figure 3.3 The Stages of Change Model
Source: Adapted from Prochaska, J.O., Diclemente, C.C. and Norcross, J.C. (1992). In search of how people change: Applications to addictive behaviours. *American Psychologist,* 47, 1102–14. © 1992 by the American Psychological Association. Reprinted with permission.

The model proposes five key stages of change:

- *Precontemplation:* individuals in this stage lack awareness of the problem behaviour and have no intentions or plans to change the behaviour in the foreseeable future (e.g. I have no intention to stop smoking). They are not motivated to make any changes and may underestimate the benefits of any potential changes in behaviour.
- *Contemplation:* characterized by a growing awareness of the costs of the negative behaviour as well as their personal susceptibility.

People in this stage are out of the 'ignorance is bliss' stage and are beginning to realize that making a change could be a good idea. People in this stage may start to look for information on the subject in question, although they may lack confidence in their ability to make a change. In short, they begin to think seriously about changing their behaviour, but have not yet acted.

- *Preparation:* individuals make a commitment to change their behaviour and start to make plans as to how they can begin to change their behaviour. This stage is characterized by the preparation of oneself and one's social world for the intended change in behaviour.
- *Action:* this is when they are actually engaged in a new behaviour (stopping smoking). The behaviour change is now public. Although the risk of relapse at this stage is high, people often receive a lot of support from their family and friends because they have made a public commitment to changing their behaviour.
- *Maintenance:* this is reached when people sustain the behavioural change over time, typically six months (I will continue not to smoke). People receive less social support during this stage because they have already engaged in action, but support is still important in terms of maintaining the new behaviour.

In addition to the stages outlined above, the model places emphasis on the role of evaluating the perceived pros and cons of changing behaviour as well as taking into account one's confidence in one's ability to implement the change in behaviour. However, much of the focus of research to date has been directed at the stage elements of the model. It is because of this focus of attention that the model has come to be described as the Stages of Change Model, rather than the Transtheoretical Model.

What is the evidence for the Stages of Change Model?

Armitage (2009: 197) notes that the different stages of the model have 'great intuitive appeal' and, indeed, a number of studies have demonstrated support for the usefulness of the model, but Albery and Munafo (2008) point out that there are critics who suggest that behaviour change might not necessarily be reflected in differences in processes between the stages, but that any change might be a result of the same processes varying across the whole change-related span. Similarly, Armitage (2009) picks up on the fact that much research has focused on the stage element of the model at the expense of the model in its entirety. He argues that researchers should revisit the origins of the Transtheoretical Model and consider conducting research with a wider focus than simply that of the different stages. Nevertheless, the Stages of Change Model has been successfully applied to a vast array of health behaviours including smoking (Siru et al., 2009), condom use (Tung et al., 2009) and drinking (Bertholet et al., 2009).

A major implication for interventions that has been demonstrated is that the nature of the intervention must be matched to the stage of change of the target individuals. So, for example, supplying participants with information about the health consequences associated with a particular health-impairing behaviour is most likely to be effective for individuals who are either in a precontemplation or a contemplation stage. Once a decision to act has been taken, action or maintenance-oriented information, perhaps focused on enhancing the self-efficacy of a person with regard to changing their behaviour, will be more effective. Therefore a key feature of this model is that rather than aiming at typical members of a target population, it is targeted at individuals on the basis of their stage of change.

Applying the Stages of Change Model

DiClemente and colleagues (1991) explored the application of the Stages of Change Model to smokers recruited for a smoking cessation programme. Specifically, this explored the suggestion underpinning the Stages of Change Model, which proposes that smokers move through a series of stages as they successfully change their smoking habit. The participants (all smokers) who they recruited were in precontemplation (n = 166), contemplation (n = 794) and preparation (n = 506) and were compared on smoking history. They all completed an array of measures including:

- *Smoking abstinence measure* – assesses the smoker's level of confidence that they will not smoke in 20 challenging situations.
- *The perceived stress scale* – measures how unpredictable, uncontrollable and overloaded respondents say their lives are.
- *Physical tolerance to nicotine* – measured using the Fagerström Tolerance Questionnaire (Fagerström, 1978). This looks at number of cigarettes smoked, minutes to first morning cigarette, smoking while ill and so on, to create a picture of addiction.

- *Smoking decisional balance scale* – measures the individual's perception of the pros and cons of smoking.
- *Smoking processes of change scale* – measures the different processes of change as linked with the Stages of Change Model.

DiClemente and colleagues (1991) concluded that the Stages of Change Model was useful in terms of predicting the outcome of smoking cessation programmes. At both one and six months, those in the preparation stage were more likely to have tried to quit. Specifically, those in the preparation stage smoked less, were less addicted, had higher self-efficacy, rated the pros of smoking as less and the costs as more, and had tried to quit more often than those in other groups. Similarly, at one month, three times as many contemplators and seven times as many preparation stage smokers made a 24-hour quit attempt when compared with precontemplators. The research team concluded that the model was useful in terms of identifying where people were in the stages and, therefore, what interventions may best suit them.

Summary

The Stages of Change Model proposes a sequence through which individuals progress as they make changes in their health behaviours. Although there are some contradictory findings in the existing research literature, a key strength of the model lies in its identification of the five stages of change. Theoretically, if we can identify what stage an individual is at, we can tailor interventions that will suit that particular level of change. In matching stage of change with intervention type, we have a potentially powerful behaviour change tool.

Problems with models of behaviour change

This chapter has focused on three of the most commonly used models of behaviour change. However, there are many other models, each of which focuses on slightly different or overlapping constructs. This can lead to confusion in the research literature as to which models are appropriate or effective.

A key problem facing behaviour models is the intention–behaviour gap, highlighted earlier in the chapter. Pascal Sheeran called this the 'tiramisu effect' in his keynote speech at the Division of Health

Psychology 2005 annual conference. What he meant by this was that although you may have good intentions to eat healthily when you go out to dinner, when the puddings are explained to you, you find that you just cannot resist the tiramisu. There is therefore a need for more researchers to focus on, and increase our understanding of, the mechanisms underlying the intention–behaviour gap.

In a paper exploring the effect of life crises on subsequent behaviour change, Ogden (2007) suggests that behaviour change models emphasize behaviour change as the result of a slow process of a combination of cognitive shifts and the development and implementation of behavioural intentions or plans. It is possible, however, that these implementations and plans may only facilitate change in the short term, rather than the 'longer term sustained changes which are required if an individual's health status is to benefit' (Ogden and Hills, 2008: 421). Likewise, Sniehotta (2009) notes that research in behaviour change is largely what he calls 'shortitudinal' – in other words, studies have short follow-up periods and rely on self-report data. In a similar vein, Michie and Abraham (2008) make a plea for more scientific reporting from researchers applying social cognitive models of behaviour change. There is therefore a need for more coherent methodological and scientific reporting of the studies concerning these models.

Social cognitive models of behaviour change have achieved a degree of success in identifying the factors that are thought to be linked to whether or not we engage in behaviour change. This has been clearly shown in reviews published by Armitage and Connor (2002) and Sheeran (2002). However, as we have noted, these models also have some shortcomings. Roger Ingham (1993) described social cognition models as 'old clothes fit only for the jumble'. However, Mielewczyk and Willig (2007: 812) pick up on this theme and suggest that social cognition researchers have been reluctant to

> abandon the old clothes, preferring instead to make repeated adjustments to their darts and waistbands (i.e. to the definition and measurement of their component variables) and to dress them up with a variety of beads, baubles and bangles (in the form of supplementary variables) in the ongoing struggle to improve both their fit and appearance.

They go on to argue that one of the reasons we find it so difficult to predict health behaviour might be found in our assumption that there is such a thing as 'health behaviour'. They note that we have tended to describe health behaviours as discrete, narrowly defined, observable pieces of action. They make the exciting suggestion that health behaviours may not be such simple discrete actions after all, but are very much context specific. Thus, they suggest a key factor we need to understand when considering behaviour change concerns the participant's use of language. If we focus on the use of language, we can unpick the different meanings associated with health behaviours:

> For example, exploring the differences between 'having sex', 'making love' and 'fucking' may help us understand why condom use may be compatible with one but not another of these practices. Similarly an examination of the many different ways in which people refer to …. 'eating behaviour' (e.g. doing lunch, having dinner, sharing a meal, snacking, dining, nibbling, stuffing oneself, having a bite to eat, treating oneself, and so on) can reveal a wide range of social practices which involve food in one way or another. What is eaten and how much of it, and the extent to which people will find it difficult to implement healthy eating guidelines, may well depend upon which of these practices they perceive themselves to be engaged in at the time. (Mielewczyk and Willig, 2007: 830)

They conclude their paper by arguing that a new look for health behaviour research is required. They suggest that one way to achieve this is to

> throw out the old clothes and to embark upon the task of acquiring a new wardrobe containing a wide range of diverse articles of clothing which can be mixed and matched in order to generate a variety of different outfits to suit different occasions. (Mielewczyk and Willig, 2007: 831)

◉ Conclusion

This chapter has focused on the key models of behaviour change which have developed as a means of identifying, evaluating and changing health behaviours. Three models in particular have been described: the Health Belief Model, the Theory of Planned Behaviour and the Stages of Change Model. We have explored why there is a need for such models and have evaluated the utility of these existing models.

In a recent paper, Chris Armitage (2009: 195) stated that:

> health behaviours are not only one of the dominant causes of mortality in advance 'economy' countries, they are potentially modifiable which means that in contrast with many other remedies, behaviour change represents a potentially cost-efficient means of reducing mortality.

It is with this in mind that attention has been paid to applying these behaviour change models in the field of health promotion. The next section of this book focuses on what health promotion is and how it is planned, implemented and evaluated.

Further reading

Armitage, C. (2009). Is there utility in the transtheoretical model? *British Journal of Health Psychology*, 14, 195–210.

Mielewczyk, F. and Willig, C. (2007) Old clothes and an older look: The case for a radical makeover in health behaviour research. *Theory and Psychology*, 17(6), 811–37.

Key search terms

Health-impairing behaviour, health protective behaviour, Health Belief Model, Theory of Planned Behaviour, Stages of Change Model

Health Promotion

Chapter 4

What is health promotion?

⟨⊙⟩ Introduction

Health promotion is concerned with finding ways to encourage health behaviours. Although we may not realize it

> at some point in our lives, we have all been the recipient of some form of health promotion activity, whether it be through being exposed to health promotion leaflets in doctor's surgeries, or viewing the large-scale messages developed for television, radio or billboards. (Albery and Munafo, 2008: 199)

In this chapter, we will examine:
- What health promotion is
- Different approaches to implementing health promotion

⟨⊙⟩ What is health promotion?

Health promotion is a term that is widely used, but rarely defined by those using it. There is often an implicit assumption that we all know what health promotion means. A closer inspection of the literature shows that not only has this term been widely used, but it has also been applied in a variety of ways. This is a problem that was highlighted by Tannahil (1985), who suggested that health promotion was a meaningless concept precisely because it has been used so differently. Naidoo and Wills (2003) note that the way in which health promotion can be defined is linked to the way in which we view health. Since how we view health changes over time, so too, the definition of health promotion has altered. As such, early approaches to health promotion were very much grounded in the medical model and so had a strong focus on disease prevention. A recent example includes the development of a programme designed to minimize the impact of swine flu. This approach relies on there being an infrastructure that is capable of delivering the programme. In other words, in order to achieve the aim of preventing swine flu, such approaches rely on there being trained personnel, equipment, lab facilities, the development of an effective vaccine and so on.

Medical models continue to have relevance for specific health issues, but more recently, the focus has shifted towards encompassing the health and wellbeing of whole populations. This means that instead of health being seen as the responsibility of individuals, there is a growing recognition that social and environmental factors also have a role to play, and that they therefore need to be taken into account when planning health promotion.

Although not yet fully part of the mainstream acceptance of the need to recognize social and environmental factors, it is important at this point to highlight the field of **complementary and alternative medicine** (CAM). This is a field which is fast gaining popularity with the public, whilst steadily gaining credibility with more traditional approaches to healthcare (Hill, 2003). Indeed, it has been argued that 'health promotion in the 21st century cannot afford to ignore developments in CAM' (Hill, 2003: 270). The reasoning behind this assertion is that because many approaches to CAM have similar underlying concepts and principles to those of health promotion (Gibson et al., 1995), constructive communication between the proponents of both approaches should take place in order that the fields of healthcare and promotion can benefit (Whitehead, 1999). This is an exciting and developing area which has potentially much to offer the field of health promotion.

Definitions of health promotion which encompass a wider view include that put forward by the World Health Organization (1984), which described health promotion as a 'process of enabling people to increase control over and improve their health' and that of Milio (1986) which suggested health promotion was all about 'making the healthy choice, the easier choice'. Similarly, Marks and colleagues (2005: 393) suggested that health promotion was a 'process or activity that facilitates the protection or improvement of the health status of individuals, groups, communities, or populations'. In line with this wider view of the remit of health promotion, the World Health Organization (1984) has made explicit five key principles that take account of the variety of influences on our health which are considered essential for health promotion:

1 That it should involve the population as a whole in the context of their everyday life and should not just focus on people at risk for specific diseases.

2 That it should be directed towards the causes of health and should ensure that the total environment (which is beyond the control of individuals) is conducive to health.

3 That it should combine diverse, but complementary methods or approaches (communication, education, legislation and so on).

4 That it should aim at effective public participation and should encourage self-help groups.

5 The recognition that health professionals have a role to play in nurturing and enabling health promotion.

Thus, the field of health promotion is currently based on the understanding that the behaviours we engage in, as well as the environment that we live in have an impact on our health (Bennett and Murphy, 1997). Indeed, a key assumption which underpins the field of health promotion is that making appropriate changes in our behaviour and wider environment will result in an improvement in our health. The remainder of this chapter focuses on how such changes might be encouraged.

◉ Approaches to health promotion

There are currently three main approaches to health promotion initiatives – the behaviour change approach, the self-empowerment approach and the community development approach (Marks et al., 2005). Each approach takes a different view as to the best way to focus on changing health behaviours:

1 Proponents of the **behaviour change approach** argue that health promotion should focus on altering individuals' thinking processes (cognitions, such as beliefs about the importance of different behaviours).

2 The **self-empowerment approach** is based on the premise that changes in health behaviours are most likely to be implemented if

an individual feels that they are in control of both their social and internal environments. The more we feel in control (self-empowered), the more influence we feel we have over the decisions we make concerning our health. If we feel in control, we are more likely to take action. Self-empowerment approaches therefore encourage engagement and involvement in health-related activities by increasing individuals' perceptions of control over their social and internal environments.

3 The **community development approach** emphasizes the relationship between individual health status and the social and health context that individuals inhabit.

The behaviour change approach

At the centre of the behaviour change approach is the argument that if we know what beliefs an individual holds about the merits of taking protective action (changing or avoiding a behaviour), as well as the beliefs they hold about the risks associated with engaging in a particular behaviour, we can then work out which beliefs need to be targeted or challenged in order to bring about a corresponding change in behaviour.

Proponents of this approach aim to encourage individuals to adopt healthy behaviours which are seen as the key to attaining improved health. This is a popular approach because it sees health as a property of individuals and assumes that people can make real improvements to their health by actively choosing to change their lifestyle. Behavioural campaigns are usually directed towards changing the target behaviour in a specific direction – perhaps encouraging people to give up smoking, adopt a healthy diet or take more regular exercise. The focus of attention is on individuals who are encouraged to make the requisite changes.

A recent example demonstrating how the behaviour change approach has been put into practice was reported by Scala and colleagues (2008). They explored the application of such an approach to a group of patients who had hypertension (high blood pressure). Hypertension has important health consequences and has been linked to coronary heart disease, heart failure, stroke and renal disease. It is a target of health promotion campaigns because it can be modified *if* lifestyle changes and preventive strategies are implemented (Burke et al., 2005; Gascon et al., 2004). Lifestyle changes linked to a reduction in blood pressure include weight loss, reducing salt intake, engaging in more exercise and reducing the consumption of alcohol (Appel et al., 2003). However, Scala and colleagues (2008) note that whilst people find it relatively easy to understand the lifestyle modifications required, the process of actually implementing them is more difficult.

In order to encourage behaviour change, Scala et al. (2008) took two groups of patients, each of which had hypertension. One group acted as a control group, the other as the intervention group. Both groups completed a questionnaire and had their blood pressure measured before the **health intervention** and then again 12 months later. In terms of the health intervention, those in the control group were simply given verbal information about hypertension, whilst those in the intervention group took part in a **focus group**. In the focus group, patients were encouraged to express their ideas, beliefs and concerns about hypertension. This enabled the researcher to identify any ambiguities and incorrect beliefs held by the patients. Those in the intervention group also took part in **role plays** designed to mimic a variety of situations. Taking part in the role plays enabled the researchers to provide accurate information about hypertension that was tailored to the level of knowledge demonstrated by the patients. It also enabled the patients to act out the lifestyle changes. This process of acting enabled the patients to identify potential obstacles to the process of implementing those changes and therefore allowed them to develop strategies they could use to overcome the obstacles, if and when they faced them in their 'real' lives.

The result of the study demonstrated reductions in both groups' blood pressure levels after one year. These reductions were more significant among members of the intervention group. Scala and colleagues (2008) suggest that the changes in the control group could have been induced by the collection of their blood pressure data. The process of collecting such data might have enhanced their awareness of their own hypertension status. The authors conclude that engaging in a behaviour change approach to health promotion was a powerful and effective tool for improving this patient group's health outcomes.

One criticism of the behaviour change approach is that it does not recognize the complex relationship between health beliefs and our ability to change them. This is because the behaviour change approach assumes that if people do not take responsible action to look after themselves, then they are to blame for the consequences. Therefore, this approach does not fully take into account the fact that social and environmental factors can have a mediating effect on our ability to implement change. A further criticism of this approach has been levelled by Sutton (2002), who points out that whilst behavioural approaches specify the types of beliefs which need to be changed in order for the target behaviour to change in the desired direction, the process by which beliefs can be changed is not addressed.

The potential influence of these factors has been studied in some depth by Darker and colleagues (2007a). They explored the complex relationship by means of a series of **semi-structured interviews** focusing on walking. Walking is the most common form of lifestyle physical activity (Siegel et al., 1995). However, previous research has shown that whilst adults in the UK hold positive beliefs about walking (walking is good for exercise and stress relief), more commonly, negative beliefs such as inclement weather and a perceived lack of time are also held and have a significant impact on the implementation of walking as a physical activity (Darker et al., 2007b). Given this information, it is perhaps not surprising to learn that in the UK over 60% of adult males and 75% of adult females do not undertake enough physical activity to benefit their health (Department of Health, 2004).

The aim of Darker and colleagues' (2007a) interview-based study was to explore in depth how walking was understood and whether participants' perception of walking matched that of health promotion campaigns. They found that although walking is generally conceived and portrayed by the field of health promotion as a form of physical activity that is most accessible to a range of people, the participants in their study classified walking differently according to context. Most commonly, they tended to see walking not as a form of exercise, but as 'a means to an end' (Darker et al., 2007a: 2175). Thus, participants described walking as a form of transport that was employed to get them from one location to another, rather than as a means of gaining exercise that could lead to health benefits. Walking in urban surroundings was considered to be an unpleasant and functional activity, whereas walking in rural surroundings was considered to be pleasurable and as a means of gaining exercise and benefiting from fresh air.

Darker and colleagues (2007a) suggest that in order to maximize the impact of behaviour change health promotion messages that promote walking, there is a need to address the misconceptions held by the targets of health promotion campaigns. In addition, mismatches between the health promotion campaign directions to walk more and participants' beliefs need to be explored in more depth so that a clearer message can be created. Their study has clearly shown how individuals' understandings and beliefs, as well as the social and environmental context in which the targeted activity takes place, have an impact on the likelihood of their engaging in the target behaviour. They conclude that in order to encourage people to change their behaviour, there is a need to understand the influence of all determinants on participants' willingness and ability to engage in behaviour change. In other words, it is not enough to simply focus on behaviour in isolation, a wider focus is required.

Self-empowerment approach

Underpinning the argument of the self-empowerment approach is the notion that if an individual feels that they are in control of their social and internal environments, they are more likely to engage in health promotion activities. The feeling of being in control empowers them to take control. Proponents of this approach suggest that it is important to help people to be in a position to identify their own health concerns, and to subsequently empower them to gain the skills and, perhaps most importantly, the confidence (self-belief) in their ability to act on their health concerns. This approach very clearly links in to the World Health Organization (1984) definition which highlights the importance of health promotion enabling people to gain control over their lives.

Smoking cessation programmes provide a clear example of the self-empowerment approach. Those who give up smoking have to deal with a number of different issues, including the loss of a powerful source of support (cigarettes), changing a well-established habit, and the potential experience of withdrawal symptoms. Bennett and Murphy (1997) suggest that smoking cessation programmes which recognize these potential problems and teach participants skills to deal with them, as well as skills to guard against relapse, are likely to be the most effective. In doing so, the health promoter gives the person attempting to cease smoking a set of skills from which they can draw. Feeling confident in their newly developed skills enhances the feeling of being able to cope with the process of giving up smoking. They feel empowered and as though they have an element of control over the process. Specific examples of this tailored approach might include helping individuals to recognize what the triggers are that lead them to smoke (e.g. habit, nicotine dependence, social pressure). Individuals will also be encouraged to think ahead about potentially high-risk situations. Thinking through such scenarios can help to prepare individuals to deal with these situations should they arise. The 'high-risk situations' will vary from person to person, but might include meeting friends in the pub or following a disagreement, where the previous habitual response would be to light a cigarette. For each scenario identified, the individual is encouraged to develop alternative responses that they can implement instead. This tailored approach is very much designed to empower the individual and improve their confidence in their ability to put into practice the health behaviour concerned.

Naidoo and Wills (2003) describe the self-empowerment approach as unique because it explicitly takes a step away from the more traditional approach, in which health professionals adopt an 'expert role', and moves towards a model where health professionals act as facilitators (coaches) and work with individuals to help them achieve their health goals. This approach is clearly tailored to individual needs and is very much 'client centred', but can also be applied on a much larger scale, in the form of the community development approach.

Community development approach

The community development approach emphasizes the relationship between individual health status and the social and health context individuals inhabit. Proponents of this approach argue that individual health status is dependent on environmental causes of illness and that in order to address these environmental causes of ill health, individuals need to act collectively as a community in order to bring change to their physical and social environment.

Before we can explore this approach in further detail, it is important to first establish what is meant by community. **Community** is a concept that is often used in discussions about health and healthcare. There are many different ways of defining community, the most common being:

- *Geography:* this approach to community suggests that health promotion campaigners can be assigned 'patches' or geographically bounded areas to work in. The assumption is that people living in the same area have the same concerns. Therefore health promotion campaigns should target geographical locations.
- *Culture:* this approach to community assumes that common cultural traditions might transcend geographical boundaries and unite otherwise scattered groups of people. The expectation is that

members of the same cultural community will help each other, share resources and have similar concerns. Therefore health promotion campaigns should target cultural groups.

- *Social stratification:* this implies that members of a community share networks of support, knowledge and resources according to their social classification. Therefore health promotion campaigns should target social groups, for example the 'working-class community' or the 'gay community'.

It is important to point out that interpretations of this concept of community are not as **homogeneous** as they might first appear. For example, any geographic community will include people whose primary identity is based on different factors. Indeed, most of us cannot be neatly categorized in terms of the three definitions outlined above. Most of us belong to several different communities and may categorize ourselves differently on the basis of the area of the city in which we live, our occupation, our race and our gender. By way of example, a person could be a lecturer, a practising psychologist, a mountain leader, a white female, a member of a local choir, a daughter, a sister, an aunty and an ex-wife. They might live in Bath, but their heart lies in the mountains of Snowdonia. In belonging to more than one category, we have many different links and it is perhaps too simplistic to define community as a 'body of people united by a common thread'.

It is clear that the meaning and significance of community differs according to the variable being considered. Indeed, Crawshaw and colleagues (2003) note that community is a complex concept and suggest that its nature and viability, as both a theoretical and social construct, have been the subject of much debate. Byrne (2001: 69) notes that it is 'used to refer to the significance of place and to shared identity and interests', and Connell and colleagues (2008: 184) highlight the 'problematic and nebulous nature of the term community'.

To illustrate this further, Connell and colleagues (2008) reviewed the literature reporting on community interventions designed to improve blood pressure control among black populations. They noted that many of the studies included in their review equated community with ethnicity. This is problematic, not least because ethnicity may or may not be the main factor which influences shared views and interests. Connell and colleagues (2008) concluded that there was a great need, not just to define cultural sensitivity, but also to assess how cultural sensitivity might influence health outcomes. They also called for an exploration of the assumptions made about the homogeneity of community, as the way in which this term is applied has implications for the potential effectiveness of health promotion interventions. When employing a community approach, it is important to think carefully about how 'community' is defined, because the particular definition employed will influence how community representatives are identified and communicated with.

Notwithstanding the definitional challenges, the community development approach has been seen as the central defining strategy for health promotion. This approach focuses on bringing about physical, social and environmental change that will have the effect of promoting health. In other words, the aim is to ensure not only that a healthy choice is available, but also that it is a realistic option. Such an approach involves a move away from a focus solely on individual behaviour, towards a focus that emphasizes the role played by the social structure and environment in determining health status (Green and Kreuter, 1999). In taking this wider focus, this approach also moves away from the potential scenario of 'victim-blaming' that can occur with approaches that take a more individual focus. Community participation and involvement is understood as a way of

> facilitating collective responses to community-defined health needs and enabling powerless and disadvantaged groups to have an effective voice in the policy decisions that affect their lives and health. (Farrant, 1991: 423)

If community approaches are to be effective, there are a number of obstacles that need to be overcome. A six-step model designed to address the key obstacles was developed (Yoo et al., 2004) and more recently implemented (Yoo et al., 2009):

1   *Entrée* highlights the difficulty of gaining access to the community concerned. As outsiders, health promoters may have to deal with uneasiness stemming from a fear among the community that process, strategies and outcomes will be imposed upon them, rather than developed by the community. Such wariness can be overcome through the development of transparent modes of communication and the building of relationships.

2   *Issue identification* concerns the process of identifying issues of relevance and importance to the community concerned. This is facilitated when community leaders are identified. These leaders then encourage participation in brainstorming exercises.

3 *Prioritization* is a process where the order of importance of the issues identified is agreed upon. This is something which is done by the community, not the health promotion personnel. Group agreement is required before an issue can be identified as the top priority.

4 *Strategy development*, whereby further discussion of the top priority issues is engaged in, in order to identify exactly how the issue impacts on the community and, in turn, to identify strategies that might be implemented to address the impact of the issue.

5 *Implementation* involves the community groups putting into practice the strategies identified in step four.

6 *Transition* is the process whereby the health promotion personnel, who have acted as facilitators throughout the collaboration, formally withdraw their involvement and hand over responsibility to the community leaders.

In spite of the problems with defining the term 'community' and actually implementing community approaches, both researchers and health promoters continue to implement community health promotion campaigns. For example, Blair and colleagues (2006) reported on a community-based oral health promotion campaign which focused on the dental health of five-year-old Glaswegian children. This 'community' was focused upon because such children reportedly have the poorest dental health in Scotland. They showed that, in particular, when the campaign was directed towards those five-year-olds living in the most deprived circumstances, the most significant changes in health outcomes were noted.

Summary

There are three main approaches to health promotion, all with the same aim in mind – moving from behaviour that has a negative impact on health to that which will either protect or improve health. However, each approach has a different focus and a different idea as to how best to achieve this aim. The behavioural approach focuses on changing beliefs, the self-empowerment approach on improving individuals' feelings of control over their internal and social environments, and the community approach on collective action to change the social and physical environments. The next section focuses on a key agent of communication that all three approaches have drawn upon in order to get their messages across; that of the mass media.

◉ Mass media

The **mass media** are powerful agents of communication that can reach large numbers of people. Mass media are defined by Corcoran (2007: 74) as 'any type of broadcast, printed or electronic communication medium that is sent to the population at large'. This definition includes audio-visual media (e.g. television), print-based media (e.g. newspapers, leaflets, billboards) and electronic media (e.g. internet, mobile phones). Over 80% of the population say that the media are their most important source of health information and their use in health promotion has a long history. As far back as 1604, King James I of England made a public declaration that smoking was:

> a custom, loathsome to the eye, hateful to the nose, harmful to the brain, dangerous to the lungs and in the black stinking fume thereof nearest resembling the horrible Stygian smoke of the pit that is bottomless. (transcribed by Jones, 1985: 1763)

A royal public declaration in the 1600s would have been the equivalent of a viral email that is read and forwarded by exponentially more people until the message has spread far and wide. The mass media, then and now, are an extremely effective method for fast transmission to a wide audience (Tones and Green, 2004).

Corcoran (2007) divides mass media into four main categories: television, radio, print-based media and electronic media:

- *Television* has been identified as being the leading source of media information about health issues (Risi et al., 2004). It is used to deliver health information, for example smoking cessation information, through health campaigns, as well as by including health stories in popular soap operas. Health behaviour can then be modelled in a positive manner in the hope that viewers will learn appropriate health behaviours.
- *Radio* has also been used to promote health through advertisements, educational messages and public service announcements, as well as incorporating health messages in popular radio series. One example is the popular BBC Radio Four soap opera *The Archers*. This was started in 1950 and was produced in collaboration with the Ministry of Agriculture. It was hoped that farmers would listen for the stories, but along the way pick up messages that would help

them feed a Britain that was at the time still subject to food rationing. *The Archers* ceased to be a formal education resource in 1972, but continues to cover issues of health importance, including more recently anorexia and cancer.

- The most common form of *print-based media* is leaflets. They have shown consistent results in terms of their ability to raise health awareness, but there is less evidence to support the idea that leaflets can change behaviour. A more novel approach to the use of print-based media concerns the health messages printed on cigarette packets. O'Hegarty et al. (2006) suggest that the inclusion of such information has promoted interest in smoking cessation. They also suggested that the inclusion of graphic warning labels might be more effective then a reliance on text alone.
- The use of *electronic media* in health promotion is appealing and is increasingly being used in healthcare. For example, Corcoran (2007) notes that populations are encouraged to use modern technology as a means of accessing health information. The vast amount of information available on the internet can be accessed by anyone who has access to a computer. This approach has been called **e-health**.

A key advantage of the use of information technology (IT) is that rather than being a passive recipient of health information, there is scope for the IT user to be actively engaged in seeking information. As access to the internet has grown, so too have health-seeking behaviours, as patients look for information that can help them to manage their conditions, or in some cases seek information that may help them to diagnose their symptoms. The internet not only provides information, but is also a resource which can be used by those seeking support as they struggle to come to terms with their particular health condition. For example, it is becoming common for patients to use online message boards (instead of joining face-to-face support groups), as a means of making contact with other people in similar health situations. Through this medium, patients can talk freely in a non-time-limited manner about issues linked to their condition. While face-to-face support groups provide members with the opportunity to help each other cope (Yaskowich and Stam, 2003), online message boards provide similar opportunities (Adams et al., 2005; Bargh et al., 2002; Harvey-Berino et al., 2002; Loader et al., 2002; Rodham et al., 2009; Woodruff et al., 2001), but also open up the possibility for discussion of taboo topics and forms of self-expression that are often unavailable in the everyday offline life of users (Adams et al., 2005; Bargh et al., 2002).

As such, the internet is a useful resource which can be used to convey health information. However, a note of caution is needed, for just as the internet is considered to be a useful resource because it is so easily accessed, this accessibility may also be problematic. Anyone can put information on the internet, and at times it can be difficult to determine the reliability and accuracy of information posted – there is much scope for misinformation.

Indeed, the internet is a relatively new form of health communication which is useful both for healthcare professionals and laypeople (Winefield, 2006). It has the potential to be a powerful resource, one which meets patients' health information needs as well as their need for support (Berland et al., 2001). Whilst online information can encourage the adoption of healthier lifestyles and behaviours, detect potential medical problems early and provide information about effective treatments, it can also be a means for leading patients to develop destructive beliefs, harmful treatments and false medical understandings (Mittman and Cain, 1999).

Planned and unpaid mass media opportunities

Most campaigns which employ mass media are carefully planned and budgeted for by health promotion personnel. Such campaigns are designed, developed and targeted in order to meet specific objectives. Examples of such campaigns include National No Smoking Day or World AIDS Day, both of which aim to raise awareness about preventive health behaviours and to educate the public about the implications of engaging in health-damaging behaviour.

In contrast, occasionally a news item fortuitously highlights a health issue. When this happens, health promoters can view this as a positive opportunity and use the news story as a means of publicizing a health promotion message. Such unpaid publicity has the advantage of low cost and greater credibility because messages are not seen as being sent directly from health promotion organizations. However, it can be hard to sustain a high level of coverage for more than a few days because the mass media have no responsibility to promote health and tend to quickly move on to the next story.

When the mass media do publicize a health-promoting message, it may be because the issue has become newsworthy because it involves a celebrity. For example, Wallack and colleagues (1993) note that media coverage of AIDS in America was relatively sparse until media celebrities (such as the basketball player 'Magic' Johnson) were diagnosed as being HIV positive, at which point media coverage soared. The media may also promote a healthy message when an issue is of interest because of the unusual story. For example, in 2006, the BBC News website reported the story of two top officials from Japan's Health Ministry who were put on a public diet as a means of getting the ministry's message on obesity across. These two ministers pledged to shed at least 5 kg each and were pictured with their shirts raised as they had the midriffs measured. They agreed to chart their progress on a blog on the ministry's website over the following six months, detailing the amount of exercise they had taken each day. The ministry aimed to highlight the dangers of a poor diet. Obesity is increasing in Japan and officials fear a rise in related illnesses such as diabetes. This story gave health promoters the opportunity to raise the profile of the 'obesity problem' in the UK.

Finally, mass media will publicize stories which highlight dramatic or tragic issues. An example of such a story in the UK was that of Leah Betts, who had taken ecstasy and subsequently collapsed at her eighteenth birthday party. Her parents released photographs to the British media of her connected to a life support machine, in order to highlight the dangers of the popular use of drugs among teenagers. Leah died four days after she collapsed. A billboard campaign was later introduced with the tag line 'Sorted – just one ecstasy tablet took Leah Betts.' In addition, a short film entitled *Sorted* was produced and shown to up to half a million British schoolchildren in the aftermath of Leah's death as a means of raising awareness of the potential effects of drug use.

One problem with unplanned media coverage is that health promoters have not influenced the message being portrayed. This can be problematic when incorrect information is publicized and can result in serious negative consequences in terms of health outcomes. For example, in 1995, the regulatory authority in the UK issued a warning about an increased risk of blood clots in the veins of women taking a specific kind of oral contraceptive (the pill). This was done before formal publication of the scientific papers involved, and resulted in a huge media 'pill scare'. The manner in which the information was released has been criticized, as has the way in which the media reported the information. The result of the scare was a loss of confidence in the oral contraceptive pill in general. The loss in confidence led many women to cease taking the pill and there was a corresponding rise in abortion rates (Szarewski and Mansour, 1999).

Advantages and disadvantages of mass media

Having highlighted the key forms that health promotion approaches employing mass media can take, we now focus on the debate in the literature concerning what it is possible for health promotion campaigns employing mass media to achieve. There is consensus that such approaches can achieve relatively inexpensive wide coverage (Randolf and Viswanath, 2004), which can be employed locally, nationally and, indeed, internationally. It is therefore a powerful tool for reaching a large number of people simultaneously. For example, Atkin (2001) suggests that campaigns which employ mass media are most likely to influence behaviour change if their focus is on behaviours that are already receptive to change. Corcoran (2007) suggests that this might include maintaining a behaviour that is already being performed, such as using sun cream to protect against burning and skin cancer. Similarly, a smoker who has begun to consider giving up is more likely to be prompted to take action, compared to a smoker who has no intention of giving up.

Mass media can also convey simple information and single messages such as 'put babies to sleep on their backs' (Naidoo and Wills, 2003: 254). Such simple messages are thought to change behaviour if **enabling factors** already exist. Thus, a message encouraging physical activity five times a week could change the behaviour of someone who already had a subscription to a local gym and who currently exercised three times a week. Their behaviour could be influenced, for two reasons:

1 A habit was established – exercising regularly – indicating a likelihood that such a person would hold beliefs positively disposed towards the health-promoting message.
2 Given that the person already had a subscription, there would be no further financial implications for them of increasing the number of sessions they engaged in.

Mass media campaigns can also increase knowledge through the provision of simple health educational messages. However, increasing knowledge does not automatically result in a corresponding change in behaviour. Nevertheless, in providing information, mass media can be a conduit for raising health issues in the general public consciousness. As I write, the mass media are currently being used as a means of providing information highlighting the rate at which fertility decreases for women after the age of 30 years. The information offered suggests that more and more women are making the decision to start a family at a later stage in life, but are then discovering that they have fertility problems. Many are then embarking on what can be an emotionally and physically (not to mention financially) draining process of fertility treatment, which has a small likelihood of success. The intention behind this education and awareness raising is to encourage women to consider the issue of fertility at an earlier, rather than a later life stage.

Thus, mass media have been used extensively as tools to promote health (Noar, 2006) and are considered to result in behaviour change, providing the targeted behaviour change is something that the recipients of the health promotion message are receptive to, and enabling factors are present. These caveats make clear the limitations of the mass media as tools for influencing behaviour change. A key issue concerns the influence of factors which may be outside the individual's control. Therefore social, environmental or political factors might restrict ability to implement the health behaviour being promoted. If such barriers exist, the success of the health promotion campaign will be severely limited. Finally, mass media cannot convey complex information or messages and consequently they cannot be used to teach skills which may facilitate behaviour change. Therefore, whilst mass media campaigns undoubtedly reach a wide audience, it is not possible to provide a tailored message which can be adapted to individual levels of knowledge or types of health belief held. It is also impossible to provide one-to-one support which may further facilitate behaviour change. However, as Corcoran (2007) notes, campaigns have more recently begun to include helpline numbers and website addresses, which can increase the level of support available.

Multimedia: the solution to the limitations of mass media?

Clearly, campaigns utilizing mass media can achieve a number of objectives. The wise health promotion campaigner must be aware of the limitations of mass media. In order to overcome these limitations, researchers and practitioners suggest that rather than relying on one method, a combination of methods should be employed. In this way, mass media can play a key role in health promotion. This integrated approach is known as 'multimedia'. By way of an example, Corcoran (2007) suggests that in a student population, flyers, email messages, induction packs and on-campus stalls may be considered more likely to be effective than simply relying on one method such as posters.

◉ Legislation

Legislation can have a powerful and immediate impact on health behaviours. As such, Bennett and Murphy (1997) note that legislation is an efficient way of affecting the environment and context in which health behaviours are implemented. Legislative approaches tend to focus on measures that act to create barriers which reduce the cues to unhealthy behaviours. These measures include restricting availability, taxation and restricting advertising:

- *Restricting availability:* The government has tried to reduce health risks through legislation. In 2007, for example, it introduced laws banning smoking in public places, and it also became illegal to sell tobacco products to anyone under the age of 18 (previously 16) in England (Abraham et al., 2008), which was followed in 2009 by increased sanctions for the persistent selling of tobacco to people under the age of 18 years.

- *Taxation:* As the price of something increases, this impacts on the level of consumption. Taxation in relation to health promotion has tended to focus on the issues of smoking and alcohol. Jeffery and colleagues (1990) pointed out that the public response to such changes tends to be supportive when the focus is on widely accepted harmful products such as alcohol and cigarettes but is a far less popular option when it is directed towards unhealthy foods.

- *Restricting advertising:* When a product is advertised widely, this process raises awareness of the product concerned and can therefore act to establish social norms, which can be interpreted as a source of social approval, which in turn can reinforce unhealthy behaviours (Bennett and Murphy, 1997). Therefore restricting advertising may have an impact on consumption. For example, Bennett and Murphy (1997: 89) note that bans on advertising smoking have been accompanied by significant falls in consumption. Similarly, Smith and Foxcroft (2009) reported an association between exposure to alcohol advertising and subsequent alcohol consumption.

👁 Conclusion

Health promotion is the process of positively influencing the health behaviours of individuals, groups, communities and populations. To further illustrate these points, I draw from the work of Naidoo and Wills (2003: 84), who state that:

> It is easy for practitioners to confine their health promotion role to offering information and advice on how to adopt a healthier lifestyle. However, for people to make such changes, the factors and situations which led them to adopt 'unhealthy' behaviours need to be addressed. People may smoke because of stress, even though they know it is bad for their health. Others may use an illegal drug because it is widely used by their peer group and is part of their social life. Equally, it is easier for some people to make healthy choices than others. It is easier to eat a diet with fresh fruit and vegetables for people with reasonable incomes who have easy access to supermarkets or high street shopping. Some factors affecting individuals' health are outside individual control: inadequate housing, busy roads, lack of child care.

This chapter has described the field of health promotion. In particular, the different approaches to implementing health promotion have been outlined and examples of each approach provided. In addition, a key method for transmitting the health promotion message has been examined. The next chapter explores how health promotion approaches can be evaluated.

👁 Further reading

Corcoran, N. (ed.) (2007). *Communicating Health: Strategies for Health Promotion*, Sage: London.

👁 Key search terms

Health promotion, health behaviour, behaviour change

Chapter 5

Planning and evaluating health promotion

◉ Introduction

Having explored the theoretical underpinnings and implementation of health promotion campaigns in Chapter 4, we now turn our attention to the planning and evaluation of health promotion campaigns. The process of designing a health promotion campaign is something which requires care, thought and attention to detail. Throughout the whole planning process, it is of paramount importance to keep the question of evaluation at the forefront of all considerations.

In this chapter, we will examine:
- What evaluation is and why it is important
- Factors influencing the success of health promotion campaigns
- The process of planning health promotion campaigns
- How we can know if a health promotion campaign has had the desired effect

◉ What is evaluation and why is it important?

Evaluation has been defined as being the process by which we judge the worth or value of something (Ryechetnik et al., 2002). Naidoo and Wills (2003) argue that at its simplest level, evaluation is a process of appraising and assessing the work activities of the health promoter. However, the practicalities of evaluating health promotion campaigns are not so straightforward. Indeed, a complex process is involved which relies on the careful assessment and critical appraisal of the campaign in question, leading to a judgement as to the impact of the campaign and the development of suggestions for future action (World Health Organization, 1981). Thus, evaluation is used to demonstrate that the health promotion campaign in question has had a positive impact on the **health outcomes** of the **target population**. Put simply, Peberdy (1997: 269) suggests that evaluation consists of two elements:

1 identifying and ranking the criteria
2 gathering the kind of information that will allow you to assess whether the criteria are met.

The evaluation of health promotion campaigns is important, not least because evaluating whether or not campaigns achieved their aims helps to inform the development of future campaigns. If we cannot identify what it was about a campaign that was or was not successful, we will be unable to repeat the success, or avoid the pitfalls, in future health promotion activities. Furthermore, the process of evaluation enables health promoters to inform colleagues of the effectiveness (or otherwise) of different strategies. In sharing the outcomes of evaluation, a knowledge base is built which enables health promoters to make informed choices about which strategies or methods they employ in their own campaigns. In addition to the desire to learn lessons that will improve practice, there are likely to be financial pressures that encourage or demand evaluation. As such, it is also important to identify whether the desired outcomes of the health promotion campaign were achieved in the most economical manner. However, while the question 'Can the costs of the campaign be justified when compared to the impact of the campaign?' appears to be simple, the process of putting a monetary cost on the outcomes of campaigns is actually extremely difficult.

By way of example, in the medical field, evaluation of interventions usually consists of randomized controlled trials (RCTs), which are used to carefully compare alternative forms of intervention in order to identify which is most effective for most people. However, Naidoo and Wills (2003) point out that although RCTs are considered to be the 'gold standard' evaluation tool, they are not appropriate for use in the field of health promotion. This is because it can be difficult to isolate the exact effect of the intervention. It is also the case that behaviour change (the target of health promotion campaigns) is often subjective, takes place over the long term, and may be related to many factors outside the influence of the health promotion campaign. Whitelaw and Watson (2005) pick up on this problem in their paper, which reports a review of the evidence base for health promotion events. They suggest that at present, the evidence base demonstrating that health promotion has an impact is weak and inconsistent. They make some important points which we will pick up on throughout this chapter.

What factors influence the success of health promotion campaigns?

In this section we focus on some of the factors which have been shown to have an impact on the success of health promotion campaigns. The ability to communicate the core message of a health promotion campaign is of paramount importance. Characteristics of the person/body communicating the message, as well as how the message is put together can influence the effectiveness of the communication process.

Source characteristics

Research has consistently shown that the characteristics of those providing information can impact on its effectiveness. These characteristics include the credibility, perceived attractiveness, perceived power and similarity to the target audience. Bennett and Murphy (1997: 101) note that sources that are liked and considered to be similar to the person receiving the health promotion message are more likely to be considered attractive and to improve recall and attitude change than disliked or dissimilar sources. They suggest that we might be more likely to change our resistant attitudes and/or behaviours if we are asked to do so by people we consider to be attractive and credible, indeed, this is why many health promotion campaigns encourage popular celebrities to endorse the message being promoted. It is thought that these 'figureheads' enhance the perception of expertise and trustworthiness of the campaign. By way of example, Hoffner and Ye (2009) explored young adults' responses to news about using sunscreen and cancer. They reported that although the perceived similarity of the person portrayed in the health information to the adolescents was clearly an important factor which influenced adolescents' receptivity to the health message, more research is needed to clarify the process underlying this influence. In other words, they highlighted that while we can see that perceived similarity is important, we do not yet know why this is so. In particular, they call for more research looking into the process of how people compare themselves to those individuals who are depicted in health promotion messages, and how that process of comparison might impact on the perceived credibility of the message.

Message content

The way in which messages are couched can have a significant impact on how they are received. For example, messages that provide arguments from both sides of an issue are more effective than one-sided messages for individuals who are at the stage of contemplating behaviour change (the Stages of Change Model was discussed in Chapter 4), with those who have higher levels of education or those who know that the issue is complex and controversial. Furthermore, if an issue being addressed is complex, messages that have a conclusion or recommendations are more effective than those that do not. In contrast, if the issue is relatively straightforward, leaving the audience to make up their own minds can be a more effective approach (e.g. Amalraj et al., 2009; Edwards and Hugman, 1997; Mansoor and Dowse, 2006):

> Effectively communicating even the simplest and most welcome of messages to a dispersed and disparate audience is a substantial challenge. (Edwards and Hugman, 1997)

Fear arousal and message framing

Some health promotion messages use fear as a means of stimulating behavioural change. The idea is that the fear aroused in the target population will motivate them to change their behaviour and their attitudes (Albery and Munafo, 2008). However, research suggests that this underlying assumption does not always hold true. Some researchers have questioned the effectiveness of evoking fear when trying to persuade people to change (Ruiter et al., 2001).

One way in which fear can be generated is when messages emphasize that the risks are more likely to occur if a person does not act in a protective manner. This is called 'negative framing'. It is also possible to frame health messages in a positive manner by emphasizing the benefits of engaging in a health protective behaviour. Such outcomes are called **framing effects**. By way of an example, manipulating the way in which the risk of dying is framed can have an impact on how participants view the risk of death:

Positive frame: 99,991.7 out of 100,000 will not die
Negative frame: 0.0083% probability of dying

In the above example, the same information is presented; one framed positively, the other negatively. Whilst the data presented (risk of dying) is identical, the way in which it is framed influences the perception of the information. Thus, the positively framed data led to lower estimates of risk of death than the negatively framed data (Halpern et al., 1989). Similarly, people have been shown to be more likely to opt for treatment if they are told that there is a 95% chance of survival than if they are told there is a 5% chance of dying.

Interestingly, positive framing has also been shown to improve people's understanding of the information being presented. Armstrong and colleagues (2002) presented risk information using survival or mortality curves and found that people who received survival curves were significantly more accurate in answering questions about the information, as well as being significantly more likely to opt for the treatment in question than those who received mortality curves.

This is not to say that it is *always* better to frame information positively, sometimes it can be better to frame in terms of loss. For example, telling people about the risks of not being screened (loss framing) has been shown to lead to a greater uptake of the recommended behaviour than telling them about the benefits of being screened (Abood et al., 2005). Similarly, Sherman and colleagues (2006) explored the influence of framing on a message focusing on flossing. Participants completed a questionnaire designed to measure their orientation on two issues: their concern over the possibility of bad occurrences and their desire to move towards positive occurrences. Participants were then randomly assigned to either a gain-framed or a loss-framed flossing article. In the gain-framed article, the possible benefits of regular flossing were emphasized. In the loss-framed message, the potential dangers of not flossing were emphasized. What Sherman and colleagues (2006) found was that both those who had higher levels of desire for positive occurrences and who received a gain-framed message, along with those who had higher concerns over the possibility of bad occurrences and who received a loss-framed message, were more likely to subsequently report engaging in flossing than those who received messages which did not match their orientation. This study seems to demonstrate that it is not simply the way in which a message is framed which has an influence on individuals' subsequent behaviour; the data suggests that it is also important to take into account the fact that people who have a stronger focus on moving towards positive occurrences are more likely to respond to gain-framed health messages, whereas those with a stronger focus on the possibility of bad occurrences will be more likely to respond to loss-framed health messages.

Message context

Context also influences people's interpretations. For example, Parducci (1968) noted that a student might think that if her contraceptives failed on 5% of occasions, this would be 'quite often', whereas if she were absent from 5% of her lectures, this would be 'almost never'. Thus, Fox and Irwin (1998) suggest that the social, informational and motivational context in which beliefs are constructed and statements formulated provides a myriad of additional cues that influence what is expressed by speakers and what is understood by listeners.

Unrealistic optimism

The term **unrealistic optimism** refers to a person's appraisal of the likelihood that they will experience a particular health threat. If an individual thinks that they are personally at risk, they are more likely to engage in behaviour to counteract that risk. However, research has demonstrated that we as individuals tend to be unrealistically optimistic. This means that people show a tendency to believe that they are less likely to encounter or experience negative health and life events when compared to other people. Engaging in unrealistic optimism (Weinstein, 1987) can mean that health promotion messages are not acknowledged, and has been linked to numerous health and life events, including sexually transmitted diseases (e.g. Gerrard et al., 1996), heart disease (e.g. Marteau et al., 1995) and drink driving (e.g. Albery and Guppy, 1995). Such overoptimism is likely to impact on individuals' willingness to engage in appropriate health protective behaviours and is something which should be addressed in health promotion campaigns (Bennett and Murphy, 1997: 41).

Summary

We have shown that it is not easy to unpick the influence of the health promotion campaign from that of other environmental and social factors which might also play a role in changing behaviour. In this section, we have focused on the importance of the communication process. In particular, we have emphasized the potential impact that message content and source characteristics can have. It is therefore of paramount importance that these issues are also considered at the planning stage of any health promotion campaign.

⊙ The process of planning health promotion campaigns

The process of planning health promotion campaigns hinges on three key questions:

1 What am I trying to achieve?
2 What am I going to do?
3 How will I know whether I have been successful?

'What am I trying to achieve?' concerns the process of working out what the needs and priorities are and then being clear about your aims and objectives. 'What am I trying to do?' can be broken down into smaller steps – choosing the best way of achieving your aims, identifying the resources you are going to use, and setting a clear plan of action of who does what and when. Finally, 'How will I know whether I have been successful?' means that you need to include plans for evaluation as an integral part of your overall plan and *not* as an afterthought.

What am I trying to achieve?

The process of planning a health promotion campaign begins with a consideration of the reasons why an intervention is being considered. This process involves the consideration of two central issues: the identification of needs and priorities, and the setting of aims and objectives.

Identification of needs and priorities

Identifying needs is a complex process. There is potentially a bottomless pit of health needs and only a finite amount of resources available to meet them, so difficult choices have to be made. The choices made will be influenced by how the need is identified. A useful distinction to make is whether you are being reactive or proactive when identifying needs. Being reactive means responding to the needs and demands which people make. In contrast, being proactive means taking the initiative and deciding for oneself the area of work to be done. For example, the health issue concerned might be a local, national or international priority. Another reason might be that epidemiologists (as discussed in Chapter 2) have identified a link between a health behaviour or a health issue and a high morbidity or mortality rate. Alternatively, colleagues might have identified a gap in an existing health service, or health practitioners might have identified a problem among a particular group of their patients. However this happens, once a need has been identified, the next step is to develop the focus of the intervention. This process begins with the setting of aims and objectives.

Setting aims and objectives

Setting **aims** and **objectives** is often a lengthy process. It is an important task to get right, because the choice of aims and objectives will influence every other stage of the health promotion process. Different aims and objectives lend themselves to different approaches to health promotion as well as to different strategies for implementing the intervention. This, then, has implications for the means by which the evaluation of an intervention can take place. This is because different strategies require different types of intervention. It should therefore be clear that the setting of aims and objectives is pivotal to the success or otherwise of the developing campaign.

Aims are broad statements of what it is you are trying to achieve, whereas objectives are much more specific and are concerned with the desired end state that should be achieved within a specific time period. For example, a psychologist may have noticed during follow-up appointments with her patients that they were finding it difficult to put into practice the skills and techniques she had taught them. The psychologist might therefore decide that she wants to improve the information she gives to them. Thus her aim would be to improve patient compliance with their treatment plans, and her objective would be to improve patients' understanding of the treatment plans. Her action plan might then be to develop a patient information leaflet.

The process of identifying aims and objectives enables the clarification not just of what will be done and to whom, but also why it is needed. Clarity on these points leads to the development of strategies that will focus on achieving the aims and objectives. In contrast, failure to appropriately engage in this process means that health promoters waste time and energy ploughing ahead with what seems like a good idea, only to realize too late that what they are doing is not actually achieving what they want. Thus, having developed the aims and objectives of the proposed health promotion campaign, the next step is to consider the second key question: 'What am I going to do?'

What am I going to do?

The process of answering this question involves the consideration of three key issues. Having identified the aims and objectives of the health promotion campaign, the next step is to decide how you will be able to achieve them. This will involve consideration of the resources you will need to access. Finally, you will need to spend time considering how you will be able to evaluate the health promotion campaign you have devised.

Decide the best way of achieving aims and objectives

Sometimes there might be only one possible way of accomplishing your aims and objectives, but usually there will be a range of options. You therefore need to be able to work out what is the best option for you. There is not usually one 'best buy' for health promotion as a whole, so there is much you should take into account. For example, you should review the published research and think about how the data presented relates to the campaign you are planning. You will also need to think about the specific strategies and their strengths and limitations. For example, in Chapter 4, mass media were shown to be effective for raising awareness but not for behaviour change. Improving knowledge might be best achieved by one-to-one teaching sessions, distributing leaflets or running a poster campaign. In contrast, working on empowering individuals might involve group work, **social skills training**, or role playing. A focus on the community might involve pressure groups, the development of advocacy schemes or the encouragement of organizational change (Ewles and Simnet, 1995). Table 5.1, although not comprehensive, summarizes how different aims might require different approaches, using smoking cessation as an example.

Smoking cessation	
Aim	Strategies
Health awareness	Articles in papers
	Exhibition on impact of smoking
	Posters on smoking cessation
	Programmes on radio/television
Community change	Ban smoking in public places
	Improve access to smoking cessation programmes
Behaviour change	Smoking cessation groups
	One-to-one support for patients wishing to give up
	Suggestions for coping with withdrawal from nicotine
	Suggestions to help avoid engaging in smoking habits, such as smoking after a meal
Increase knowledge	Introduce lessons on impact of smoking in schools
	Advice and instructions to patients
	Talks on smoking cessation in the community
Attitude change	Group work
	One-to-one work

Table 5.1 Comparison of health promotion aims and strategies

Having identified the strategies you intend to employ in order to achieve your aims and objectives, the next step is to identify the resources you will need in order to implement your strategy.

Identify resources

In addressing this issue, you will need to think about what resources are already available to you as well as those resources that you will need to buy in or acquire. Possible resources include:

- *You:* your experience, knowledge, time, skills, enthusiasm and energy.
- *Your colleagues:* your colleagues might have relevant experience and expertise and could advise you. Your organization might have secretarial staff who could contribute to administrative tasks, or perhaps there are technicians who could help with audiovisual equipment or with developing electronic resources.
- *Your clients:* your clients also have knowledge, skills, enthusiasm, energy and potentially time which you can harness and build on. An ex-client can be a valuable resource too – perhaps someone who has successfully lost weight, given up smoking or learned to cope with

pain can be a big help to current clients struggling with similar problems and experiences.

- *Policies and plans:* there might already be a policy on the issue that your health promotion campaign is going to address. Can you use the policy to back up the work you plan to do? Does your proposed work fit into existing national strategies for health?
- *Facilities and services:* what facilities already exist, are they fully used? Are you able to access them or will you need to hire a venue in order to implement your campaign?
- *Material resources:* these include leaflets, posters and display materials. If you are planning group work, you'll need to think about things like rooms, space, seats, audiovisual equipment and teaching materials.

Having audited the availability of existing resources and identified those resources you need to access or buy in, the next step is to concentrate on planning how you will be able to evaluate your campaign.

Planning evaluation methods

This stage is focused upon working out how you are going to measure the success of your campaign. Evaluation must focus explicitly on the aims and objectives you have set. This sounds simple, but in practice it can be difficult. For example, if your aim is to improve awareness of an issue, you need to think about how you can gain a **baseline measure** of awareness levels, as well as identifying how you will be able to demonstrate that your campaign has raised levels. Similarly, if your aim is to change behaviour, you need to consider how you can capture any changes that occur.

Perhaps more important is the need to consider how you can be sure that any changes that occur following the implementation of your campaign can be directly linked to being a result of the campaign's influence. Health-related knowledge, attitudes and behaviour are constantly changing, regardless of health promotion campaigns. Societies are also changing in response to many different factors. As a consequence, Naidoo and Wills (2003: 383) ask: 'How can the changes due to health promotion be isolated from everything else?' In other words, how will you know whether your campaign has been successful?

How will I know whether I have been successful?

In the field of health promotion, it is impossible to implement a campaign under laboratory conditions where all the factors except the one being studied are controlled. The real world does not work like this. As noted above, it is difficult to unpick the impact of the campaign from all the other variables that might also be having an impact. Naidoo and Wills (2003) suggest the adoption of a **quasi-experimental approach** where a control group of people who are similar to those receiving the campaign are also monitored. Any changes that are noted in the group receiving the campaign are then compared to those found among the control group – the assumption being that any changes found in the campaign group, but not the control, can be attributed to the influence of the health promotion campaign. This too is an imperfect approach because it is difficult to isolate different groups of people, which means it is difficult to be sure that the control group did not also come across the health promotion campaign materials. However, it is a pragmatic approach to this thorny issue and does allow health promoters to be more confident of the impact of their programme than they could be if they did not make use of a control group.

An example of a campaign: 'Folic Acid – One of Life's Essentials'

This campaign was used as an example of how to plan, develop and deliver a health promotion campaign in the publication *Campaigning for Health* (Health Promotion Agency, 1998), which was produced for health and social care teachers. The campaign was implemented in October 1998. It was developed in response to a review of the research which demonstrated that if women increased the amount of folic acid taken before and during pregnancy, the number of babies born with neural tube defects could be greatly reduced. A review of public knowledge, attitudes and behaviour in relation to folic acid in Northern Ireland was undertaken by the agency in 1996. This showed that while awareness of the existence of folic acid was high, knowledge of the benefits of taking folic acid supplements was limited and, in addition, there was some confusion over when these supplements should be taken. In response to these findings, in February 1998, the agency was commissioned to prepare and implement a public information campaign on folic acid for Northern Ireland.

The agency proposed targeting both women aged 16–45 years and health professionals. Its aims were to increase knowledge of the benefits of folic acid, to encourage a positive attitude to taking it, and to promote behaviour change so that more women would take sufficient folic acid both before becoming pregnant and in the early weeks of pregnancy. Breaking the aims down into objectives (the desired outcomes of the intervention), the agency identified the following objectives:

- To increase the number of women who recognize that folic acid is safe
- To increase awareness of the importance of taking folic acid
- To increase awareness about the need to take folic acid before conception and up to the end of the twelfth week of pregnancy
- To increase awareness that a daily folic acid supplement is needed
- To increase the number of women who would take folic acid during pregnancy
- To not make anyone feel guilty or responsible if they have a child with a neural tube defect or cause anxiety among women who are already pregnant and have not taken folic acid because they did not know about it.

The campaign was launched in October 1998 and comprised television and cinema advertising, leaflets, posters and the production of a magazine. In addition, guidance notes for professionals were produced. The television and cinema advertisement highlighted that folic acid is a vitamin that helps prevent conditions such as spina bifida and should be taken before becoming pregnant and until the twelfth week of pregnancy. The leaflets and posters gave information on the importance of taking folic acid and were distributed to health service facilities, pharmacies and supermarkets.

The agency recognized that women who were not thinking about pregnancy would be unlikely to pick up a leaflet about folic acid, so a magazine in the style of popular women's magazines was produced. The magazine was entitled *It's You*, and contained celebrity interviews, real-life stories, puzzles and general features on health as well as information on folic acid. It was inserted into local newspapers and sent to hairdressing salons, dental surgeries and health centres for their waiting areas.

The guidance notes produced for health professionals included sources of folic acid/folate, dosage and timing information, questions and answers and contact addresses for specialist advice. The guidance notes were sent to GPs, practice nurses, pharmacists, family planning staff, health visitors, midwives and dieticians.

In February 1999, 1,000 adults were interviewed in order to evaluate the 1998 campaign. A similar survey that had been conducted in 1996 allowed for pre- and post-campaign comparison. Whilst the evaluation did not measure whether behaviour changed as a result of the campaign, it did indicate that awareness of folic acid had risen from 45% pre-campaign to 73% post-campaign. Knowledge of the benefits of folic acid had also risen from 60% to 83%. The campaign was considered successful and was recommended for a national award in 2001.

Summary

In this section, we have considered the process of planning and evaluating health promotion campaigns. It has become apparent that there are many factors outside the control of the health promotion campaign which might also influence whether or not the aims and objectives of the campaign are achieved. In the next section, we focus in more detail on the process of identifying whether a health promotion campaign has had the desired effect.

How can we know if a health promotion campaign has had the desired effect?

Given all the information presented in this chapter, you might very well be asking yourself, how then can we know whether our campaign has had an impact? Naidoo and Wills (2003) suggest that the following dimensions that should be considered: effectiveness, acceptability and appropriateness:

- *Effectiveness* – did an activity achieve what it set out to do? Were the aims and objectives of the health promotion campaign achieved fully?
- *Acceptability* – interventions must be perceived by the intended recipients as 'acceptable'; however, an intervention that has been acceptable to a particular population may come across difficulties if rolled out in a different geographical, cultural or economic context. For example, much of the early UK health education material on HIV/AIDS depicted it as originating in African and developing countries (also identified in the literature as the 'third world'). This reinforced racist stereotypes and offended many black and minority ethnic groups. The portrayal of where AIDS came from left many

groups angry and not prepared to take part in HIV/AIDS education programmes. Similarly, Young and Oppenheimer (2009) highlight the problems experienced during the 2003 SARS epidemic by health promoters, who attempted to get across the message that the risk of contracting SARS whilst on a plane was low. The public reacted to the information with alarm, rather than reassurance and the health promotion campaign backfired badly.

- *Appropriateness* – is an activity appropriate to the particular health needs of the people being targeted? Would funding an expensive campaign encouraging cyclists to wear helmets be appropriate if the area targeted was one with few cyclists, but one that needed meals on wheels? Evaluations therefore might need to distinguish between people's own perceptions of their needs and those held by others, such as doctors or health workers who are drawing on a different understanding or model of health. What this means is that the more you know about the intended recipients of a health promotion campaign, the more likely it is that you can ensure that the message is relevant and appropriate for the population concerned (Kreuter and Wray, 2003).

In addition, you should remind yourself why you are planning to engage in evaluation. Is it to improve your own practice next time you do something similar? Is it to help other people improve their practice? Is it to justify the resources that went into the project? Working out the answer to this question is important because it will affect the way you do the evaluation as well as the amount of effort you put into it.

Similarly, knowing who will be using the data you generate from your evaluation will determine the questions you ask, how much depth and detail you go into, and how you present the information. So if you are assessing how a health education session went for your own benefit so that you can change it next time you run a similar session, you will probably rely on your own observations about the session and the reactions of the learners. If, however, you are writing a report for your manager, or for a body that you want to fund your work, you will need to think about the kinds of questions these people will expect to be answered and the amount of detail they will need.

Perhaps most importantly, deciding how to assess the outcome will involve a consideration of the kinds of changes that might be reflected in the methods you employ to assess or measure those changes. For example, if your aim was raising health awareness, you might decide to measure the amount of interest shown by consumers in your campaign by recording how many people took up offers of leaflets, monitoring changes in demand for health-related services, or analysing the amount media coverage. On the other hand, if your aim was to improve knowledge levels, you might be interested in recording changes in what clients say or do by observing how clients show their new knowledge through the administration of written tests/questionnaires.

Finally, consideration will need to be given to who should evaluate the health promotion campaign. Much evaluation of health promotion activities is done by the very people who carry out the health promotion. An external evaluator could be more fair and objective, but might also take longer to understand the issues and establish contacts. You could argue that if people evaluate their own practice, they can learn more easily what they can improve and how, but this will only happen if they are committed to improvement rather than self-justification. Perhaps it is best to capitalize on the strengths of both types of evaluator. It can also be useful to gauge the opinion of the target population as to the impact and effectiveness of the campaign. Such people provide a unique perspective and may provide health promoters with useful insights as to how their campaign was received.

⊙ Conclusion

In spite of the considerable length of time that health promotion campaigns have been taking place, there is a lack of definitive evidence that demonstrates the impact that such activities have on health outcomes. Many of the findings are contradictory and it is difficult to unpick the influence of the campaign from the potential influence of other factors. Consequently, there is a need for more research that draws on high-quality, methodologically sound approaches to the process of evaluating health promotion.

What we can conclude from the evidence to date is that health promotion campaigns have been shown to be successful at securing an intent to change health behaviour (e.g. Health Education Authority, 1997), that knowledge can be shown to have increased as a consequence of campaigns (e.g. Tilford et al., 1997; Whittle et al., 1994), but that such campaigns have had a limited impact on changing behaviours and attitudes (e.g.

Smith et al., 2002; Yzer et al., 2000). Such findings reflect the intention–behaviour gap, explored in Chapter 4.

Whitelaw and Watson (2005) suggest that rather than being based on clear **evidence-based practice** indicating effectiveness, health promotion campaigns tend to be implemented based on three shaky principles:

1 From a general faith in their effectiveness rather than as a result of any formal appraisal
2 In the context of a fear of taking a different approach to that taken traditionally – 'we have always done health promotion in this way'
3 As a political cover used to suggest action is being taken.

These are disheartening conclusions to draw. However, Whitelaw and Watson (2005) suggest that there are strategies which do appear to contribute to health promotion. It is these strategies that have been outlined in this chapter. What is required now is that health promotion professionals adopt and implement these strategies in a more consistent and rigorous manner. The words of Whitelaw and Watson (2005: 222) are a fitting conclusion to this chapter:

> Events should have a highly defined purpose with clear and measurable aims and objectives, be consistent, sustained and repeated; not operate in isolation, but rather have some degree of interactivity and are combined with community, small group and face-to-face skills based interventions and contextualized in existing structures like the family, the community or the school. Likewise, optimal content should variously be: positively orientated, realistic; relevant and salient to target groups; perceived as familiar, attractive and credible; build on the audience's existing motives, needs and values.

Having examined health promotion, we move to the last section, where we focus on two health issues, namely, stress and coping with stress, and eating behaviour and eating disorders.

◁◉▷ Further reading

Edwards, A., Elwyn, G., Covey, J. et al. (2001). Presenting risk information: A review of the effects of 'framing' and other manipulations on patient outcomes. *Journal of Health Communication*, 6, 61–82. A useful paper reviewing the process of presenting health risk information.

Whitelaw, S. and Watson, J. (2005). Wither health promotion events? A judicial approach to evidence. *Health Education Research: Theory and Practice*, 20(2), 214–25.

◁◉▷ Key search terms

Health promotion, health behaviour, behaviour change, evaluation, measurement, planning

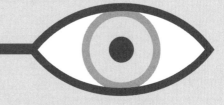

Examples of Health Issues

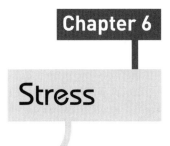

Chapter 6

Stress

Introduction

Stress is a ubiquitous term which is used in our everyday conversations. We all use the term freely: 'That was really stressful', 'It really stressed me out', 'Don't stress' and so on, but if asked to define what we meant by the term, we would each be likely to come up with different definitions.

In this chapter, we focus first on how the term stress is defined in the field of health psychology. We then turn our attention to the ways in which stress has been shown to operate within the different systems in our bodies. Having provided an overview of these different systems, we explore how stress has been measured. Finally, the chapter concludes with an exploration as to how stress might impact on us.

In this chapter, we will:

- Define stress
- Outline the key bodily systems through which stress is thought to operate
- Identify sources of stress
- Explain how stress can be measured
- Identify the ways in which stress might impact on us

How can we define stress?

As we have noted above, the term 'stress' is used widely in many different situations and environments. The word 'stress' can be used to refer to:

- a situation (e.g. an exam)
- an object or a person causing stress

- the outcomes (behavioural, cognitive or physiological) that occur as a reaction to a stressful event.

As such, stress can have many different meanings depending on who is using the term and how they are using it. Some people will see stress as something that is positive, whereas others will be very clear that stress is negative and something to be avoided at all costs. Researchers such as Montoro and colleagues (2009: 41) have highlighted that 'stress is curiously difficult to define despite the fact that it is a widely used and apparently simple term'. They argue that the very fact that the term is used so widely results in it being 'banalized' and wrongly applied. They suggest that because our tendency is to use the word 'stress' to describe any situation that generates brief anxiety or nervousness, we are actually applying the term to situations that are not truly 'stressing'. However, whilst this provides us with a good explanation of how the word 'stress' is used, the definition of stress is still unclear.

Curtis (2000: 123) suggests that we use the terms 'stressors', 'stress-responses' and 'stress' as a means of distinguishing the different ways in which the term 'stress' is used:

- A **stressor** is an event that a person interprets as endangering their physical or psychological wellbeing
- A **stress-response** refers to the reactions to the stressor
- Stress is the state that occurs following the reaction to the stressor and stress–response.

In employing this terminology, we can agree that stress, or the stressor that causes it, triggers a response in our bodies. This response is designed to cope with the situation and it is through the process of (not) coping with the situation that we come to experience stress. Stress can therefore be defined as a:

> general bodily response to initially threatening external or internal demands, involving the mobilisation of physiological and psychological resources to deal with them. (Nieto et al., 2004, cited in Montoro et al., 2009)

This definition takes into account the fact that stress may be evoked as a response to physical, environmental and psychological stressors and also suggests, in the use of the term 'threatening', that an element of interpretation is required. This is an important distinction, because, as we shall see later, not everyone reacts in the same way to stressors. In the next section, we explore the different physiological and psychological pathways through which stress is thought to be operationalized.

👁 How is stress operationalized?

Stress has been operationalized through two different perspectives: physiological and psychological. Many researchers have focused on how the impact of stress is felt in our bodies and in particular have explored the role of the nervous system. However, remembering that the definition of stress we outlined above incorporates an element of interpretation, it is also important to consider how stress might be operationalized psychologically. Therefore, we first focus on the physiological explanations and outline the nervous and endocrine systems. We then turn our attention to the psychological pathway.

Physiological explanations: stress and the nervous system

The nervous system is really the communication network for our bodies (Figure 6.1). Its role is to monitor internal and external conditions. The nervous system essentially splits into two major divisions: the central nervous system (CNS) and the peripheral nervous system (PNS). The CNS is made up of the brain and the spinal cord, whilst the PNS consists of sensory and motor neurons that are involved in the transmission of chemicals known as 'neurotransmitters', which act as messengers and take information about internal and external conditions to different parts of our body. The PNS itself consists of two key parts, the somatic and the autonomic nervous systems. The somatic nervous system transmits messages sent from the skin and muscles to the brain. However, researchers consider that it is the autonomic nervous system (ANS) which is primarily involved in the stress response.

The ANS is also divided into two systems: the sympathetic nervous system (SNS) and the parasympathetic nervous system. Without getting too complicated (whole textbooks are devoted to each of these systems), the SNS is activated during emergencies, or what are perceived as emergencies. The result of the activation of the SNS is increased vigilance, arousal and mobilization. This response is often called the 'fight or flight' system, whereby our body prepares itself either to fight the stressor or to flee from it. This means that the body needs to be prepared for major activity. The effects we would notice when this system is activated include an increase in our heart rate, an increase in our breathing and an increase in the activity in our sweat glands. In contrast, the parasympathetic system works to calm the body's response, to relax and bring our body's systems back to stable, normal functioning. These two systems work together to maintain balance, rather than one being in operation, followed by the other. For more detail about the nervous system and its role in relation to stress, Robert Sapolsky's (1998) book *Why Zebras Don't Get Ulcers* explains this in an extremely user-friendly format. However, for the purposes of this book, we will focus briefly on different elements of the SNS, each of which consists of a 'chain reaction' in response to a stressor. We focus on this system because it is the SNS which activates when we interpret a situation or event as being a potential stressor.

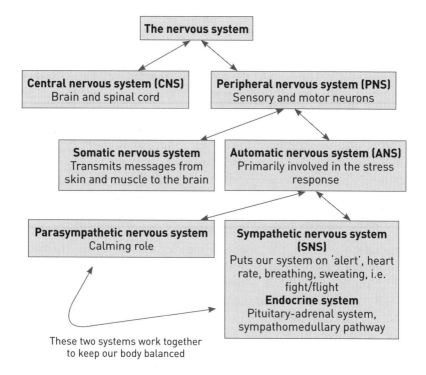

Figure 6.1 A representation of the nervous system

Stress and the endocrine system

The endocrine system is a system of glands that are also involved in the stress response. Endocrine glands, which are found on the top of each kidney, make different hormones which they put into the blood system so that they can be sent all around the body.

Stress and the pituitary-adrenal system

The adrenal glands are also found on the top of each kidney, along with the endocrine glands. Adrenal glands also make hormones in response to stress. This happens as a result of a chain reaction of messages which start in the brain. When we interpret something as being a stressor, parts of our brain are activated to send messages that can prepare our body to deal with the stressor. The area in the brain responsible for the first stage in this process is known as the 'hypothalamus'. This sends a message in the form of the hormone 'corticotrophin-releasing factor' to another area in our brain called the 'pituitary gland', which in turn sends a message to the adrenal glands. This message is in the form of adrenocorticotropic hormone (ACTH). When ACTH reaches the adrenal glands, they, in turn, are activated to produce glucocorticoid hormones, the most common of which is called 'cortisol'. Cortisol is sometimes called the 'stress hormone'. The release of cortisol acts as a message to prepare the body to deal with the stressor. This system is known as the hypothalamic-pituitary-adrenocortical system.

Stress and the sympathomedullary pathway

The adrenal medulla (part of the adrenal glands) is responsible for releasing two hormones into the body called 'adrenaline' and 'noradrenaline'. Americans call these hormones 'epinephrine' and 'norepinephrine' respectively. The prime responsibility of these two hormones is to increase blood pressure and heart rate. The sympathetic nervous system works very fast and evolved as a means of getting us out of dangerous situations as fast as possible.

It is clear from these brief descriptions of the physiological response to stressors that our bodies have evolved to respond in a series of chain reactions when a threat or stressor is detected. What these models and explanations of the stress response do not address is the issue of how we interpret a stimulus as being stressful. It is to this aspect that we now turn.

Stress and psychological factors

Early models put forward to explain how we respond to stress tended to focus on the body's physiological response to stressors and, in doing so, failed to take into account the role of psychological factors.

One such model is known as the **General Adaptation Syndrome** (Selye, 1956). The General Adaptation Syndrome (GAS) suggests that we automatically respond to stressors in three stages:

1 The *alarm* stage is when we mobilize our resources in order to meet with and/or resist the stressor.

2 The *resistance* stage involves our efforts at coping with the stressor as we attempt to reverse the alarm stage.

3 The *exhaustion* stage is reached when we have been repeatedly exposed to the initial stressful situation and are now unable to resist it further.

The GAS assumes that we all respond in the same way to stressors and, as such, has been criticized for failing to consider the very human tendency to interpret and perceive the same event from a number of different perspectives, thereby inducing a different response to the same stressor.

Another approach to explaining stress was developed by Holmes and Rahe (1967), who developed the 'life events' scale. This consisted of a list of life changes and life events, such as 'death of a spouse', 'son or daughter leaving home', 'pregnancy' and 'vacation', which was given to participants so that they could indicate which of the events/changes they had experienced. Originally, an individual's level of stress was scored by simply counting the number of events experienced. The reasoning was that someone who had experienced more events or changes would be more stressed. However, this approach did not take into account differences in perception of different life events, and so someone who had experienced the death of a spouse and the death of a close family member would score two, as would someone who had recently been on two holidays. It is of course possible that the second individual may have had two awful holidays, but it would be difficult to argue that levels of stress for the different events were similar. Furthermore, this approach fails to take into account differences in individual perceptions, so, for example, an individual might have experienced the death of a spouse and view it as a terribly upsetting and stressful situation, whereas another person who had perhaps been nursing their spouse through a terminal illness may see the death as a release and so view it as a less stressful event. Similarly, divorce can be a complex experience, or it can be a liberating and positive event, which symbolizes the closure of an unsatisfactory relationship. Perception is therefore of great importance in the process of identifying stressors.

Taking into account these notions of interpretation and perception, Lazarus and Launier (1978) described stress as resulting from a lack of 'person–environment fit'. What they meant by this was that if an individual is faced with a particularly trying situation (a stressor), the amount of stress they feel is determined by their interpretation of the demands of the stressor. In other words, a calculation is made as to how stressful the situation is combined with how confident an individual is in their ability to cope with the stressor. This calculation then determines the stress-response, which in turn influences the amount of stress felt. A good person–environment fit therefore results in little or no stress, whereas a poor person–environment fit results in the experience of higher stress.

Building further on this work, Lazarus and Folkman (1984) put forward a **transactional model of stress**, which emphasized the perception of potential harm, threat and challenges combined with the level of confidence in dealing with these stressors. They suggested that it was the interpretation of stressors that was more important than the events themselves, and described stress as a relationship between the person and the environment that is perceived as exceeding their resources. This approach to stress represents a transactional approach, in that the interaction between the person and their environment is what results (or does not result) in stress. Three types of appraisal were identified as playing a role:

1 *Primary appraisal:* where we first interpret our situation in terms of how we think it is affecting our wellbeing. Following such an appraisal, we may decide that the situation is 'irrelevant', 'benign-positive', 'harmful and a threat', or 'harmful and a challenge' to our wellbeing.

2 *Secondary appraisal:* Lazarus has argued 'that an event needs to be appraised as stressful before it can elicit a stress-response' (quoted in Ogden, 2007: 227). Having assessed the situation that we find ourselves in as being stressful, we then engage in a process of asking ourselves how we can best deal with it. This second stage concerns working out what resources we will need in order to deal successfully with the situation and evaluating whether we have these resources as well as the confidence to deploy them.

3 *Reappraisal:* finally, we make another appraisal of our situation and our responses to it by incorporating new and changing information as it becomes available.

Lazarus and Folkman's (1984) approach takes into account and provides a role for an individual's psychological state. Its central assumption is that stress will be experienced when perceived harm or threat is high, but perceived coping ability is low. Stress results when there is a mismatch between perceived demands and resources.

Summary

It can be seen that both physiology and psychology play an important role in stress, which is a difficult-to-define concept. Both physiology and psychology are interrelated; we have shown how the physiological processes only begin once the brain has interpreted the cues from a situation. The way in which we interpret cues is related to our psychological processes of interpretation and perception. In the next section, we turn our attention to identifying potential sources of stress.

⊙ Sources of stress

If we remember that how we perceive events can influence whether or not we interpret them as being stressful, the potential sources of stress are limitless. However, before considering the potential sources of stress, it is first necessary to briefly highlight the difference between acute and chronic stress:

- *Acute stress* is that which tends to be imminent and relatively short term in nature. This might include exams, as well as natural disasters, such as earthquakes, tornadoes and bushfires.
- *Chronic stress* is much longer term in nature. It might be experienced, for example, in response to long-term illness.

Researchers have paid much attention to the potential sources of chronic stress, indeed, Gurung (2006) notes that researchers have tended to focus on three different areas: relationships, work and the environment, and it is to these three areas that we now turn.

Relationship stress

Interacting with others can be stressful. In the course of our lives, we interact with family, friends, partners, lovers, spouses, colleagues, neighbours and so on. Conflict in any of these relationships can result in us feeling stressed. Much research has been conducted focusing on the marital relationship, for example Kiecolt-Glaser and colleagues (2003) took physiological measures from 90 couples during the first year of their marriages and then followed them up 10 years later. They were able to show that the measures could be linked to measures of marital satisfaction and break-ups all those years after the initial measures had been taken.

Work stress

Nearly all the working population will feel job-related stress, which can be as a result of having too much work to do as well as the converse (not having enough to keep you occupied). Alternatively, perhaps you are experiencing discrimination or bullying, perhaps promotion eludes you, or perhaps you lack control over what you have to do at work. These different factors can be classified as 'job demands' – conditions that affect performance – and 'job autonomy' – how much control an individual has over the speed or the nature of the decisions that are made at work. All these factors have been linked to the experience of job stress. Thus, in the same way that stress is thought to arise from a mismatch between perceived demands and resources, a similar model is proposed to explain work stress. Researchers have put forward theories which explore the 'person–environment fit'. Such theories propose that if the demands of the job exceed the skills of the person employed, stress will result.

If we are stressed at work, the consequences can be far-reaching, not just for us, but for our colleagues and also our families and relationships outside the work environment. For example, Doumas and colleagues (2003) asked couples to keep a diary over a period of 42 days. After analysing the diary entries, they were able to show that the spouses reported more positive interactions with one another on the days when they worked less, showing how the experience of feeling stressed at work can 'spill over' into other areas of our lives.

Environmental stress

The environment that we inhabit can cause us to feel stressed or can facilitate our relaxation. Living or working in a noisy environment can increase the stress we experience, particularly when the noise is unpredictable. Other factors include not having enough personal space as well as high levels of pollution, both of which can cause individuals to become stressed and frustrated. Researchers have also explored the impact of natural disasters, such as flooding, earthquakes and hurricanes, on survivors. A third type of environmental stressor which has been researched is known as a 'techno-political stressor' and can include chemical plant accidents, wars and acts of terrorism.

Summary

Stress (both acute and chronic) arises from a number of different sources. Much research has focused on chronic stress, and, in particular, attention has been directed towards relationship, work and environmental stressors in an effort to discover the potential impact of experiencing long-term stressful situations. The next section turns to the issue of how we can measure these physiological and psychological processes that are employed when we face stressors.

◉ How can we measure stress?

When considering the question of how to measure stress, it is important to think about the environment in which stress is being measured. Some researchers measure stress in naturalistic settings, in other words, 'real-world' settings. In order to do this, they may measure stress responses to events such as before and after examinations, during a job interview or perhaps whilst engaging in physical activity. However, much stress research is conducted in the laboratory setting. This involves bringing people into a controlled setting and inviting them to complete a stressful task. The advantage of laboratory settings is that they can be controlled. This means that any changes in the stress-response recorded can be attributed to the individual rather than the stressor itself. As always, there are advantages and disadvantages for whichever approach is employed and what is important is that the potential limitations are recognized and where possible controlled for.

In terms of the types of stressful task that researchers have employed in the laboratory setting in order to induce a stress-response, examples include exposing participants to an unpleasant event such as a loud noise, and asking participants to plunge their arm into a bucket of freezing cold water and keep it submerged for as long as possible (known as the 'cold pressor test'). Alternatively, people have been asked to engage in memory tasks, spelling tests, public speaking, or mathematical tasks that activate a loud buzzer when participants give an incorrect answer.

Physiological measures of stress

Physiological measures are mostly used in the laboratory because they often involve the participant being wired up to different devices in order that, for example, their blood pressure, respiration rate, heart rate or galvanic skin response can be measured. In addition, blood or saliva samples can be taken in order to measure the level of changes in the nervous system, for example through measuring changes in cortisol levels.

Self-report measures of stress

There are a range of self-report measures that enable researchers to measure stress. Some researchers continue to use life event measures such as the Holmes and Rahe (1967) scale, which measures the number of self-reported life events experienced in a particular time period. Other measures take more account of individuals' perceptions of stress. These include the Work–Life Balance Scale (Gröpel and Kuhl, 2009), the Stress Arousal Checklist (MacKay et al., 1978), the Positive and Negative Affect Scale (PANAS) (Watson et al., 1988), and the Daily Hassles Scale (Kanner et al., 1981).

Work–Life Balance Scale

The Work–Life Balance Scale measures perceived sufficiency of time available for work and social life respectively. Items include: 'I often visit my friends and acquaintances', 'Because of my work, I have no free time', 'In my free time, I still deal with my work duties'. Gröpel and Kuhl (2009) argue that the integration of work and social life is critical and that balancing work and social roles becomes a strong contributor to how we feel. In short, when we experience problems in balancing our different life demands, we experience stress. Thus, it is suggested that a measure of work–life conflict equates to a measure of stress.

Stress Arousal Checklist

The Stress Arousal Checklist provides participants with a list of 19 words, such as 'tense', 'worried' and 'jittery', and the following response categories: 'definitely feel', 'slightly feel', 'cannot decide' and 'definitely do not feel'. The idea behind this scale is that participants are asked to complete it whilst also experiencing a lab-induced stressor. Participants are asked to indicate whether they feel any of the emotions whilst they are completing the checklist. The more items the participant agrees they are feeling, the higher the levels of stress recorded.

Positive and Negative Affect Scale (PANAS)

Although the PANAS scale is not typically considered to be a stress measure, Dijkstra and colleagues (2009) used it in their study exploring changes in stress in younger and older adults. They explain that although the PANAS is a measure of mood, relationships between perceived stress scores and decreased positive affect, as well as with perceived stress scores and increased negative affect, have been recorded by Simpson and colleagues (2009). Dijkstra and colleagues argue that stress can therefore be assumed if participants score low on positive affect and high on negative affect.

Daily Hassles Scale

Mark Forshaw (2002: 61) notes that 'life is made up of "big things" that happen to us, and "little things"'. Usually, when we review the things that have happened to us, we experience a few 'big things' and many 'little things'. Indeed, a lot of our stress comes from the little things that we experience. Little things might be things that test our patience, such as waiting in queues, waiting for buses, leaving your umbrella behind on a rainy day and so on. It is not the 'daily hassle' itself, but its frequency, duration and intensity that provides the stressor. Thus, unlike major life events such as those focused upon by Holmes and Rahe (1967), hassles tend not to require a large adjustment on the part of the person experiencing them. Nevertheless, the impact of hassles was thought to induce stress if they were frequent, chronic or repeated over time. In order to measure this idea, Kanner and colleagues (1981) designed the Hassles Scale, which was subsequently developed by DeLongis and colleagues (1988) into the Hassles and Uplifts Scale. This invited participants to rate events as to whether they were a hassle and then as to whether it was what was termed an 'uplift' or positive event. The scale was found to be strongly associated with 'negative mental and physical outcomes, even when major life events were taken into account' (Morrison and Bennett, 2009: 320). One problem with the scale is that it is retrospective and relies on participants being able to remember things accurately. A further problem with the daily hassles approach is that it is impossible to work out whether the hassles caused our stress, or whether our stress levels caused us to view the hassles as stressful. Furthermore, when the scale was tested, the results demonstrated that two different people could experience the same number of events, weight them equally, but then experience different health outcomes. This leads to the question of whether there are other factors which moderate our response to stress, and this an issue which we will return to in Chapter 7.

Combined approach to measuring stress

Many researchers take a combined approach to measuring stress, preferring to take measures of both physiological and self-report measures. However, Ogden (2007) notes that although stress is considered to reflect both the experience (perception, interpretation) and the underlying physiological changes such as heart rate and cortisol levels that take place, curiously the two sets of measures do not always tally. She highlights work by Lohaus and colleagues (2001), who found poor relationships between the physiological and perceived measures of stress they recorded from their participants. Ogden (2007: 234) suggests that this might actually be a reflection of the type of stressor. She proposes that:

physiological measures might only match self-report measures when the stressor that individuals are exposed to is perceived as being controllable by them, or when it is considered a threat rather than a challenge or when the individual draws upon particular coping strategies.

Summary

There are a plethora of measures of stress, many more than we have covered in this chapter. Each method has advantages and disadvantages and, to date, none used in isolation are capable of capturing the full complexity of stress. We have seen that physiological measures record the different ways in which the body reacts to a stressful event, perhaps by recording changes in hormones or blood pressure, whereas psychological measures assert a role for measuring interpretation and perception. As Morrison and Bennett (2009: 344) note: 'a vast amount of research is conducted in this field that acknowledges that since stress is a subjective experience, measuring it cannot expect to be an exact science'. Bearing in mind the limitations of our ability to define and measure stress, we now turn our attention to the work that researchers have conducted in order to try and understand how stress might affect us.

How might stress impact on us?

Having highlighted the different ways in which we can measure stress, we now turn to exploring the potential impact that stress can have upon us. Researchers have typically focused on three different areas: cognition (our ability to think and reason); behaviour (the way in which we act when under stress); and physiology (how our body's reactions might increase the likelihood that we experience illness).

Cognition

Our ability to think straight when under stress has been explored by researchers. This can be manifest, for example, in our ability to remember important pieces of information, the way in which we think about ourselves and the ways in which we go about making decisions.

Negative self-evaluations

Among students, there is a tendency to be hard on themselves when they fail to reach a valued goal. Neely and colleagues (2009) noticed that their students were sometimes unforgiving of their failings. Many of their students also seemed to be unable to see that they were not working towards one goal in isolation, but that in life we are all working towards a number of different goals and are juggling competing demands. It is inevitable therefore that some goals must be relinquished in order to attain other goals. As teachers, Neely and colleagues (2009) wanted to explore whether they could teach their students how to identify and regulate competing goals and, in doing so, modulate their reactions to the stress of juggling competing demands.

Self-compassion, sometimes called 'self-kindness', has been defined by Neff (2003) as a healthy form of self-acceptance, which involves a tendency to treat oneself kindly in the face of perceived inadequacy. Neely and colleagues (2009: 89) explain that individuals who are self-compassionate have the ability to 'face their own painful thoughts without avoiding or exaggerating them, managing their disappointment and frustration by quelling self-pity and melodrama'. Self-compassion is therefore potentially a form of regulating our reactions to stressful situations. Neely and colleagues (2009) explored whether individuals who were adept at self-compassion managed stress better than those with less ability to be self-compassionate. They found that self-compassion was indeed an important skill to have when experiencing stressful situations. In the context of their study, they asked students to complete questionnaires exploring how well they coped when a goal they were working towards was not achieved – not achieving goals was considered a stressful experience. Neely and colleagues (2009) found that students' self-compassion scores predicted their evaluations of how they described their reactions to real-life events. They concluded that, in fostering self-compassion, individuals can more easily divest efforts from stated goals and redirect them towards new, more salient goals. This, they argue, 'may be healthier than tenaciously pursuing a goal at significant physical and psychological cost … and the ability to bring in self-compassion when facing disappointments may help students to enjoy higher levels of well being' (p. 96).

Decision-making

Porcelli and Delgado (2009) note that people are often forced to make decisions when under stress. They cite stockbrokers who make important financial decisions under extreme time constraints whilst working in a noisy, distracting and competitive environment. They were interested in exploring whether being under stress would lead decision-makers to take more risks, or whether the typical style engaged in by decision-makers would become exaggerated when under stress. They exposed their participants, who were university students, to memory and financial decision-making tasks under normal or stressful (cold pressor task) conditions. They found that stress interfered with participants' ability to complete the tasks effectively. They suggest that whilst more research is needed, their findings imply that a person's environment might interfere with their ability to make decisions, and that if, as they suggest, risk-taking biases become exaggerated under stress, then decision-makers might become unreliable.

Behavioural

Much attention in health psychology is directed at the way in which we react when under stress and in particular whether we engage in health protective behaviours or health-damaging behaviours, such as sickness absence and unhealthy eating habits.

Work-related stress and sickness absence

High workload combined with perceived high psychological and physical demands has been linked to higher stress levels, symptoms of illness and increased sickness absence (Lidwall and Marklund, 2006; Stansfield et al., 1999; Vingård et al., 2005). In particular, physical and mental demands that are perceived as being greater than an individual's capacity, along with high work stress and a lack of control over working hours, have been linked to greater levels of sickness absence (Ala-Mursula et al., 2005).

In their cross-sectional study, Holmgren and colleagues (2009) investigated the prevalence of work-related stress and its association with perceived health and sickness absence in a general population of employed working women. In the study, 424 women had a half-day health examination, which included an interview, questionnaires, physical examinations, measurements and blood tests. At the end of the examination, the participants were given a questionnaire which they were asked to complete and return to the researchers. Measures of work characteristics and perceived stress were included in this questionnaire.

Workplace issues which participants reported as being stressful included indistinct organization and conflicts at work, individual demands and commitment, low influence at work, and work interfering with leisure time. All these categories of work-related stress were significantly associated with increased odds of the women showing high levels of illness symptoms and an increased probability of risk of sickness absence. The authors conclude that work-related stress among this population is an important public health issue.

In a study with a similar focus, Munch-Hansen and colleagues (2009) investigated the relationship between overall satisfaction with psychosocial work conditions and sickness absence. Their assumption was that high satisfaction would reflect objectively favourable psychosocial work conditions, which would be health promoting, whereas low satisfaction would be a reaction to poor work conditions, which would in turn have adverse health effects – the implication being that an increase in satisfaction will reduce stress and therefore reduce levels of illness. They took measures of employee satisfaction with psychosocial work conditions and recorded levels of sickness absence for the six months prior to the assessment of workplace satisfaction as well as for the six months following this assessment. They found a strong relationship between the two variables: as satisfaction increased, sickness absence decreased. They argue that it is possible that even a small improvement in satisfaction might considerably reduce sickness absence.

Unhealthy eating and obesity

Research has shown that when we are stressed, we often change our diets, both in terms of quality and quantity (Louis et al., 2009). Most of us will reduce the amount we eat when we are stressed (e.g. Adam and Epel, 2007; Ogden and Mitandabari, 1997; Pollard et al., 1995), but some individuals respond to stress by eating much more than usual (e.g. Ingledew et al., 1996). It is thought that the experience of stress changes the kinds of foods to which we are usually attracted. For example, Wardle and colleagues (2000) showed that stressed people are more likely to crave high-density foods that are rich in energy, fats and sugars.

Rutters and colleagues (2009: 72) took this a step further and noted that obesity results from a chronic deregulation of energy balance, with energy intake far exceeding energy expended; this is an issue now considered to be of epidemic proportions. Furthermore, they suggested that obesity 'may be caused in part by stress, because in Western society high levels of ambient stress are abundantly present'. In their study, Rutters and colleagues (2009) used the 'eating in the absence of hunger' paradigm reported by Fisher and Birch (2002). This is a way of describing the behaviour we engage in when we are faced with an array of large portions of palatable foods, even when we are not hungry. In their study, participants consumed a standard lunch, and then completed either a stress or a control task, after which all participants had free access to snacks (including chocolate, sweets, crisps and nuts) for 30 minutes. Participants were told that they could eat as much as they liked of any of the foods. Throughout the 30-minute snack period, every 10 minutes, participants completed a questionnaire designed to measure their mood state. Rutters and colleagues (2009) found that those with increased state anxiety induced by the stress task ate more in the absence of hunger than those in the control group.

However, de Vrient and colleagues (2009) reviewed the existing literature on the topic of stress and obesity and concluded that, whilst chronic stress has a potential role in the cause of obesity by interacting with both mechanisms of energy intake and energy expenditure, our understanding of the underlying mechanisms is not yet sufficient to fully comprehend why this might be so. It is, however, extremely important to continue to research this topic, because, as noted by Louis and colleagues (2009), a healthy diet is beneficial throughout the life span, whereas poor nutrition is linked to retarded development, life-threatening illnesses and earlier mortality.

Physiological: stress and the immune system

There is some evidence to suggest that our immune systems do not work so efficiently when we are experiencing stress. The immune system, like the nervous system, is distributed throughout the body. It is the immune system which is activated when our body is required to fight off infection. The means by which our body fights off infections is through white blood cells known as 'leukocytes'. One means of exploring the potential impact of stress on our immune system has been to expose participants to the common cold virus. Cohen and colleagues (1993) looked at two groups of people; those who reported having experienced a number of significantly stressful life events, and those who had not. Under controlled conditions, both groups were infected with the cold virus. They found that those who had experienced more stressful life events had a more extreme reaction to the virus than those reporting fewer stressful life events. Their work provides convincing evidence to suggest that there is a relationship between chronic stress and the common cold.

This field of study is known in health psychology as **psychoneuroimmunology** (PNI). Its underpinning assumption is that there is a relationship between the mind and the body. In other words, psychoneuroimmunologists assume that the immune system can be affected by the workings of the mind. This is especially important in the field of stress, where it is accepted that interpretation or perception of stressors is as important as the stressors themselves. One area that PNI researchers have focused on is wound healing. In order to be able to measure the process of wound healing, researchers need to be sure that each participant has an equivalent wound. They therefore use a 'punch biopsy', which removes a uniform small piece of skin and tissue from participants, ensuring that each participant has the same 'wound'. Kiecolt-Glaser and colleagues (1995) used this technique to explore the impact of the stress of being a carer to a spouse with Alzheimer's disease on the speed of wound healing, compared to a control group. Carers were focused on because the role of caring for someone who has a serious progressive illness is in itself a stressful and emotionally charged task. Kiecolt-Glaser and colleagues (1995) found that the wound healing among the carer group was much slower than in the control group. They therefore concluded that immune function was adversely affected as a consequence of the stress linked to the role of being a carer.

This study and others are helping to piece together the ways in which the mind and body might interact. PNI is a fast-growing area in health psychology and shows great promise for increasing our understanding of the relationship between physical health and illness, and social, environmental and psychological factors.

⊙ Conclusion

In this chapter we focused on how the term 'stress' is defined in the field of health psychology. We then turned our attention to the different ways in which stress has been shown to operate within the different systems in our bodies. Having provided an overview of these different systems, we explored the different ways in which stress has been measured. Finally, we looked at how stress might impact on us. This process is outlined in Figure 6.2.

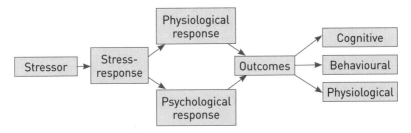

Figure 6.2 A representation of the stress-response

We have shown that researchers are in agreement that there is a clear link between stress and ill health, although what is not completely clear is the mechanism by which stress impacts on our health. It appears that stress can impact on us through physiological as well as psychological means, and, most likely, through a combination of both routes working in parallel. This is perhaps why, when researchers and clinicians have considered the problem of how to manage stress, both pathways have been explored. Morrison and Bennett (2009: 346) note that 'there is still some way to go before full understanding of how stress operates, and in particular how it operates in real environments'. There is a need for longitudinal studies of people in their 'natural' environment (as opposed to the laboratory setting) that will enable us to gain insight and understanding of the potential impact of stress in terms of our health outcomes. One way in which we can mitigate against the impact of stressors is to learn how to manage them. In the next chapter, we focus on coping with stress and the practice of stress management.

Further reading

Sapolsky, R. (1998) *Why Zebras Don't Get Ulcers: An Updated Guide to Stress, Stress-related Diseases, and Coping.* New York: W.H. Freeman.

Key search terms

Stress, stressor, nervous system, work stress, relationship stress, environmental stress

Chapter 7

Managing and coping with stress

👁 Introduction

In the previous chapter, we explored what stress was, how we could measure it and how it might impact on us. In this chapter we turn our attention to the process of managing, or coping with, stress.

We focus first on how coping is defined and explore the main coping styles and strategies that researchers have identified. We then focus on the links between personality, social support and coping, before turning our attention to the process of coping with stress.

In this chapter, we will:
- Define coping
- Describe coping styles and coping strategies
- Explore the relationship between personality and coping
- Explore the relationship between social support and coping
- Identify approaches to coping with stress

👁 What is coping?

There are a lot of approaches within the field of health psychology that focus on interventions which are aimed at improving wellbeing by means of enhancing coping. Underpinning this is the assumption that the more effective our coping strategies are, the better we will cope with stress. Furthermore, it is considered that better stress management leads to better health outcomes (Gurung, 2006: 142).

Coping has been defined as anything that people do to manage problems or emotional responses (Carver and Scheier, 1994). Others have described the process of coping as a conscious response or reaction to external stressful or negative events (e.g. Kohn et al., 1994). In other words, the process of coping consists of the 'thoughts and behaviours that people use to manage the internal and external demands of situations that are appraised as stressful' (Lazarus and Folkman, 1984, quoted in Folkman and Moskowitz, 2004: 746). Gurung (2006) further elaborates this definition by splitting the process of coping into two categories: **coping styles** and **coping strategies**. Essentially, coping styles equate to general predispositions to dealing with stress. This means that, as individuals, we tend to adopt a particular approach when we face a stressful situation, and we tend to use this approach over and over again in a variety of situations. Coping styles tend to be described as 'approach' or 'avoidant'. People who take an **approach style** to coping are more likely to monitor their environment, to face issues 'head on' and to engage in problem-solving strategies to deal with the stressors they are facing. In contrast, those who engage in an **avoidant style** prefer to avoid the stressor if at all possible, and focus on addressing their emotional reaction to the stressor, rather than dealing with the stressor itself. The term 'coping strategies' refers to the specific behavioural and psychological efforts we make as we try to master, tolerate, reduce or minimize stressful events (Gurung, 2006: 144). Coping strategies have tended to be categorized as being either problem or emotion focused:

- **Problem-focused coping** involves directly facing the stressful situation and then working to find a way to resolve it. Examples of this kind of coping include making a plan of action or focusing on the next step (Folkman and Moskowitz, 2004). It is generally considered that problem-focused coping is most likely to be effective when there is something that can be done to control or address the stressor.

- **Emotion-focused coping** involves dealing with the emotions surrounding the stressor. This might involve attempts to positively reappraise the stressor in order to see it in a more positive light. Alternatively, an individual taking an emotion-focused approach might try to accept the situation, look for emotional support, vent their emotions or engage in spiritual activities, for example meditation.

Such approaches are considered to be more effective when there is nothing that can be done to control or address the stressor.

Summary

Conceptually and empirically, problem- and emotion-focused coping are intertwined. Thus, they suggest that the two forms of coping actually work to facilitate each other:

> Looking for the positive in a grim situation, for example, may encourage the person to engage in problem-focused coping. Conversely, effective problem-focused coping can lead to positive re-appraisal of the individual's competence, or it may lead to the appreciation of another person's contribution to the solution.
>
> (Folkman and Moskowitz, 2004: 753)

It is also important to recognize that coping strategies are not inherently good or bad. What makes the difference is the context in which they are implemented. This means that while a coping strategy may be effective in one instance, it might not work in another. Furthermore, it is important to remember that as we face situations in our lives, the context is not static, but is dynamic and may change, thereby requiring us to engage in a reappraisal of our situation. Folkman and Moskowitz (2004) give the example whereby it might be adaptive to engage in problem-focused coping before sitting an exam, for example completing the learning and revision necessary to prepare for the exam, and to engage in an emotion-focused strategy of 'distancing' once the exam is over and you are waiting for your results.

👁 Personality and coping

Gurung (2006) suggests that a person's personality characteristics provide some good clues as to how they will cope with a stressor. In this context, the term 'personality' refers to an individual's unique set of consistent behavioural traits. In 1987, McCrae and Costa developed a five-factor model of personality, which has come to be known as the **Big Five**. Gurung (2006) suggests the acronym OCEAN as an aid to remembering what the Big Five are:

- *O – Openness:* includes daring, nonconforming and imaginative characteristics, in other words 'open to new experiences'
- *C – Conscientiousness:* includes ethical, dependable, productive, purposeful characteristics, in other words 'responsible'
- *E – Extraversion:* includes talkative, fun-loving, affectionate characteristics, in other words, 'sociable'
- *A – Agreeableness:* includes sympathetic, warm, trusting characteristics, in other words, 'cooperative'
- *N – Neuroticism:* includes anxious, insecure, guilt-prone, self-conscious characteristics, in other words, 'tense'.

Morrison and Bennett (2009) note that much published research has focused on the neuroticism dimension. Individuals who have high levels of neuroticism often have anxious beliefs and engage in behaviour which is disproportionate to the situation (Suls and Martin, 2005). Individuals classified as high on neuroticism have also been shown to have an avoidant coping style which employs emotion-focused coping strategies (Semmer, 2006). Gurung (2006) mentions a study by McCormick and colleagues (1998) which showed that neuroticism was highly related to avoidant coping, agreeableness was negatively related to problem-focused coping, and conscientiousness was positively related to problem-focused coping and negatively related to avoidant coping. This research suggests that our personality traits are linked to the style and strategy of coping we employ when faced with stressors.

Defence mechanisms

One way of coping with a stressor is to employ psychological barriers, also known as **defence mechanisms**. There are four types most commonly referred to in the literature: repression, regression, rationalization, and denial, which we briefly outline:

1 **Repression** is a defensive coping style that works by protecting the individual from negative memories and anxiety-producing thoughts by preventing them from reaching consciousness (Morrison and Bennett, 2009: 262). For example, Ward and colleagues (1988) demonstrated that 'repressing' chemotherapy patients were found to report fewer physical symptoms than those who did not engage in repression.

2 **Regression** is a defensive coping style that is employed when an individual reverts to behaviours that are more appropriate to an earlier level of development. Milliken (1998: 268) offers a number of examples of regressive behaviour. These include elderly patients who have been bedridden for some time, lying in the fetal position and refusing to respond to their surroundings; or young children who have mastered the art of drinking from a cup, but then demand a bottle when a new brother or sister is born. Dependence on others for personal care when one is capable of self-care is another example.

3 **Rationalization** is sometimes also called 'intellectualization' and works by the individual explaining away the stress to themselves. In other words, they rationalize or intellectualize the stress, rather than accepting it as reality.

4 **Denial** is a defensive coping style that works by an individual refusing to believe that the stressful event is happening at all. Druss and Douglas (1988) note that diverse forms and degrees of denial have been described in the literature, ranging from clear-cut disavowal of illness, to avoiding talking or thinking about the stressor. It has been argued that the concept of 'denial' can subsume the repression, regression and rationalization styles. Indeed, Weisman and Hackett (1961), as quoted by Druss and Douglas (1988: 165), went so far as to define denial as 'the conscious or unconscious repudiation of part or all of the total available meaning of an event to allay fear, anxiety or other unpleasant effects'. More recently, Vos and colleagues (2009) investigated the relation between denial and physical outcomes among lung cancer patients. They concluded that a moderate or increasing level of denial was consistently related to improved patient-rated physical outcomes. Specifically, lung cancer patients displaying more denial reported a better overall perception of health as well as better physical functioning. Vos and colleagues (2009) suggest that denial may be an adaptive response in lung cancer patients and might be something which should be respected in clinical settings. They suggest that it is possible that through avoiding confrontation with some aspects of their disease and treatment, patients can protect themselves from an uncontrollable reality.

⊙ Social support and coping

The way in which we cope with stress is often influenced by how much support we receive from those around us. It is important to point out that while the amount of support available to us is important, perhaps of greater importance is our perception of the level of support we have. People who believe that they have **social support** feel 'loved, cared for, esteemed, valued' (Morrison and Bennett, 2009: 382). Gurung (2006) describes the evidence showing the usefulness of social support as 'astounding'. Social support is essentially emotional, informational or practical support from others and has been linked to better health and faster recovery from illness, and to reducing psychological distress and improving emotional wellbeing.

Morrison and Bennett (2009: 383) highlight that social support is incorporated within the model of stress and coping put forward by Lazarus and Folkman (1984) in the form of a 'resource variable'. In other words, if social support is perceived as being available, it will affect how individuals appraise and respond to stressors. Those who perceive their social support as high are more likely to appraise events as being less stressful than those who do not feel they have support.

Several researchers have explored the influence of social support on those experiencing chronic illness and disabilities. For example, Levy and Heiden (1990) and Temoshok (1985) demonstrated that for cancer patients, social support was associated with an enhanced quality of life and better disease outcome. Furthermore, Burgoyne and Saunders (2000) showed that support from spouses and partners was especially influential among those who were chronically ill. Lichtenthal and colleagues (2003) wanted to explore this further. They noted that much of the previous work in the field had relied on patient self-reports about the support their partners provided. Whilst this approach provides valuable information about the importance of our perceptions of the level of support available to us, it does not tap into whether how patients perceive support matches the support partners think they are providing. In other words, although partners might think they are providing excellent support, unless patients also perceive the support offered in a positive manner, they will rate it poorly. There is therefore a need to gain insight into whether there is a match between both parties' perceptions of the support provided and received.

In exploring the relationship between patient and partner reports of social support, Lichtenthal and colleagues (2003) found a lack of fit between patient reports of the support they said they received and partners' reports of the support they said they had provided. This finding suggests that whilst partners think they are providing support, they are not perceived as doing so by their ill spouses. Given the weight of evidence highlighting the potential benefits of social support, this study provides important information and suggests that clear communication between partners, where one is ill and the other is providing support, is crucial; partners wish to provide appropriate support and patients could be empowered to be able to ask for the kind of support they require if what is being provided does not meet their needs.

King and colleagues (2006: 902) describe social support as 'one of the most important factors affecting how people adapt to adversity'. They explored the importance of social support at crucial transitions in life. They interviewed 15 individuals aged 30–50 years of age who had chronic, non-progressive disabilities, such as a physical disability or attention deficit disorder. They concluded that social support played a significant role in the adaptation of their participants to challenging events and experiences in their lives. Social support

> made them feel good about themselves (emotional support), gave them tools and strategies to address their issues (practical support) and helped them to feel not alone in their situations and experiences (cognitive support). (King et al., 2006: 915)

These studies provide evidence for the importance of social support in terms of coping with stress as well as health outcomes; however, we have not yet covered how the process of social support is thought to produce these effects. Two main theories have been put forward to explain how social support might operate: the direct effects hypothesis and the buffering hypothesis:

- The **direct effects hypothesis** suggests that social support is beneficial to us, regardless of the amount of stress we experience, and vice versa, a lack of social support is detrimental to our health, even in the absence of stress (Morrison and Bennett, 2009: 384).
- The **buffering hypothesis** suggests that social support works by protecting the individual against the negative effects of stress. Social support acts as a buffer either by influencing the way in

which a person thinks about the situation (their appraisal), or by modifying the coping strategy adopted by the individual, in other words, they seek help from others in order to cope with the stressor (Morrison and Bennett, 2009: 384).

Summary

Whether social support acts as a buffer or with direct effects, there is clear evidence to suggest that it has an important role to play in terms of how we manage stress.

◉ Managing stress

Having defined coping and explored some of the mechanisms which have an impact on coping, we now turn our attention to how the ways in which we cope might impact on our ability to manage stress. Health psychologists have identified two main approaches to the management of stress. The first approach focuses on relaxation techniques and the second focuses on a more cognitive behavioural technique.

Relaxation approaches

Most of the stressors we experience today in the West are related to thinking. As Gurung (2006: 161) puts it: 'our worrying about problems and anticipation of threats causes the most havoc'. Generating these worries and focusing on them activates our stress–response (described in Chapter 6). Relaxation-based approaches aim to reduce our focus on these thoughts, which lessens our stress–response.

There are a number of different approaches to relaxation, including progressive muscle relaxation, biofeedback, systematic desensitization, exercise and drug therapy, all of which are briefly described below.

Progressive muscle relaxation

Individuals learning **progressive muscle relaxation** (PMR) are first taught that having tense muscles results in tension which increases the feeling of being stressed. In learning to relax their muscles, they can reduce the level of stress they are experiencing (Curtis, 2000). A person implementing PMR would either be lying down or sitting comfortably. They begin by breathing deeply and exhaling slowly. Following this, they tense a muscle in their foot, for example, and hold the tension for 10 seconds. They then release this tension slowly and focus on the feeling of relaxation as the tension in that muscle fades away. The sequence is repeated for each muscle group (toes, feet, calves, thighs, stomach, hands, arms, shoulders, neck, forehead and so on) as they gradually work their way up their body. The process of first tensing and then relaxing muscles helps an individual to learn to recognize and distinguish between a tensed muscle and a completely relaxed muscle. With this simple knowledge, it is then possible for the individual to bring about physical muscular relaxation at the first sign of the tension that accompanies anxiety.

Biofeedback

Biofeedback involves the use of equipment which can track our physiological responses, for example our pulse, and provides us with feedback about it if it changes. So, when you are wired up to the equipment and are faced with a stressor, your high pulse will be indicated to you, perhaps by a sound or an image on a screen. The idea is that as you practise your relaxation strategies, you receive instant feedback concerning how effective they are, the sound slows or the image alters as you lower your pulse. The provision of feedback helps to reinforce your relaxation strategies.

Systematic desensitization

Systematic desensitization is a form of **classical conditioning**. Classical conditioning is the process which actively pairs up actions and their reactions (Forshaw, 2002). In the case of coping with stress, stressful thoughts or events are paired with relaxation. The theory is that if two events are linked enough times, a trained response can develop. Gurung (2006) uses the example of public speaking. If you were anxious about speaking in public, your first task would be to make a list of the things that scare you when you think about speaking in public, with the scariest thing at the top and the least scary at the bottom. You then focus on the bottom (least scary) item on your list and think about it while practising relaxing. You do this until you can think of that item without getting anxious. You repeat this with the next scary item until that no longer scares you, and so on. Once you have established a link between the thought and the relaxation, the idea is that speaking in public will not be so stressful.

This approach has been applied in other contexts, particularly in the field of phobias. To take the example of spiders, a person who is afraid of spiders may first be asked to look at a cartoon picture of a spider, then, once they are no longer anxious, a picture of a real spider may be used. The next step could be a video of a spider, followed by observing a spider in a transparent box, followed by holding the box with the live spider, followed by taking the lid off the box, followed by holding the spider. This form of desensitization is called a **titration methodology** (Gilroy et al., 2003), which involves individuals moving forward with the task containing the object of their phobia until anxiety is experienced, moving back and onwards until the anxiety disappears. For an example of titration methodology using a wooden spider toy to help spider phobics overcome their anxiety, see Chamove (2007).

Exercise

Increasing our physical activity can be an effective tool to cope with stress. Research has shown that people who exercise on a regular basis tend to be less depressed and less stressed (e.g. Salmon, 2001). Exercise helps us to cope with stress because engaging in exercise influences the release and processing of stress hormones and also varies the way in which the nervous system reacts to stress. For example, Throne and colleagues (2000) worked with firemen; half were assigned to an exercise condition, and half to a 'no-exercise' condition. Both groups were then stressed with a fire drill. Throne and colleagues (2000) found that those who were 'exercise-trained' reacted with lower pulse rates than those in the no-exercise condition. Other researchers have also found that exercise helps individuals to cope with stress (e.g. Babyak et al., 2000; Ker and Kuk, 2001). Gurung (2006: 166) concludes that 'the next time you feel stressed with work, it may be worth the effort to exercise even if you only take a quick paced walk outside'.

Drugs

We highlighted in Chapter 6 the physiological ways in which stress can impact on us. It follows that some approaches to stress management have targeted the physiological reactions that take place in our bodies – the assumption being that if the physiological reactions (symptoms of stress) can be reduced, the impact of stress will also be reduced. Thus, drugs which focus on reducing the physical symptoms of stress, such as increased heart rate and high blood pressure, are sometimes prescribed to those suffering from stress. Drugs which are prescribed to deal with stress belong to the benzodiazepine family. Benzodiazepines affect the levels of a neurotransmitter called GABA in the brain. GABA works to quieten down the physiological processes that we described in Chapter 6, thereby reducing physiological arousal and so resulting in the individual feeling calmer.

The key issue to remember with drug therapies for stress is that they address the symptoms, but not the cause of the stress. They are therefore perhaps of greatest benefit as a tool for helping someone through a stressful situation (in the immediate aftermath of the death of a loved one, or to help an individual reduce their stress before a public performance) but they do not offer a long-term solution. As a worst-case scenario, individuals could become reliant on the drugs prescribed, and, with prolonged use, their tolerance to them increases, which means that stronger doses will be needed in order to reduce the physical symptoms of stress. Thus, in the longer term, psychological therapy aimed at dealing with the issue concerned would be more effective in helping the individual to develop more effective coping strategies to deal with the stressor concerned.

Summary

There are a plethora of approaches to coping with stress. In this part of the chapter, we have focused on those that take a relaxation approach and so emphasize the importance of the influence of physical relaxation on the stress response. However, an alternative approach is to focus on calming the interpretation of stressors by targeting our cognitive, behavioural and social reactions. In so doing, it is envisaged that they will bring about a calming effect on our physiological reaction to stress. These are known as 'cognitive behavioural approaches'.

Cognitive behavioural and social approaches

Cognitive behavioural approaches are designed to help an individual learn to label the stressor, discuss the emotions associated with it and find a way to solve it. Mechanisms employed under this approach include cognitive behavioural therapy, emotional expression, music, humour, and mindfulness-based stress reduction, all of which are detailed below.

Cognitive behavioural therapy

Cognitive behavioural therapy (CBT) emphasizes the importance of changing cognitions and behaviours. The assumption is that by changing an individual's perceptions and thoughts about a stressor, this may in turn influence their emotional and physiological reactions to the stressor. Thus, a key principle of CBT is that the way in which a person interprets events and experiences has a major effect on that person's mood and behaviour. Some individuals develop automatic patterns of thinking that are considered to be distortions of reality. These patterns may result from states of depression, anxiety or stress (Hawton et al., 2006: 153). In CBT, the therapist aims to help the individual to identify their distorted patterns of thinking and the way these thought patterns influence their mood and behaviour. Once this link has been identified, the therapist then helps the individual to focus on changing the way in which they interpret events and experiences. For example, Antoni and colleagues (2009) explored the use of CBT with women undergoing treatment for breast cancer. They note that women are faced with adversity as they try to adapt to the diagnosis of and treatment for breast cancer. It has been shown that women who have poor cognitive coping skills and a negative outlook (e.g. Carver et al., 1993) and fewer social resources (Alferi et al., 2001) experience greater anxiety and distress during the stressful period of treatment. In a brief review of the literature, Antoni and colleagues (2009) demonstrate that psychosocial and relaxation-based interventions have been shown to be helpful in terms of improving emotional adjustment and quality of life in cancer patients undergoing medical treatments (e.g. Luebbert et al., 2001). In particular, CBT interventions have been shown to improve depression, anxiety and quality of life in cancer patients (e.g. Kissane et al., 2003; Trask et al., 2003).

Emotional expression

Schüler and colleagues (2009) state that there is broad empirical evidence showing that expressing stress-related emotions and thoughts can improve health and subjective wellbeing. They note that emotional expression has been found to be associated with enhanced immune functioning (e.g. Petrie et al., 1995), fewer visits to the physician (e.g. Lepore and Greenberg, 2002), lower blood pressure (e.g. McGuire et al., 2005) and improved psychological health (e.g. Sloan and Marx, 2004). An unusual exploration of emotional expression was reported by Stephens and colleagues (2009) who found that swearing generally increased their participants' tolerance for pain.

The notion of emotional expression was developed by Pennebaker (1993) and his colleagues. The method they developed involved asking participants to write down their deepest thoughts and feelings about an extremely important emotional issue that has affected them and their life (Pennebaker et al., 2001). The mechanism underlying this process concerns the disclosure of emotions. Disclosing emotions is thought to change the emotional and cognitive processing of a stressful experience in such a way that thinking about the stressful experience loses its ability to disrupt emotions and trigger physiological stress reactions (Lepore et al., 2002). Pennebaker and Seagal (1999: 1248) summarize this process: 'Once a person has developed a new meaning of the stressful experience, the event can be summarised, stored and forgotten more efficiently.'

Music

Nilsson (2009: 201) suggests that healing environments 'help patients refocus from negative stimuli to something more pleasant and familiar, allowing them to escape into a world of their own'. She further suggests that a key feature of such an environment can be soothing music. Music has been shown to be closely linked to both emotions and arousal. Indeed, Bernardi and colleagues (2006) reported that listening to music modulated emotional arousal; Nilsson (2008) showed that soothing music inhibited stress by reducing anxiety and sedative use; and Nilsson and colleagues (2005) and Cepeda and colleagues (2006) showed that listening to music reduced pain and therefore had a positive impact on stress.

Other researchers have focused their attention on adolescents. Listening to music is described by Miranda and Claes (2009) as a 'paramount source of enjoyment and entertainment in adolescence'. Other researchers have established that adolescents use listening to music as one of their most important coping strategies (e.g. Larson, 1995). One reason put forward to try to explain this is that listening to music helps to regulate emotions. It is thought that this can happen through one of three means:

1 distraction from unwanted moods
2 solace and validation of personal issues
3 catharsis in relation to negative moods (Schwartz and Fouts, 2003).

Confirming these findings, Miranda and Claes (2009) found that adolescents in their sample reported deliberately using listening to music as a means of coping with daily stress. Although Miranda and Claes (2009) suggested that listening to music can take the form of a problem-solving approach, for example by playing songs with lyrics that offer solace and advice for the issues adolescents are experiencing, listening to music is primarily considered to be an emotion-focused approach to coping.

Humour

Some researchers working in the psychoneuroimmunology field have suggested that humour or laughter might have a positive effect on health through moderating the production of stress chemicals. Martin and Dobbin (1988) tested this theory using a sample of college students to see if sense of humour might act as a moderator of daily hassles and concluded that although they could find no direct relationship, a sense of humour might act as a buffer against daily hassles. More recently, Bennett and Lengacher (2009) have reviewed the literature exploring the influence of humour and laughter on physiological and psychological wellbeing. This particular branch of research is replete with difficulties, not least because how we define humour is subjective, some subjects exposed to a humorous stimulus do not laugh, or do not find it funny. It is also difficult to choose a neutral stimulus to use with control groups. Researchers have also used different conceptualizations of humour and different methodologies to examine the effect of humour, which makes it difficult to summarize the body of research conducted. As a consequence, Bennett and Lengacher (2009) conclude that findings are, to date, little more than tentative and more work is needed before broad claims can be made for humour having an impact on health outcomes.

Mindfulness-based stress reduction

Mindfulness-based stress reduction (MBSR) is a psycho-educational training programme in mindfulness and its applications to daily life (Biegel et al., 2009). Mindfulness involves giving close attention to stimuli that enter our awareness, without engaging in discursive thought about them. MBSR encourages individuals to develop an attitude of acceptance or non-judgementality towards events and experiences (Shapiro et al., 2006). The idea is that we do not ignore unpleasant thoughts or sensations, but try to embrace these thoughts as they occur. As thoughts enter our consciousness, we are encouraged to observe them non-judgementally. This process is thought to help us to gain insight into how we interpret the world, as well as into the drives that motivate us. In gaining insight, we should be able to relax through this process of self-discovery (Curtis, 2000).

Biegel and colleagues (2009) argue that there is a growing body of research which suggests that mindfulness-based psychosocial interventions are effective for a wide range of mental and physical health disorders. For example, Miller and colleagues (1995) demonstrated that at a three-year follow-up, after having completed MBSR, a cohort of patients had maintained the clinical improvements they had achieved on completion of the MBSR training. The study also showed that these patients continued to practise MBSR techniques regularly. Furthermore, Davidson and colleagues (2003) showed that mindfulness meditation enhanced antibody production following influenza vaccination. Similarly, Baer (2003) reviewed the use of mindfulness training as a clinical intervention and showed that MBSR had been widely used with patients with chronic pain. She found that the research demonstrated significant improvements in the rating of pain, other medical symptoms as well as more general psychological symptoms. Having reviewed the MBSR literature, she concluded that there was evidence to suggest that mindfulness-based interventions might help to improve psychological functioning.

Summary

Health psychologists have identified two main approaches to the management of stress. Both approaches acknowledge the causal link between our physiological and psychological responses to stress. Relaxation approaches target the physiological response, whereas cognitive behavioural approaches target the psychological response; both approaches suggest that in focusing on one element of the response to stress, you are also indirectly influencing the other.

◉ Conclusion

This chapter has provided an overview of the field of coping, with particular attention being paid to the process of coping with stress. We have shown that there are a variety of influences on, and approaches to, the process of coping. It has become increasingly clear that there are many different variables which influence the relationship between a stressor and our response to it. Indeed, Morrison and Bennett (2009: 387) note that 'biological, psychological and social factors work together in the stress-illness experience'.

We have highlighted the evidence in the literature which demonstrates the utility of both emotion-focused and problem-focused coping. We have also shown that there appear to be some situations where engaging in defence mechanisms, traditionally viewed as a negative strategy, can have positive health outcomes. It is therefore reasonable to suggest that effective coping is characterized by the flexibility to react appropriately to different situations (Wenzel et al., 2002). What is considered appropriate is likely to vary from person to person and context to context. This has been highlighted by Folkman and Moskowitz (2004), who noted that a given coping process may be effective in one situation, but not another. Therefore, one stressor may require us to call on our social support network, perhaps for practical or emotional support, another situation may require us to face the problem and work out ways of dealing with the challenges it presents, and still other situations may require us to address the emotional reactions we have in response to the stressor.

So, we can conclude that coping with stress requires an individual to react appropriately to stressors, and that different coping strategies are required for different situations, stressors and contexts. We suggest that effective coping requires us, as individuals, to develop a 'toolbox' of strategies that we can use for different situations, thereby developing the flexibility referred to above by Wenzel and colleagues (2002).

◉ Further reading

Kabat-Zinn, J. (2005). *Coming to our Senses: Healing Ourselves and the World through Mindfulness.* Piatkus: London.

◉ Key search terms

Stress, coping, social support, personality, emotion-focused coping, problem-focused coping

Chapter 8

Eating behaviour

👁 Introduction

Eating is something we all do, but it is also something we rarely pay attention to. Many of us do other things when we eat; we listen to the radio, watch television or carry on working while we eat at our desks. Without food, we cannot function. Food is of fundamental importance for health, not simply in terms of getting enough food to give us energy, but also in terms of getting the right combination of foods to give us the nutrients we need to function well (Steptoe and Wardle, 2004). It is therefore not enough to eat, we also need to pay attention to eating healthily if we are to reduce our risks of becoming ill.

In Jerome K. Jerome's *Three Men in a Boat* (1889), one of the lead characters reports how he has recently been reading a medical book which describes the symptoms for various maladies in great detail. He goes through this book reading about ailments from A to Z and concludes he has the symptoms for everything except housemaid's knee. He says:

> Gout, in its most malignant stage, it would appear, had seized me without my being aware of it; and zymosis I had evidently been suffering with from boyhood. There were no more diseases after zymosis, so I concluded there was nothing else the matter with me.

He began to wonder how long he had to live and decided to visit his doctor. He explained in detail to his doctor how it was that he came to be suffering from all diseases known to man (except housemaid's knee). His doctor examined him and then wrote a prescription. The prescription read:

1 lb. beefsteak, with
1 pt. bitter beer, every six hours.
1 ten-mile walk every morning.
1 bed at 11 sharp every night.
And don't stuff up your head with things you don't understand.

This example illustrates how our conception of what constitutes healthy eating behaviour has changed over time. In the 1880s, eating red meat regularly was considered healthy, whereas today we are more commonly advised to reduce our intake of red meat. Current recommendations include eating a wide variety of fruit and vegetables every day along with high-fibre carbohydrates. Meat, fish and dairy products should be eaten in moderation, whilst fatty and sugary foods should be eaten infrequently and in small amounts (Ogden, 2007: 128).

What we eat and how we eat plays an important role in our long-term health (Morrison and Bennett, 2009: 63). Researchers have demonstrated links between diet and heart disease as well as some forms of cancer. In this chapter we focus on the different factors that are thought to influence our eating behaviour. The different theories that have been proposed to explain our eating behaviour are outlined. Finally, we turn our attention to the issue of dieting.

> **In this chapter, we will examine:**
> - Health concerns, eating behaviour and culture
> - Biological explanations for eating behaviour
> - Evolutionary explanations for eating behaviour
> - Psychological explanations for eating behaviour
> - Dieting

Health concerns, eating behaviour and culture

Our food choices and our eating behaviour are very much linked to our health. Our diet can have an influence on whether or not we stay well or succumb to illness. In some instances, a particular diet can make us more or less likely to develop certain diseases, similarly, the kinds of food we eat (or do not eat) can help us to manage chronic conditions such as diabetes or coronary heart disease. If we are lacking nutrients, our body will not function as efficiently as we would like, and in particular, our immune system might be weakened, making us more susceptible to infections. In other words, our eating behaviour should be a health concern of ours. However, whether or not we engage in healthy eating is affected by many variables, some of which will be explored in this chapter.

Different cultures have different beliefs and attitudes towards food. For example, in traditional Chinese medicine, health equates to the balance of yin and yang, which are described as the two complementary forces in the universe (Kaptchuk, 2000). Yin and yang are translated into hot and cold qualities (not temperatures) found in foods. To be healthy, it is thought that you should balance 'hot' and 'cold' foods. This idea is common in many different cultures, including Chinese, Indian and Mexican (Gurung, 2006). Examples of 'hot' foods include garlic, ginger, chicken, alcohol and sour foods, and examples of 'cold' foods include cabbage, celery, honey, milk and melon.

There are also differences in the way in which cultures view food. In the West, an 'epidemic' of food worrying has been identified by Becker (1986). Rozin and colleagues (1999: 164) suggested that there is a 'sense among many Americans that food is as much a poison as it is a nutrient, and that eating is almost as dangerous as not eating'. This extreme attitude contrasts starkly with a much more relaxed, pleasure-oriented attitude to food among the French (Stearns, 1997). It is clear, then, that the culture in which we live will influence what foods are considered palatable, desirable and healthy, as well as the attitudes we hold towards our food and the concerns we have about our eating behaviour.

This is illustrated in a study designed to explore cultural differences in terms of attitudes towards food and the role it plays in everyday life. Rozin and colleagues (1999) compared people from America, France, Belgium and Japan and found that the Americans in their sample were most likely to report health concerns, worrying about their diet as well as modifying their diet in the direction they perceived as healthy. They were also the cultural group least likely to consider themselves to be healthy eaters. In contrast, the French participants worried least and had the most positive attitude towards food. Stearns (1997) suggests that these disparities could be explained by the differences in traditional eating patterns in the two countries; with a French emphasis on moderation and high quality, and an American emphasis on high quantity. Rozin and colleagues (1999) conclude that there are substantial differences in concerns about diet and health in different countries. Furthermore, they suggest that there could be a link between this and food-related stress and, as a consequence, call for more research exploring this link between food/health attitudes and patterns of food intake. In the final sentence of their article, they suggest that 'on the psychological level, Americans may have something to learn from the French' (Rozin et al., 1999: 179), thereby highlighting the influence culture might have on our attitudes and behaviours where food is concerned.

The influence of the mass media on health promotion was explored in Chapter 6. In the context of eating behaviour, the mass media exert a considerable influence and can serve to make eating behaviour a health concern that we take note of. For example, Gough (2007) notes the status of food in popular Western culture is evidenced by the high number of successful cooking programmes as well as the many cooking columns, recipes and restaurant reviews in magazines and newspapers, which Chamberlain (2004) has coined 'gastro-porn'. Food-related activities (shopping, cooking, eating, dieting) enjoy a similarly high profile to that given to food itself. Such activities are conventionally portrayed in Western society as female centred (Caplan et al., 1998). Similarly, there is a widespread assumption that men tend to rely on women for advice and support on food and health (e.g. Courtenay, 2000).

The idea that women traditionally buy, prepare and cook food, whilst men are thought to be less knowledgeable about the benefits of particular foodstuffs (Nutrition Forum, UK, 2003), that men report eating less fruit and vegetables than women (Baker and Wardle, 2003) and that food and health have traditionally been associated with femininity led Gough (2007) to direct his attention to exploring the role the media plays in influencing men's diet. He analysed a database of UK national newspapers and searched for articles relating to men and diet. He identified three different styles of media reporting:

1 *Warning! Male diet kills:* male eating habits were implicated in the onset of serious illness, especially cancer, but also heart problems, obesity and sexual dysfunction. The clear message of these kinds of articles was that men should change their ways in order to protect their health.

2 *Men cooking, but in a 'masculine' way:* these articles report on men engaging in cooking, but the terminology employed highlights the masculine way in which such a task is approached. Military and sporting metaphors abound.

3 *Real men don't diet:* these articles establish dieting as a female domain, an irrational place, which is now beginning to attract more

men. Where diets are directed at men, they are once again constructed in stereotypically male-friendly ways, emphasizing toughness and endurance.

Gough (2007) concludes that the media representation of men and diets is done in a stereotypically masculine manner. Diet continues to be something which is construed as women centred and therefore non-masculine. Gough concludes that until the media representation of men and diet changes, it is unlikely that males will be encouraged to take up healthier eating behaviours. Specifically, he suggests that

> media features will need to recognize diversity between men, entertain the possibility that some men are actively interested in what they eat and how it affects their health and produce advice tailored to specific groups of men so that particular concerns and constraints are taken into account. (Gough, 2007: 336)

Gough does not, however, offer solutions as to how his suggestions might be implemented.

Having outlined some of the issues which impact on whether or not we see eating behaviour as worthy of being a health concern, we now turn our attention to three accounts that have been put forward to explain our eating behaviour.

Biological explanations for eating behaviour

Food intake and energy expenditure are controlled by complex neural systems which we describe in this chapter in a simplified manner. Lenard and Berthoud (2008) note that there has been much progress in identifying the important role of the various hormonal and neural mechanisms by which the brain acts to create a state of **homeostasis** (or balance) through regulating our eating behaviour. The main part of our brain involved in regulating our appetite is the hypothalamus. The lateral hypothalamus triggers feelings of hunger, whereas the ventromedial hypothalamus triggers a sense of feeling full, and is often called the 'satiety centre'. It is the interaction between these two parts of the hypothalamus that Nisbett (1972) focused upon in the development of set-point theory.

Set-point theory

Set-point theory was put forward by Nisbett (1972), who argued that body weight is determined by a set-point, which regulates weight in the same way that a thermostat regulates the temperature of a radiator (Stroebe et al., 2008). Nisbett (1972) suggested that different people had their weight set at different levels. Stroebe and colleagues (2008: 176) note that 'in our culture, obese individuals face the unfortunate situation that their weight is set far above the cultural norm'. The underpinning argument is that, as individuals, we will fight to defend our body weight against any pressure to change, and that this might be why overweight and obese individuals have trouble achieving what society deems to be 'normal' weight. This theory has been criticized for lacking empirical support (e.g. Pinel et al., 2000; Stroebe, 2008), but it has had a lasting impact on thinking about eating behaviour, particularly in the field of obesity.

The role of neural mechanisms involved in controlling eating and satiation

Towards the top of the hypothalamus the paraventricular nucleus (PVN) can be found. The PVN works to integrate signals that influence metabolic and digestive processes. A key signal is the peptide neurostransmitter known as neuropeptide Y (NPY). NPY has the main function of increasing food intake and decreasing physical activity. It also increases the proportion of energy stored as fat. NPY is released by the hypothalamus in response to decreased levels of the hormone leptin.

Leptin is a hormone that is secreted by fat cells and sends messages to the brain about the amount of fat which is stored in the body's fat cells (known as adipocytes). Lean individuals secrete less leptin than fatter individuals. Leptin has an indirect effect on our satiety. As the levels of stored fat increase, more leptin will be secreted, the brain interprets the rising levels of leptin as signalling the need to eat less, consequently we feel full (satiated) sooner. In contrast, if we engage in dieting, as the levels of stored fat decrease, so too do the levels of leptin. This reduction in leptin signals to the hypothalamus that there is a need to increase food intake and NPY is secreted.

Working alongside this process, as we eat and become full, our stomach and intestinal tract distend. As these stretch, they send signals to our brain and when food arrives in the stomach, the peptide cholecystokinin (CCK) is released into the blood system by the small intestine. CCK works to send a message to neurons in the lower brainstem that control digestion, as well as to other neurons in the forebrain which inhibit the intake of food (Greenough et al., 1998). Serotonin is also thought to play a role in regulating our eating behaviour, in particular with decreasing our food intake. Its role in carbohydrate craving is discussed in more detail later in this chapter.

Evolutionary explanations for eating behaviour

> A scientist from another planet observing human feeding habits would be quick to notice four things: the remarkable variation in food habits within and between populations, the fact that in many populations food is farmed rather than hunted or gathered, the importance of cultural traditions and ritual in relation to food, and the fact that food is often processed – e.g. by cooking or other means – before it is eaten. It is this last of these that is completely human. (Krebs, 2009: 707)

So begins the review article written by John Krebs, in which he states that whilst it is tempting to argue that human food preferences are shaped by culture and individual experience, it is also important to recognize our evolutionary heritage. The importance of this heritage is, he notes, underlined by our physiology and anatomy. For example, researchers studying human remains have been able to ascertain that our early ancestors were **omnivores** – they ate both plants and animals. Researchers have even been able to estimate that the diet of our ancestors was approximately 75% fruit and leaves and 25% meat. Omnivores are adapted to eat a variety of foods in relatively small quantities, which in turn minimizes possible toxicity (only a small amount is ingested) and maximizes nutrition (if one source of food is low in a particular nutrient, eating a variety of foods ensures that the nutrient will be gained elsewhere). Remick and colleagues (2009) conclude that our omnivore status – our preference for a variety of foods – is advantageous for humans.

Other evolutionary evidence for our eating preferences and behaviours has come from the study of the use of spices in food. In response to the question 'Why are spices, which are potentially toxic, as well as costly, added to food?', two key nutritionally based answers have been offered:

first, that spices contain important nutrients and second, that they have **antimicrobial properties** and can therefore kill or inhibit the growth of microorganisms such as bacteria (Sherman and Billing, 1999). A third suggestion, which we include for completeness sake, is that because spices were (and still are) expensive, adding them to your food was a way of letting other people know you were wealthy. However, of more relevance to this chapter, researchers have noticed that more spices are used in hotter climates, and that the spices that tend to be used are those that inhibit bacterial growth in meat dishes (Sherman and Hash, 2001). The suggestion is that through cultural evolution, we have learned to harness the natural protective aspects of these spices and have incorporated them into our diets and food preferences.

A further strand of evolutionary research has focused on our genetic evolution. One theory put forward is the idea of **thrifty genes** (e.g. Diamond, 2003). Krebs (2009) explains that in the past, we were genetically selected to cope with periods of famine and feast. This meant that our human ancestors who possessed the thrifty gene, and were therefore 'programmed' to have large appetites, combined with the ability to take up energy quickly, would have had an advantage. In other words, thrifty genes enable individuals to efficiently collect and process food to deposit fat during periods of food abundance. However, the influence of the thrifty gene is not so advantageous in today's era of relative plenty and could potentially explain the rise in obesity levels we are currently experiencing. Indeed, this idea is picked up on by Ulijaszek (2002), who notes that our ancestors would have chosen to eat energy-dense foods as a means of maximizing their energy intake because they did not know for sure when they would next be able to eat. In other words, food availability was less certain. In contrast, our present-day eating behaviour is characterized by the consumption of high energy-dense diets which are no longer linked to seasonal cycles of food availability. This means we continue to prefer energy-dense foods, even though our need for them has lessened. Thus, whilst it is possible that the way in which we have evolved, physically, anatomically and genetically, plays a role in our eating behaviour, Krebs (2009) explains that the picture is a complex one and reminds us of the importance of taking into account other variables as we seek explanations for our eating behaviour. Although our evolutionary background

> may help to explain our food preferences and our responses to food, as well as variation in these responses, this does not downplay the

crucial importance of environmental, developmental and cultural influences. (Krebs, 2009: 710)

👁 Psychological explanations for eating behaviour

Psychologists have approached the task of explaining our eating behaviour from a variety of perspectives. For example, much work has explored the relationship between food and mood, and, more specifically, on why it is that when our mood is low, we often turn to carbohydrates. Other researchers have taken a more developmental perspective and explored how the processes of exposure to food and social learning can impact upon our eating behaviour. Finally, the notion of 'mindless eating' put forward by Wansink (2007) is explored.

Mood

Much of the work conducted on food and its relationship with mood has focused on the impact of negative mood and in particular on the consumption of carbohydrates. **Carbohydrate craving syndrome** is characterized by an almost irresistible desire to consume sweet or starchy foods in response to negative mood states (Wurtman, 1990). It has been suggested that eating carbohydrates triggers mood improvement, and that eating such foods can be considered a form of self-medication (e.g. Wurtman and Wurtman, 1995). One potential explanation for the carbohydrate craving syndrome is that people crave carbohydrates when their brains are low in a neurotransmitter called 'serotonin'. Serotonin is responsible for reducing appetite, alleviating irritability and raising moods (Wurtman and Wurtman, 1995). Cavallo and Pinto (2001) explain why carbohydrates are important in this process. Carbohydrates act through the hormone insulin, which in turn stimulates the levels of tryptophan in the brain, which is then converted to serotonin. When our levels of serotonin are low, we tend to feel depressed, irritable or tense and eating carbohydrates indirectly raises serotonin levels, creating a euphoric effect (Fernstrom and Wurtman, 1971).

Carbohydrate craving syndrome was recently investigated by Corsica and Spring (2008) in their placebo controlled, double-blind trial. In their three-part trial, overweight females who met strict criteria for carbohydrate craving took part. Participants reported their mood before and at several time points after having their mood lowered (otherwise known as **dysphoric mood induction**). After their mood was lowered, on day one, they were served a carbohydrate drink, on day two, they were served a protein-rich drink. Both drinks had been 'taste matched', meaning they tasted the same. The drinks were also calorie matched and only differed in their nutrient content. On the third day, participants were presented with both drinks and asked to choose the one they preferred, based on how it had made them feel in the earlier tests.

Results showed that, when their mood was lowered, carbohydrate cravers chose the carbohydrate drink significantly more often than the protein-rich drink and reported that they had chosen it because they felt it had produced greater mood improvement. The carbohydrate drink was perceived as being more palatable by the carbohydrate cravers, although before the trial, independent 'taste testers' did not report a difference between the two drinks. Corsica and Spring (2008) concluded that their study supported the existence and positive impact on mood of carbohydrate craving syndrome.

Lyman (1989) suggests that the relationship between food and mood is bidirectional, that is, in the same way that our choice of food might affect our mood, our mood can affect our choice of food. Similarly, Christensen (2001) suggested that a cyclical relationship exists between food and mood in emotionally distressed individuals. This was elaborated on by Christensen and Brooks (2006: 294), who state that

> emotional distress, especially symptoms such as depression and fatigue, generates cravings for sweet carbohydrate- and fat-rich snacks, such as ice cream, candy bars and desserts. The cravings cause a search for and consumption of these snack foods, which results in a temporary mood improvement. Because the improvement is temporary, the negative mood state returns and the cycle starts again.

Other researchers have also linked craving behaviour with emotional eating (e.g. Hill et al., 1991) and with mood (e.g. Christensen and Pettijohn, 2001). Similarly, Sayegh and colleagues (1995) demonstrated that drinking a sweet, carbohydrate-rich drink reduced reported depression, anger and confusion in women who had severe menstrual symptoms.

To further explore the hypothesized cyclical relationship between food and mood, Christensen and Brooks (2006) set out to investigate the effect of simulated distressing and non-distressing events on individuals' beliefs about the type of food they would eat. Participants were asked to read a 'happy' or 'sad' vignette, put themselves in the situation described and picture themselves experiencing and feeling the events and emotions described. After reading the vignette, they reflected on what they thought they would do if they had actually experienced the events described, and then completed a food questionnaire in which they were asked to rate the likelihood of eating each of the foods listed. Although the study can be criticized on methodological grounds – participants were all introductory psychology students and therefore perhaps not representative of the wider population, and the scenarios were vignettes rather than 'real' – the findings of this study provided support for other published studies. Christensen and Brooks (2006) suggest that they have provided further evidence that food selection is influenced by mood.

Exposure

We need to eat a variety of foods in order to have a balanced diet, but, paradoxically, we show fear and avoidance of novel food stuffs. This is called **food neophobia**. Neophobia means fear (phobia) of new things (neo), in this context, new things are foodstuffs. Defined by Pliner and Hobden (1992) as the 'reluctance to eat and/or avoidance of novel foods', food neophobia influences everyday human food choices, both in terms of willingness to try novel foods, as well as expected liking and sampling behaviour for these foods (Hursti and Sjödén, 1997; Raudenbush and Frank, 1999).

Food neophobia is typically seen in young children, but can also be seen in adults and is thought to reduce as individuals are exposed to more novel foods (e.g. Birch and Marlin, 1982; Pliner et al., 1993). The process of **exposure** is thought to work because the individual discovers that eating the food has not resulted in any negative consequences. Flight and colleagues (2003) found that exposure to diverse cultures and higher socioeconomic status increases knowledge of a wide variety of stimuli, including food, and therefore may reduce food neophobia. Similarly, Olabi and colleagues (2009) found that when comparing Lebanese college students with their American counterparts, those students who had taken trips outside their country, who had regularly eaten 'ethnic' foods or who had not had a history of sickness after eating a new food were least likely to be neophobic.

Other researchers have suggested that urbanization reduces food neophobia, again through a process of greater exposure to a wide variety of different foods. Thus, Tuorila and colleagues (2001) found that, in Finland, the level of food neophobia decreased with an increased level of urbanization. Similarly, Flight and colleagues (2003) compared rural and urban Australian high school students and found that rural adolescents were more neophobic than their urban counterparts. In addition, rural students have been shown to have higher levels of suspicion towards novel foods compared to those with an urban identity (Bäckström et al., 2004).

Olabi and colleagues (2009) argue that the study of food neophobia is of particular importance because of its impact upon our food preferences and, in particular, the potential that it results in a more restrictive diet (Tuorila et al., 2001). It is through understanding these influential factors that we have the opportunity to develop, implement and promote positive changes in our food preferences. Olabi and colleagues (2009) also call for more cross-national studies to help unpick the cultural and national variables that influence food choices. For example, earlier in this chapter, the influence of 'hot' and 'cold' foods on what is considered a balanced diet was introduced. Similarly, Ritchley and colleagues (2003) found that American and Finnish adults were equally food neophobic, but were more food neophobic than Swedish adults. Information obtained from such cross-national studies can further inform our understanding of the variables that influence food neophobia and thus help with the development of interventions aimed at altering eating behaviour.

Social learning

Social learning is the process of observing other people's behaviour and the impact this has on our own behaviour. Social learning is usually discussed in the context of the development of children's preferences by means of learning from their parents or significant others in their environment. For example, Lowe and colleagues (1998) demonstrated that children who had a history of food refusal improved their food preferences after watching a video of older children ('food dudes') enthusiastically consuming the food which had been refused by the younger children. However, social learning can also take place in adulthood. Hermans and colleagues (2009) suggest that modelling (or social learning) is beneficial for various reasons, but its social function might be of particular importance. They suggest that the primary force behind modelling among humans is a desire to be like others and belong to others (de Waal, 2001). Furthermore, Chartrand and Bargh (1999) showed that individuals who *were* modelled (the object of the modelling) liked the other person (the person *doing* the modelling) more and indicated that interactions between the two had been more smooth and harmonious. A further means of implementing social learning is the mass media, discussed earlier. Here, we note that television and food advertising is both ubiquitous and influential, and, indeed, Macintyre and colleagues (1998) concluded that the media have a major impact upon what people eat and how they think about foods.

Mindless eating

Wansink (2007) draws on psychological theories in his work and argues that most of us are 'blissfully unaware of what influences how much we eat'. In fact, he goes so far as to say that what we usually do is engage in a process of **mindless eating**. He has formed this conclusion after conducting many studies observing what it is that influences our eating behaviour. Such studies have included giving five-day-old popcorn (stale, but safe to eat) to unsuspecting cinema goers and measuring how much of it they ate – and they ate a lot (Wansink, 2007: 18). Other studies involved an elaborate 'bottomless soup bowl' (Wansink et al., 2005). In this innovative study, Wansink and colleagues (2005) developed a way of refilling soup bowls without diners realizing. They then invited participants to eat soup and at the end of 20 minutes to estimate how many calories they had eaten. Some participants' bowls were the special 'bottomless bowls' and others had normal bowls. Wansink and colleagues (2005) found that those eating from the normal bowls ate about 9 oz of soup, whereas those eating from the bottomless bowls ate an average of 32 oz. Both sets of participants estimated that they had ingested a similar amount of calories, but those eating from the bottomless bowl were unaware that they had eaten more than three times as much as their counterparts. This was largely because they were relying on external cues (when the bowl was empty), rather than relying on internal cues (when they were full) to stop eating. Wansink's work explores the psychological underpinnings of our eating behaviour in novel and accessible ways and exposes the many and often subtle ways in which our eating behaviour can be influenced.

Summary

This section of the chapter has explored some of the key psychological theories put forward to explain eating behaviour. These have included the relationship between food and mood, the influence of being exposed to novel food and how this impacts on food neophobia, the mimetic influence of social learning and the possibility of 'mindless eating'. We now turn our attention to the issue of dieting.

◉ Dieting

The relative abundance of food in the West, combined with an increasingly sedentary lifestyle, has led to what Steptoe and Wardle (2004: 31) have called an 'epidemic of over consumption, not only of energy, but also of fat, sugar and salt'. At the same time, our consumption of high-fibre, nutrient-rich foods has fallen. These changes in our diet and our activity have been linked to epidemic increases in obesity (Kumanyika et al., 2002; Strauss and Pollack, 2001), and changes in our physical, cultural and social environment have come to be termed the 'obesogenic' environment (this term is explored in greater detail in Chapter 9). As Ard (2007: 1058) notes:

> the availability of high energy dense, palatable, inexpensive food is only surpassed by the mechanized labor-saving and entertainment devices designed to keep us from moving too much. We have evolved from a society of hunter-gatherers to a society of drive-through picker-uppers.

Thus, the obesogenic environment is characterized by an abundance of easily accessible food, which is high in fat, coupled with a lifestyle which does not require a large expenditure in energy.

In addition to this general increase in our size and decrease in our physical activity, there have been parallel changes in the cultural norms concerning body size and shape. More commonly this has concerned the female form. For example, Strahan and colleagues (2006) note that images of thin women are ubiquitous in the media, and women's magazines contain many messages about physical attractiveness (Malkin et al., 1999). Indeed, the National Eating Disorders Association (2002) highlighted the fact that whereas the average American is 5 ft 4 in tall and weights 140 lb, the average American model is 5 ft 11 in tall and weighs 117 lb. This means that the standards of physical attractiveness set by models are unrealistic for the average woman to strive for. Interest in the influence of the media's portrayal of the male form and the effect this is having on men is also increasing.

This means that we have a general increase in the size and weight of the population, an epidemic of obesity, the availability of high-density, energy-rich food, combined with cultural norms for body shape which increasingly emphasize the importance of being thin. This combination of influences leads many to consider dieting, or, as it is increasingly known as, **restrained eating**. Indeed, the prevalence of restrained eating is increasing (Offer, 2001). Of those who do engage in restrained eating, some may be overweight and wish to lose weight for health reasons, others may be overweight and wish to lose weight for social reasons – to conform to the social norm created by the media in order to feel more accepted – and another group may not be overweight at all, but perceive that they are because of the influence of unrealistic media images. Unfortunately for those individuals who engage in dieting, evidence increasingly shows that restrained eating is not effective. For example, Ogden (1992: 55) made the stark claim that dieting does not work:

> Whether they are obese, overweight or simply see themselves as being fat, dieting does not help them to become thinner. Initial weight loss may occur, but this is very often regained, making further weight loss difficult.

The success or failure of dieting

The success or failure of dieting depends on a number of factors. For example, environmental factors, including the increased availability of food regardless of its seasonality, and the increase in portion sizes of meals served encourage overeating in everyone. Indeed, Young and Nestle (2002) note that 'from 1970 to 2000, the number of new larger-sized [food] packages increased tenfold'. Furthermore, the way in which we perceive food has been shown to influence our levels of consumption. This was explored in depth by Provencher and colleagues (2009), who wanted to investigate whether calling a snack 'healthy' or 'unhealthy' would have an impact on the amount eaten. Participants were assigned to a 'healthy' or an 'unhealthy' condition, but were presented with identical cookies. What differed was how the cookies were described. The 'healthy' cookies were described as a new high-fibre oatmeal snack made with healthy ingredients that were low in saturated fat and free from trans-fat (unsaturated fat), whereas the 'unhealthy' cookies were described as new 'gourmet' cookies made with fresh butter and old-fashioned brown sugar that made them a great treat with a pleasant sweet taste. Participants were asked to rate the palatability of the cookies on a variety of issues and were told to eat as many as they needed to in order to achieve accurate ratings. The researchers found that participants who believed that the cookies were 'healthy' ate more than those offered the 'gourmet' cookies, demonstrating that if we believe a food to be healthy, we are likely to eat more of it. Other researchers have reported similar findings, for example customers dining in restaurants labelling their foods as healthy underestimate the calories in the foods being offered, or tend to choose more high calorie side dishes to accompany the 'healthy' meal (Chandon and Wansink, 2007).

Restraint theory explored the impact of imposing cognitive restraint on eating and showed that, paradoxically, trying to eat less often results in overeating (Herman and Mack, 1975). As a means of trying to explain this, Herman and Polivy (1984) developed the **Boundary Model**, which brought together physiological and cognitive perspectives relating to food intake. This model suggests that food intake is triggered by a physiologically determined boundary and stopped by a physiologically determined satiety boundary. In other words, we eat because our physiology tells us we are hungry and we stop eating because our physiology tells us we are full. We therefore regulate our intake by a process of biofeedback. However, the model also suggests that restrained eaters use cognitive boundaries in place of physiological boundaries. This means that their food intake is no longer regulated by physiological cues, but relies on cognitive control. Ogden (2007: 147) explains that the cognitive control, known as the 'diet boundary', represents the dieter's selected imposed quota for consumption on any given occasion. This quota is decided upon before the meal and is not related to physiological cues for hunger or satiety. Taking such a cognitive approach means that it removes our attention from our body's signals. We decide how much to eat before we put any food in our mouths and then we eat the quantity of food we have chosen, until it has gone, rather than simply eating until we are full.

Transferring attention from physiological to cognitive control equates to transferring internal cues (hunger and satiety) to external cues and might provide an explanation for the failure of dieting. For example, the work of Wansink (2007), discussed earlier, clearly demonstrates that we are not adept at monitoring our intake when we neglect our physiological messages and rely instead on external cues. Wansink and colleagues (2007) explored the differences between French and American eating behaviour, because French women are stereotypically considered to be thinner than American women. They demonstrated that one explanation for the smaller body size of French women could be that they paid attention to their internal body cues when they ate, such as whether they felt full, and less attention to external cues, such as the amount of food on a plate. The French participants reported that they stopped eating when they no longer felt hungry, whilst the American women reported that they stopped eating once their plate was empty.

Whilst much of the evidence in this field suggests that dieting is an ineffective method for achieving weight loss, there are some studies that suggest a small proportion of dieters do manage to lose weight and, crucially, to maintain their weight loss. Ogden and Flanagan (2008) suggest that an individual's beliefs can play a key role in this success. Using the theory of 'coherence', whereby a person's beliefs about causes and solutions are consistent with one another, Ogden and Jubb (2008) showed that beliefs in biomedical causes of a problem tended to result in the endorsement of more medical solutions, whereas a belief in behavioural causes was associated with beliefs in a more behavioural solution. If we extrapolate this to the issue of dieting, it follows that those who are dieting who subscribe to a psychological model of obesity are more likely to endorse and subscribe to a behavioural solution (dieting) to their problem. This study suggests that it is of paramount importance to explore an individual's beliefs concerning the causes of their weight as well as their reasons for wishing to lose weight. The notion of coherence in terms of beliefs about causes of weight gain and solutions for weight loss is one which requires further research.

Consequences of restrained eating include hunger and subsequent overeating (Provencher et al., 2009). Other outcomes include regaining weight lost, increases in appetite (e.g. Doucet et al., 2000), and an increase in obsessive thoughts about food and eating (e.g. Hart and Chiovari, 1998). Jane Ogden (1992) concludes her book *Fat Chance: The Myth of Dieting Explained* with the following words, which are, perhaps, an apposite summary for this section of the chapter:

> Dieting aims to result in eating less, but paradoxically can cause overeating. Giving up dieting takes away this problem. Initially, you may eat as a response to the new found non-dieting freedom, but gradually food will no longer play a central role in your life. Stop dieting and you will think about food less. You will eat when you are hungry, not when your craving for food becomes too strong to

ignore. You will no longer wish for platefuls of cakes and high calorie foods because knowing that you can eat them whenever you want stops them from being so attractive. Cream cakes everyday seem wonderful on a diet, but as a reality will become boring. Stop dieting and eating will become less important to you. (Ogden, 1992: 100)

Conclusion

This chapter began with an illustration of how our conception of what constitutes healthy eating behaviour has changed over time as our understandings of the link between diet and health have grown. Our eating behaviour plays a significant role in our long-term health. It is therefore of prime importance that we understand what it is that drives our health concerns and our eating behaviour in order that we can help individuals and populations maximize their health. As such, biological, evolutionary and psychological explanations for eating behaviour have been presented. We have demonstrated that the consumption of food has implications beyond that of simply providing us with the nutrients and energy that we need to survive. Therefore, when we think about this topic, we must recognize the complex interplay between evolutionary, biological, social, cultural and psychological influences that are exerted on our eating behaviour.

Further reading

Wansink, B. (2007). *Mindless Eating: Why we Eat More than we Think.* Bantam Books: New York.

Key search terms

Eating behaviour, dieting, obesity

Chapter 9

Eating disorders

Introduction

The previous chapter focused on eating behaviour in general and outlined the biological, evolutionary and psychological explanations for eating behaviour. The subject of dieting and the factors which influence the success or failure of restricted eating was also covered. In this chapter, we turn our attention to specific examples of disordered eating:

> Eating disorders are of great interest to the public, of perplexity to researchers and a challenge to clinicians. They feature prominently in the media, often attracting sensational coverage. Their cause is elusive, with social, psychological and biological processes all seeming to play a major part. (Fairburn and Harrison, 2003: 407)

As Forshaw (2002: 81) notes, 'the term "eating disorder" generates thoughts and images of people with anorexia nervosa ... However, any problem of eating is really an eating disorder.' In other words, the term 'eating disorder' includes all extremes of eating behaviour, ranging from those who eat too much and become obese, to those who eat so little that they are defined as being anorexic. There has been a dramatic increase in anorexia nervosa and bulimia in the West, and we are also, ironically, in the midst of what some people have termed an 'obesity epidemic' – thus both extreme 'thinness' and extreme 'overweightness' are becoming increasingly common in Western populations.

There are three important issues to highlight in this introductory section. The first is that eating disorders also affect males. In a paper entitled 'What about the boys?', Soban (2006) points out that the number of anorexia nervosa cases found among men is rising. Similarly, Drummond

(2002) called for resources to be developed for health professionals who work with men who have eating disorders. Both researchers highlight the fact that the assumption that anorexia nervosa is a 'female problem' hinders males from accessing help and support.

The second issue is to make clear that the word **anorexia** simply means lack of appetite. As Forshaw (2002) points out, most of us have experienced anorexia when we lose our appetite at times when we are unwell. Few of us will have experienced anorexia nervosa, which literally means lack of appetite because of nerves.

The third issue concerns the fact that, traditionally, the conditions anorexia nervosa and bulimia nervosa have fallen under the remit of clinical psychologists because of their link to mental health. This does not mean that health psychologists are unable to play a role, in fact, Gurung (2006: 213) has argued that given the 'strong psychological and social components to eating disorders, the biopsychosocial approach of health psychologists to illness can be a great aid in preventing eating disorders and helping those with them'. Thus, these two conditions will be addressed in this chapter along with the topic of obesity which is itself recognized as being a major challenge for health psychologists.

In this chapter, we will examine:
- The causes, consequences and management of anorexia nervosa and bulimia nervosa
- The causes, consequences and management of obesity

Anorexia nervosa and bulimia nervosa

Anorexia nervosa is defined by Carter and colleagues (2009: 202) as a 'serious psychiatric disorder'. For someone with anorexia nervosa, the pursuit of weight loss is paramount. Fairburn and Harrison (2003) note that this loss of weight is mainly the result of severe and selective restriction of food intake, but can also be combined with overexercising, purging and the misuse of diuretics and laxatives. Foods that an anorexic perceives as fattening are excluded from their diet. Fairburn and Harrison (2003) highlight the various motivations for engaging in such behaviour, which include psychological influences such as asceticism, competitiveness and a wish to punish themselves. Perry (2002) describes the 'typical' anorexic as having an obsessional interest in their personal appearance, to the point where they believe themselves to be overweight, even though to those around them, they may be severely underweight. **Bulimia nervosa** is distinguished from anorexia nervosa in that attempts to restrict food intake are punctuated by repeated **binges** – episodes of eating where there is a sense of loss of control and an unusually large amount of food is eaten. Fairburn and Harrison (2003) note that the combination of undereating and binge eating results in body weight being generally unremarkable. Most people who have bulimia nervosa are distressed by their loss of control over their eating and often feel ashamed of their behaviour.

Causes

Anorexia nervosa and bulimia nervosa usually develop in adolescence (Salbach-Andrae et al., 2009), with the onset of bulimia nervosa typically later than that of anorexia nervosa. Both are thought to be conditions that manifest in Western industrialized cultures. Indeed, Perry (2002) suggests that in developing countries where food supplies are often scarce, anorexia nervosa is extremely rare. It tends to be associated with females, but males can also present with anorexia nervosa. In addition, much research indicates that it is females from wealthier families (e.g. social classes 1 and 2) who are mostly affected (Fairburn and Harrison, 2003). The onset of anorexia nervosa and bulimia nervosa has been linked to family background, genetic and psychological factors.

Family background

The potential influence of parenting styles and family background has been widely debated within the literature. Shoebridge and Gowers (2000) suggested that events which have occurred in a person's early years might influence their susceptibility to developing anorexia nervosa or bulimia nervosa in later life. They also linked parental overconcern to the development of anorexia nervosa. Shisslak and colleagues (1990) reported that people with bulimia nervosa tended to describe their childhood as being characterized by a chaotic lifestyle. A chaotic lifestyle included conflict within the family accompanied by a lack of parental warmth and care. Overconcern on the part of parents has also been linked to the onset of bulimia nervosa, for example Rorty and colleagues (2000) described higher levels of what they termed 'maternal invasion' during the adolescent years, limited privacy, parental intrusiveness and overconcern with their daughter's shape and weight.

Genetic factors

Research focusing on identical and non-identical twins has been conducted to explore the potential influence of genetics on the development of eating disorders. Higher rates of bulimia nervosa have been found in monozygotic (identical) twins when compared with dizygotic (non-identical) twins (e.g. Hsu et al., 1990). Similar conclusions have been drawn from twin studies focusing on anorexia nervosa (e.g. Bulik et al., 1998; Klump et al., 2001; Kortegaard et al., 2001). Although this suggests that genetic factors may at least be partly responsible for the onset of anorexia nervosa and bulimia nervosa, the influence of the environment, social and psychological factors have not yet been ruled out.

Psychological factors

Fairburn and Harrison (2003) summarize the psychological approach to explaining the onset of eating disorders and suggest that the most influential approaches have been cognitive behavioural theories. These suggest that the restriction of food intake which characterizes the onset of both anorexia nervosa and bulimia nervosa has two potential origins. First, a need to feel in control of life which is transformed into a need to control eating (Fairburn et al., 1999), and second, an overevaluation of shape and weight. As the dietary restriction begins, the resulting weight loss is highly reinforcing.

Evolutionary factors

Much of the work conducted on eating disorders takes a psychosocial or biomedical stance. However, some researchers have considered the possibility that anorexia nervosa might be best explained using an evolutionary perspective. Although Gatward (2007) suggests that, from an evolutionary, perspective anorexia nervosa is a puzzling condition, Guisinger (2003: 745) argues that anorexia nervosa's distinctive symptoms of 'restricting food, denial of starvation and hyperactivity are likely to be evolved'. Gatward (2007: 2) quotes Voland and Voland (1989: 224), who state that 'at first glance, it appears absurd that anorexia nervosa could have evolved as an adaptive feature. How can temporary or permanent sterility, or under extreme conditions, self-sacrifice, pass the test of **natural selection?'**

However, one of the key theories underpinning the evolutionary perspective is that of the **adapted to flee famine hypothesis** (AFFH). This proposes that the symptoms of anorexia nervosa (restricting food, hyperactivity and denial of starvation) reflect an adaptive mechanism that was once instrumental in helping migration in response to local famine (Guisinger, 2003). This means that when local food resources were scarce, local inhabitants did not have enough to eat and consequently experienced extreme weight loss. Individuals who were perhaps better placed to survive were those who were able to seek out new food resources. In order to be able to move towards potential new sources of food, individuals would need to feel restless and energetic. Furthermore, maintaining morale in such difficult times would also have been important. This might have been achieved by optimistically denying that one was dangerously thin.

In excellent review papers, Guisinger (2003) and Gatward (2007) present convincing arguments to support this evolutionary perspective. However, whilst Gatward (2007) notes that a major strength of the AFFH is that it explains features of anorexia nervosa that other models do not address well, it is not a model which is easy to prove or disprove. The most we can expect from such a model, he argues, is that it has the potential to provide us with a novel way of regarding eating disorders, and, in so doing, perhaps it will provide us with a means of finding more successful ways to help people with anorexia nervosa to recover.

Problems

The process of starving the body has a huge impact on different body systems, with potentially serious implications. Anorexia nervosa has been linked to a number of health problems, including cardiac dysfunction, central nervous system abnormalities, musculoskeletal problems, fluid and electrolyte imbalances, and dental problems, which we briefly describe.

Cardiac dysfunction

Moodie and Salcedo (1983) found that young anorexics had reduced heart size, with particularly small left ventricles. In a healthy heart, the left ventricle is responsible for maintaining the circulation throughout the rest of the body and any deterioration in this function has potentially serious consequences.

Central nervous system abnormalities

When the brain is starved of vital nutrients, it is less able to produce energy for its own requirements. Some studies suggest that a consequence of anorexia nervosa is cognitive impairment. For example, Kingston and colleagues (1996) showed that anorexics performed poorly across a range of cognitive tasks.

Musculoskeletal problems

Cases of severe anorexia nervosa have been associated with a loss of bone mass. During normal development in puberty, bone mass intensifies in order to prepare the bone structure for the stresses of pregnancy and labour. The deposit of calcium during this time is therefore of considerable importance. As a consequence, girls who develop anorexia nervosa during puberty, thus depriving their bodies of the calcium and vitamin D vital for skeletal development, face a potentially devastating impact because loss of bone density is thought to be irreversible. This was evidenced in a follow-up study, which showed that even when women had recovered to within 20% of their ideal body weight (e.g. Rigotti et al., 1991), bone density levels did not improve.

Bulimics also suffer from musculoskeletal problems and their bone density is similarly affected (Rigotti et al., 1991). For example, Newton and colleagues (1993) compared bulimic women with control participants and found that bulimics were far more likely to have reduced bone density, which is thought to be irreversible and has serious long-term consequences. However, in addition, bulimics often make use of emetic agents in order to purge themselves after they have engaged in binge eating. Use of these products can have serious health consequences, which include fluid and electrolyte imbalances and dental problems.

Fluid and electrolyte imbalances

Where vomiting and laxative abuse are frequent, the normal balance of **electrolytes** within the body can be upset. Electrolytes are chemicals which regulate our body's systems. Frequent vomiting can disturb the pH (the balance between alkali and acidity) levels of our body's fluids and is associated with low levels of potassium and chloride. Low levels of these electrolytes are associated with fatigue, muscle weakness and constipation (e.g. Thompson, 1993). Researchers have established links between vomiting and laxative use (typically employed by bulimics) and electrolyte imbalances (e.g. Turner et al., 2000).

Dental problems

Bulimics often suffer from dental problems. Toothache is common and their tooth enamel may become eroded. Enamel erosion is thought to be accelerated if an individual cleans their teeth immediately after vomiting, but is primarily a consequence of the persistent contact of the teeth with the acid contents of the stomach (e.g. Mitchell et al., 1997).

Management

In terms of approaches to managing anorexia nervosa and bulimia nervosa, the outcomes are mixed. For example, Steinhausen (2002) reviewed 119 follow-ups of anorexia nervosa over 10 years and found that 57.1% recovered, 25.9% showed improvement, 16.9% chronicity and 1.8% mortality. In contrast, Salbach-Andrae and colleagues (2009) found that at one-year follow-up, almost 60% of their sample showed a poor outcome and only 28% had a good outcome. Gowers (2008) reported similarly pessimistic findings, and Salbach-Andrae and colleagues (2009: 703) conclude that 'for many patients, anorexia nervosa is a troublesome part of their life for many years'.

The most common approach to managing disordered eating is by means of cognitive behavioural therapy (CBT). Fairburn and Harrison (2003) reviewed the evidence and concluded that, for bulimia nervosa, the most effective treatment was a form of CBT which focused on modifying the specific behaviours and ways of thinking that maintain the disordered eating (e.g. Fairburn, 1981; Fairburn et al., 1993). They explain that CBT typically takes the form of about 20 individual treatment sessions over a period of five months, with a third to half of the patients making a complete and lasting recovery. Although not described as a panacea, Fairburn and Harrison, (2003) note that CBT can be of great benefit to many patients. They bemoan the situation in the UK, where it seems few patients actually receive such therapy (Mussell et al., 2000).

For anorexia nervosa, Fairburn and Harrison (2003) argue that there is less evidence for the efficacy of treatment approaches. This is echoed by Carter and colleagues (2009), who state that there are remarkably few randomized controlled treatment studies of anorexia nervosa. Of the four they found, two focused on psychological therapy and two on medication approaches to treatment. One study found no difference between individual versus family therapy (Eisler et al., 1997) and the other found preliminary evidence in support of CBT versus nutritional counselling (Pike et al., 2003). For the medical approaches, the findings were inconsistent (Kaye et al., 2001; Walsh et al., 2006).

Fairburn and Harrison (2003) suggest that generally there are three key aspects of the management of anorexia nervosa:

1 *Recognition of the need for help:* the first step is to help patients to recognize that they need help. This is crucial, because anorexics tend to be extremely reluctant to change.

2 *Weight restoration:* this second goal is concerned with an attempt to reverse the malnutrition and restore the weight lost. Fairburn and Harrison (2003) note that once achieved, this usually results in a substantial improvement in the patient's overall state.

3 *Overevaluation of shape and weight:* there is no one way to achieve this aim, but it involves addressing the individual's body image, identity, eating habits and general psychosocial functioning.

For younger patients, family-based treatment seems to have been successfully implemented (Russell et al., 1987), whereas CBT is more commonly used for older patients. However, as we noted above, the efficacy of CBT for people with anorexia nervosa has not been widely documented. Recently though, Carter and colleagues (2009) published a study which provided clear support for the use of CBT when treating anorexics, both in terms of improving outcome and preventing relapse. When the success of CBT approaches with bulimics is taken into consideration, researchers are optimistic that similar successes will be achieved with anorexic patients.

Summary

Anorexia nervosa and bulimia nervosa are both complex conditions about which we still have much to learn. Whilst these conditions primarily affect adolescent girls, there is evidence that an increasing number of males are also affected, so there is a need to consider whether approaches to managing these disorders require a gender-specific perspective. There is also a need for more longitudinal studies of the different treatment approaches in order to identify which approaches work best. It seems clear that a multidimensional approach to research is required, which takes into account genetics, biological, psychological, social, environmental and evolutionary perspectives.

◁⊙▷ Obesity

Obesity is a major challenge for health psychologists. The European Commission (1999) estimates that 31% of the EU adult population is overweight, with a further 10% reaching weights that are defined as clinically obese. Ogden (2007: 336) notes that in the UK, rates of obesity are on the increase. She highlights that, in 1980, 6% of men and 8% of women were classified as obese, whereas these rates had risen to 13% and 16% in 1994, and 18% and 24% respectively in 2005. In the USA, the figures are worse, with roughly half of Americans considered to be overweight and a third are obese (Ogden et al., 2007: 336).

Obesity is generally measured in terms of a person's **body mass index** (BMI), which is worked out by calculating a person's weight in kilograms, divided by their height in metres squared. If an individual's BMI falls between 25 and 29, they are considered to be overweight. A BMI of between 30 and 39 is considered to indicate an individual is moderately or clinically obese, whereas a BMI of over 40 is considered to indicate severe obesity.

Another form of measuring obesity involves measuring a person's waist circumference. Such a measurement enables the identification of where fat is stored. This is important because some physical problems can be predicted by abdominal fat rather than lower body fat (Ogden, 2007: 334). Lean and colleagues (1995) suggested that if a person's waist circumference was greater than 102 cm in men and 88 cm in women, weight reduction should be recommended.

A third approach to defining whether or not someone is obese is to measure the percentage of body fat they have. Good health tends to be associated with the amount of fat, rather than weight per se. The percentage of body fat can be measured using skinfold thickness, usually around the upper arm and lower back, but has also been measured using more sophisticated means of **bioelectrical impedence**, which involves passing an electrical current through a person's body tissues. The more the current is impeded, the more body fat is stored (fat is an insulator and does not conduct electricity). Using this measure, the overall percentage of body fat can be calculated.

Causes

Having identified how obesity is defined, we now focus our attention on theories which attempt to explain how obesity is caused. Physiological, behavioural and evolutionary theories have been suggested. Physiological explanations include genetic theories, metabolic rate theory and fat cell theory. Behavioural explanations tend to focus on the obesogenic environment, but some researchers have also explored the role of beliefs and their influence on behaviour. Evolutionary theories suggest that in the past, we were programmed to have a large appetite and to favour energy-dense foods, so that we would have reserves to draw from in times of food scarcity.

Physiological explanations

Genetic theories

Researchers have explored the possibility that obese people are obese because of their genetic inheritance rather than their behaviour. For example, Garn and colleagues (1981) reported that if one member of a couple was obese, there was a 40% chance of producing an obese child, whereas if both members of a couple were obese, the chance rose to 80%. Conversely, the chance that a couple who are both thin will produce an obese child is small, approximately 7%. However, because both the parents and their children will share the same environment as well as genetic constitution, it is difficult to unpick whether obesity is genetic or environmentally influenced.

To address this problem, twin studies have been conducted. Researchers have been especially interested in studying twins who have been reared apart from one another, who have not therefore experienced the same environmental influences. Results have generally shown that identical twins reared apart are more similar in weight than non-identical twins who have been reared together. This suggests that there could be a strong genetic component in determining obesity. In addition, researchers have also compared the weight of adopted children with their adoptive parents and their biological parents. They found that the weight of the adoptee more closely matched the weight of their biological rather than their adoptive parents. These studies add support to the notion that weight is genetically determined.

Metabolic rate theory

Our metabolic rate is the rate at which we use energy to carry out all the biological processes we need in order to stay alive. These include breathing, heart rate, blood pressure and so on. Some researchers have explored whether differences in metabolic rate may explain variations in weight. **Metabolic rate theory** argues that people who have lower metabolic rates might be more prone to obesity because when resting, people with lower metabolic rates burn up less calories. The underlying idea is that people with lower metabolic rates should require less food because their bodies naturally burn fewer calories, so if they eat more calories than they burn, they will gain weight.

Evidence for this theory is mixed, with some studies suggesting that there is a relationship between metabolic rate and the tendency for weight gain, whilst other studies have failed to demonstrate that obese people have lower metabolic rates. Ravussin and Bogardus (1989) attempted to explain this paradox by suggesting that obese people might have had lower metabolic rates to start with, which resulted in their gaining weight, and that the weight gain itself resulted in an increase in metabolic rate. Further research is clearly needed in this area before any firm conclusions can be drawn about the influence of metabolic rate.

Fat cell theory

Morrison and Bennett (2009) note that **fat cell theory**, another genetic theory put forward to explain the cause of obesity, suggests that obese individuals are born with a greater number of fat cells. However, researchers have shown that the number of fat cells in a person of average weight and in many mildly obese people is between 25–35 billion. Ogden (2007: 339) notes that although the number of fat cells in someone who is mildly obese is broadly similar to the number of fat cells in someone of average weight, the cells in the heavier person are enlarged both in size and weight. The number of fat cells found in a severely obese person is dramatically increased – up to 100–125 billion, which suggests that new fat cells are formed as a person's size increases. However, Spalding and colleagues (2008) reported that the number of fat cells stays constant in adulthood in both lean and obese individuals, even after marked weight loss. They suggest that this indicates that the number of fat cells in our body is set during childhood and adolescence and it is the volume of these cells which changes as we gain weight, rather than the number. With such mixed findings, evidence in support of this theory is currently limited.

Evolutionary explanations

Obesity can be understood by considering the influence of our evolutionary heritage. The environment inhabited by our ancestors was very different to the one with which we are familiar. Our ancestors would have been uncertain about where their next meal was coming from, they would have most probably lived in small sustainable groups feeding on a seasonally dependent diet and would have moved to new hunting grounds when local conditions deteriorated (Prentice, 2005). It is also likely that our ancestors would have experienced hunger between kills. As a consequence, it is not surprising that their bodies evolved to enable them to store fat during times of food surplus and their tastes were for energy-dense and fatty foods (Blundell and Gillet, 2001). Thus, Mankar and colleagues (2008) note that fat accumulation has classically been considered to be an efficient means of energy storage. It has been suggested that the thrifty gene (a concept introduced in Chapter 8), which enabled this process of storing fat in times of food abundance and reusing fat during times of food shortage, was favoured through natural selection, whereby those individuals possessing this gene were more likely to survive times of shortage.

Although the thrifty gene would have been advantageous for our ancestors, it is not so helpful for us. In a short time (in evolutionary terms), our environment and the way in which we have access to food has changed immensely. The evolutionary drive to seek energy-dense food to ensure our survival during times of shortage is no longer appropriate. In the West, we have an abundance of food available to us – food which is no longer dependent on the seasons. We also have the ability to preserve foods, so we do not have to eat as much as we can whenever food is available, because we can be relatively certain of where and when we will get our next meal. In our current environment, food is widely available, convenient and easily accessible. The combination of this environment and our evolutionary heritage might go some way to explaining the current obesity problem. We explore the influence of our obesogenic environment in the next section.

Behavioural explanations

A simple explanation of obesity is that it is a condition that occurs because an individual ingests far more energy than they expend (Pinel, 2003). It has been argued that engaging in this behaviour has been encouraged by the obesogenic environment which we in the West inhabit.

Obesogenic environment

The term 'obesogenic' was coined by Swinburn and colleagues (1999), who suggested that the physical, economic, social and cultural environment encourages us to eat more and exercise less. In particular, factors such as the food industry, food labelling, food advertising, the availability of energy-dense foods, and an environment which has been increasingly designed to encourage a sedentary lifestyle through the use of cars, computers and television (Hill and Peters, 1998) have been emphasized as contributing to the obesogenic environment. Ulijaszek (2007) argues that this is a problem because while the energy balance (energy intake in excess of energy expenditure equals weight gain) is simple enough to understand, avoiding the obesogenic environment is not so straightforward. Issues such as food security and convenience food exert an influence on us.

Food security

Food security is achieved when we have physical, social and economic access to sufficient safe and nutritious food. Ulijaszek (2007) notes that in poorer nations, socioeconomic status and obesity are positively related, in other words, as socioeconomic status rises, so do levels of obesity. In industrialized societies, this relationship is inverted – as sociecomonic status rises, obesity levels fall. Such findings have been linked to the energy density and energy cost of foods. This means that diets that are more energy dense cost less, are more likely to be eaten by those with lower socioeconomic status and therefore contribute to the levels of obesity.

Convenience food

Alongside changes in the way we work, the demand for convenience in food has led to the development of pre-packaged foods which have short preparation times (Schluter and Lee, 1999), as well as an increase in the amount of food which is consumed away from the home (McCrory et al., 1999). The number of fast-food outlets has also increased exponentially and has a negative impact on our weight levels. For example, Jeffrey and colleagues (2006) found that eating at fast-food restaurants was positively associated with a high fat diet, high BMI and low vegetable consumption.

Problems

Obesity has been associated with a range of physical and psychological problems including cardiovascular disease, diabetes, joint trauma, cancer, hypertension, mortality, and low self-esteem, poor self-image and depression (Ashton et al., 2001; Ogden and Flanagan, 2008; Wadden et al., 2006). Morrison and Bennett (2009) note that the relative risk of disease increases proportionately in relation to how overweight a person is. Ogden (2007) notes that where fat is stored in the body is also relevant; weight stored in the upper body, especially the abdomen, is more detrimental to health than that stored on the lower body. She also points out that although men are more likely than women to store weight on their upper bodies and are therefore more at risk if they are obese, it is women who are apparently more concerned about their weight and it is women who are more commonly studied. Given the 'current obsession with thinness, the aversion to fat in both adults and children, and the attribution of blame' towards those who are obese (American Medical Association, 2003), it is not surprising that in terms of psychological problems, low self-esteem, poor self-image and depression are most commonly found in those who are obese.

Management

Behavioural interventions

In Chapter 8, we focused at length on dieting (restricted eating) and the factors which impact on the success or otherwise of this method. Traditionally behavioural interventions for obesity have almost exclusively targeted reduction in energy intake and improvement in time spent in physical activity (Manzoni et al., 2009). Many dietary programmes have been shown to be effective in the short term in reducing body weight. However, research also shows that weight regain typically occurs after intentional weight loss. Obese individuals trying to lose weight can find that their weight is 'cycling', as they lose and then regain their weight. Maintaining weight loss is not easy (Jeffrey et al., 2000).

In Chapter 8, the link between food intake and mood was described. Emotional eating is relatively common (Bekker et al., 2004; Lindeman and Stark, 2001) and can be considered to be a form of dysfunctional coping (Solomon, 2001). Manzoni and colleagues (2009) noted that individuals who eat or overeat in response to negative emotions are more likely to be overweight or obese and suggested that if such people could decrease their emotional eating, they would be more likely to succeed at weight reduction. As a means of reducing emotional eating in a group of obese women (aged 18–60 years), Manzoni and colleagues trialled the use of relaxation training. They found that as their participants' ability to engage in relaxation exercises improved, so too did their belief in their ability to reduce their emotional eating. The study was not longitudinal, so long-term impacts of this intervention on weight loss have not been recorded, but at three-months' follow-up, those participants who had undergone relaxation training reported significantly lower numbers of emotional eating episodes compared to the control group who did not receive such training. Manzoni and colleagues (2009) are hopeful that relaxation training could be a useful tool to reduce the number of emotional eating episodes in which an individual engages.

Surgical interventions

Whilst most obese patients are managed through behavioural interventions, there is a growing body of research which suggests that many behavioural interventions fail to produce sustained weight loss. As such, some clinicians have begun to turn towards surgery. Surgery is currently an option reserved for the morbidly obese and is offered when all other attempts at weight loss have repeatedly failed (Ogden et al., 2006). The two most common forms of obesity surgery are **gastric bypass** and **laparoscopic gastric banding**. Both physically limit the amount a person can eat and so reduce the need for the individual to voluntarily restrict their own eating behaviour. A gastric bypass operation involves creating a small stomach pouch and bypassing part of the small intestine to make the digestive system shorter, although nothing is actually removed. This means that it is only possible to eat small meals and also that the body absorbs less food. Gastric banding also reduces the size of the stomach, but does so using a band so that only small meals can be eaten before feeling full.

Reports of the success of surgical interventions are positive in terms of weight loss. For example, Torgerson and Sjostrom (2001) reported an average weight loss after two years of 28 kg in a surgical group of patients compared to only 0.5 kg in the conventional treatment group. This difference was still evident at an eight-year follow-up. However, Ogden and colleagues (2006) point out that obesity surgery does not simply affect weight loss, but also impacts on psychological wellbeing. This impact has been largely positive. For example, de Zwaan and colleagues (2002) and Ogden and colleagues (2005) both demonstrated that patients reported improved quality of life post surgery. Similarly, Holzwarth and colleagues (2002) reported a decrease in antidepressant use following surgery, indicating an improvement in mood. In a study exploring the impact of surgery, Ogden and colleagues (2006) reported that the positive consequences of surgery-induced weight loss were renewed confidence, self-esteem, energy and overall quality of life. They quote one participant as saying:

> I feel more confident … I'm less embarrassed and not self-conscious anymore and body language has changed … I can just lean back in my chair and talk … I feel like I've got a new life, new chances, new opportunities. I'm a new person … It is a rebirth really. (Ogden et al., 2006: 287)

Key to these positive changes was the feeling of control that patients reported. For some, control was an externally imposed control which they welcomed as a release from their previous sense of responsibility (the surgery controlled their intake). In contrast, for others, the control was internalized (the surgery enabled them to feel that they could take control). Whichever form of control was mentioned, the result was a more positive psychological state, which Ogden and colleagues (2006) found was generalized to other areas of their participants' lives, with many feeling more in control of their lives in general. It seems that for patients who are seriously obese and for whom other interventions have repeatedly failed, surgery is a successful option.

Beliefs

There is some evidence to suggest that GPs have not given sufficient attention to the issue of obesity (Moore et al., 2003). For example, Kopelman and Grace (2004) have noted that, in the UK, most management of obesity happens in **primary care**, where the approach to obesity is uncoordinated and inconsistent. There is also evidence to suggest that GPs' attitudes to the management of obesity can influence the success or otherwise of interventions. For example, in a study exploring the views of GPs treating obesity, Epstein and Ogden (2005) reported that GPs primarily believed that obesity was the responsibility of the patient, rather than a medical problem requiring a medical solution. However, GPs also reported that they felt patients saw the issue differently, in that patients wanted their GPs to take responsibility for, and control of, the issue. They quote one GP as saying: 'he was looking to what I was going to do about his weight, rather than what he was going to have to do about it'. This conflict meant that GPs were often left feeling frustrated about their patients' apparent inability to change their lifestyle. A need to resolve this conflict led GPs to sometimes offer treatments that they believed were inappropriate, such as anti-obesity drugs.

This conflict in beliefs about responsibility and treatment options can create problems in the GP–patient relationship. This is particularly so, given the current emphasis in primary care of openness and shared decision-making (Tailor and Ogden 2009). In order to engage in shared decision-making, both parties need to come to an agreement about whose responsibility it is to manage the condition. Ogden and colleagues (2003) explored the use of language and how the choice of a particular term could impact on patients' perception of a problem. They concluded that when GPs used more medical terms (e.g. gastroenteritis) rather than lay diagnoses (e.g. stomach upset), patients had more confidence in their GP and felt that they had been taken more seriously. On the other hand, when GPs used the lay term, patients had greater ownership of the problem being discussed and felt a higher sense of blame. It was suggested that the language used by the GP might influence how patients feel about their problem.

As a consequence of this work, Tailor and Ogden (2009) explored the use of the term 'obese' in the GP–patient consultation. They found that the majority of GPs avoided the term 'obese' and instead favoured the use of euphemisms (such as 'your weight may be damaging your health'). Using vignettes with obese and non-obese patients, they found that patients believed the problem had more serious consequences when the term 'obese' was used. They also reported feeling more anxious and upset than when the same symptoms were labelled with the euphemism. However, when the findings for patients were split into obese and non-obese, it was shown that the term 'obese' had greater emotional impact than the euphemism on the non-obese patients. In contrast, obese patients found the euphemism more upsetting. Tailor and Ogden (2009) conclude that language use is potentially extremely useful in terms of influencing behaviour change, but suggest that more research in this fascinating area is required before concrete guidelines about language use can be developed.

⊙ Conclusion

There is much scope for health psychology in the field of disordered eating, not least because many people (males and females) in Western cultures have trouble establishing a positive body image. Levine and Smolak (2006) suggest that disordered eating is a major public health challenge and that regardless of their body size, people should be encouraged, among other things, to learn to accept and value what one can and cannot change about one's physical characteristics and, perhaps more importantly for health psychology, to understand how psychological and social factors can influence eating, size and shape.

Further reading

Fairburn, C. and Harrison, P.J. (2003). Eating disorders, *The Lancet*, 361, 407–16.

Soban, C. (2006) What about the boys? Addressing issues of masculinity within male anorexia nervosa in a feminist therapeutic environment. *International Journal of Men's Health*, 5(3), 251–67.

Key search terms

Anorexia nervosa, bulimia nervosa, obesity, eating disorders

Glossary

action planning The process of making a detailed plan about how, when and where the behaviour in question can be implemented.

adapted to flee famine hypothesis (AFFH) An evolutionary theory which attempts to explain anorexia nervosa by proposing that anorexic symptoms once served an adaptive function in times of famine.

aim Broad statement of what it is you are trying to achieve.

anorexia Lack of appetite.

anorexia nervosa Lack of appetite because of nerves. A mental illness where a person starves themselves in order to be thinner, mistakenly believing themselves to be fat, no matter what their size (Forshaw, 2002).

antimicrobial properties Something that has antimicrobial properties is able to kill or inhibit the growth of microorganisms such as bacteria.

approach style People who adopt an approach style to coping are more likely to monitor their environment, face issues 'head on' and engage in problem-solving strategies.

avoidant style People who adopt an avoidant style to coping are more likely to avoid a stressor if at all possible, and tend to focus on addressing their emotional reaction to the stressor, rather than dealing with the stressor itself.

baseline measure A measure of performance taken before an intervention is implemented, against which future performance measures are compared, thereby allowing the impact of the intervention to be determined.

behaviour change approach A health promotion perspective that argues that the alteration of thinking processes should be the central focus in the development of health promotion activities (Albery and Munafo, 2008).

Big Five A model of personality developed by McCrae and Costa (1987), which proposes that certain personality types can help or hinder the coping process.

binges Episodes of eating where there is a sense of loss of control and an unusually large amount of food is eaten.

bioelectrical impedence The process of passing an electric current between a person's hand and foot. The more the current is impeded (slowed), the more body fat is stored.

biofeedback A form of therapeutic process through which people can learn to alter their physiological processes by watching them change on some kind of meter (Forshaw, 2002).

biopsychosocial model The focus is on the interaction between health and body, and there is an acceptance of the range of individual differences in personality and culture which can affect health (Forshaw, 2002).

body mass index (BMI) A means of measuring obesity by calculating a person's weight in kilograms, divided by their height in metres squared.

Boundary Model This attempts to explain how we regulate our eating.

buffering hypothesis A hypothesis put forward to explain how social support can reduce stress. It suggests that social support acts as a buffer, cushioning the individual against major stressors (Forshaw, 2002).

bulimia nervosa An eating disorder. A person with bulimia nervosa will typically eat large quantities of food and then vomit or take laxatives to prevent the intake of calories having an impact on their weight.

carbohydrate craving syndrome A syndrome characterized by an irresistible desire to consume sweet or starchy foods.

case-control study A research study design used widely in epidemiology which matches groups of individuals on the basis of the presence or absence of certain characteristics (e.g. a specific disease) in order to identify other factors (e.g. exposure to an environmental factor) associated with the specific characteristic (Albery and Munafo, 2008).

classical conditioning Refers to the process of pairing up of actions and their reactions.

cognitive behavioural therapy An approach which emphasizes the importance of changing our cognitions and behaviours as a means of influencing our emotional and physiological reactions to a stressor.

cohort study A research study design which follows a group of participants over an extended period (i.e. longitudinally), in order to identify factors which predict a change in status (e.g. disease onset) (Albery and Munafo, 2008).

collective/community development approach A health promotion perspective that argues that individual health status is dependent on environmental causes of illness and that people should act collectively to change their physical and social environment (Albery and Munafo, 2008).

community A body of people who have something in common linking them together. This may be geographical location, religious affiliation, ethnic origin, or profession.

complementary alternative medicine (CAM) A term describing a wide range of medical systems, diverse therapeutic practices and alternative healthcare systems that fall outside the boundaries of conventional biomedicine (Hill, 2003).

control group A group of participants treated in an identical manner to the intervention/treatment group, except that they do not receive the intervention itself. In other words, all variables other than the intervention are kept constant (Marks and Yardley, 2004).

coping Anything that people do to manage problems of emotional responses (Carver and Scheier, 1994).

coping strategies Refers to the specific behavioural and psychological efforts we make as we try to master, tolerate, reduce or minimize stressful events (Gurung, 2006).

coping styles Coping styles are our general predispositions to dealing with stress, which tend to be dichotomized as being either approach or avoidant in style.

cross-sectional design The study of a group of participants at a single point in time.

cues to action Factors or triggers that prompt a behaviour (the term is from the Health Belief Model).

defence mechanisms Usually unconscious mental processes that help us to avoid conscious conflict or anxiety (Sykes, 1989).

denial A defence mechanism that works by the individual refusing to believe that the event is happening at all.

descriptive study A study that tries to reveal patterns associated with a specific disease without an emphasis on pre-specified hypotheses.

direct effects hypothesis A hypothesis put forward to explain how social support can reduce stress, which suggests that social support is directly good for us (Forshaw, 2002).

dysphoric mood induction The process of inducing a negative mood in another, usually achieved by encouraging them to remember a sad or difficult experience, or by asking a person to read a vignette designed to lower mood.

e-health The use of modern technology as a means of accessing or delivering health information.

electrolytes Chemicals which regulate our body's systems.

emotion-focused coping Such a strategy involves dealing with the emotions surrounding the stressor.

enabling factor A factor which has the ability to enhance the likelihood that a health behaviour will occur.

epidemiology The study of the distribution and determinants of health and illness in populations (Rugulies et al., 2004).

evaluation The process by which the worth or value of something is decided, involving measurement, observation and comparison with the programme policy/aim (Corcoran, 2007).

evidence-based practice The use of research evidence to guide practice (Corcoran, 2007).

experimental study Experimental studies manipulate (change) a condition in order to determine the effects of that condition on the outcome of interest.

exposure The process of safely exposing individuals to the issue they are afraid of.

fat cell theory The suggestion that obese individuals are born with a greater number of fat cells.

focus group A small group of people brought together to discuss a topic under the guidance of a researcher or moderator.

food neophobia The reluctance to eat or avoidance of new foods.

framing effects These concern the way in which data or information is communicated. The same information can be given a positive or a negative spin, which can have a significant impact on the way in which it is subsequently interpreted.

gastric bypass An operation which physically limits the amount a person can eat by creating a small stomach pouch which bypasses part of the small intestine.

General Adaptation Syndrome (GAS) This suggests that we automatically respond to stressors in a three-stage response: alarm, resistance and exhaustion. This model fails to incorporate the possible influence of psychological factors.

hardiness A personality type which has been characterized by three factors (Albery and Munafo, 2008): commitment (a sense of purpose in life events and activities); control (the belief of personal influence over situations); and challenge (seeing adaptation and change as a normal and positive experience).

health behaviour An action taken with the intention of maintaining, attaining or regaining good health, or in order to prevent illness.

health belief Thoughts and knowledge (not necessarily based on fact) held by individuals concerning their health.

Health Belief Model Helps to predict health behaviour based on perceptions of susceptibility to an illness, costs and benefits of the health behaviour, and environmental 'cues to action' which can trigger the behaviour (Forshaw, 2002).

health-impairing behaviour A behaviour which has a negative impact on health.

health intervention Treatment provided to improve a situation, especially medical procedures or applications that are intended to relieve illness or injury. In other words, an action taken to improve health status.

health motivation Our incentive to behave in a healthy manner.

health outcomes Changes in health following the implementation of a health intervention.

health promotion Any activity, event or process that facilitates the improvement of the health status of individuals and groups, or which stimulates behavioural change to protect against harm associated with maladaptive health behaviour (Albery and Munafo, 2008).

health protective behaviour A behaviour which has a positive impact on health.

homeostasis The process of maintaining balance.

homogeneous Of the same kind, sharing the same characteristics.

illness representations The way in which we think about illness.

intention–behaviour gap Refers to whether or not intentions to change behaviour are actually translated into action.

intervention/treatment group A group of study participants that are treated in an identical manner to the control group, but who, in addition, are exposed to the intervention itself. All variables other than the intervention are kept constant between the two groups.

laparoscopic gastric banding An operation which physically limits the amount that a person can eat by placing a band around the stomach to make it smaller.

locus of control A term encapsulating the idea of perceived control. It is suggested that people who feel that they have control over their lives have an 'internal locus of control', whereas those who tend to feel that their lives are governed by chance have an 'external locus of control'.

mass media Any type of printed or electronic communication medium that is sent to the population at large (Corcoran, 2007).

medical model Views humans as being reducible to tissues and physiological processes which are therefore the focus of any interventions. Culture, thoughts and beliefs are generally not considered as having influence (Forshaw, 2002).

metabolic rate theory The suggestion that people who have lower metabolic rates might be more prone to obesity because, when resting, people with lower metabolic rates burn up less calories.

mindfulness-based stress reduction (MBSR) A psycho-educational training programme in mindfulness and its applications to daily life (Biegel et al., 2009). MBSR encourages the development of an attitude of acceptance or non-judgementality towards events and experiences.

mindless eating A term developed by Brian Wansink to describe our tendency to eat without paying attention to physiological, environmental, cultural or psychological cues.

morbidity rates The number of cases of disease or illness that exist at a given point in time, expressed either as the number of new cases (incidence) or total number of existing cases (prevalence).

mortality rates The number of people in a population who die from a particular illness or disease (Albery and Munafo, 2008).

natural selection The process by which traits that make it more likely for an organism to survive are passed down through the generations by reproduction. In other words, if particular traits allow you to survive better in the world, you will pass these traits to your offspring.

obesity Being overweight, commonly defined as having a body mass index (BMI) of greater than 30.

objective Objectives are concerned with the desired end state that should be achieved within a specific time period.

omnivores Beings that eat both plants and animals.

perceived barriers/costs Beliefs related to the likely barriers to undertaking a recommended course of action in response to a health threat. From the Health Belief Model (Albery and Munafo, 2008).

perceived behavioural control Beliefs that relate to how much control a person thinks they have over their behaviour. From the Theory of Planned Behaviour (Albery and Munafo, 2008).

perceived benefits Beliefs related to the likely positive consequences associated with undertaking a healthy behaviour. From the Health Belief Model (Albery and Munafo, 2008).

perceived severity Beliefs about the severity of consequences of becoming ill or not undertaking a behaviour on one's health. From the Health Belief Model (Albery and Munafo, 2008).

perceived susceptibility Beliefs about how likely one is to suffer a negative or positive health outcome. From the Health Belief Model (Albery and Munafo, 2008).

placebo A harmless pill, medicine or procedure that can have a strong psychological effect on those that take it.

primary care The treatment you receive from the people you normally see first when you have a health problem, for example a doctor, dentist, optician or pharmacist.

problem-focused coping Such a strategy involves directly facing the stressful situation and working to find a way to resolve it.

progressive muscle relaxation An approach to relaxation that involves individuals learning both the technique and the benefits of relaxing their muscles.

psychoneuroimmunology (PNI) The field of health psychology which studies the relationship between the mind and the immune system.

quasi-experimental approach An approach which differs from randomized controlled trials, in that participants are not assigned to treatment/intervention and control groups by the process of random allocation.

randomized controlled trial (RCT) A method of experimentation in medicine whereby one group is given the drug or treatment in question and another group is not. Allocation to these groups is entirely random (Forshaw, 2002).

rationalization A defence mechanism that works by the individual explaining away the stress to themselves, thereby engaging in a process of intellectualizing the stress.

regression A defence mechanism that is employed when an individual reverts to behaviours that are more appropriate to an earlier level of development.

repression A defence mechanism that works by protecting the individual from negative memories and anxiety-producing thoughts by preventing them from reaching consciousness (Morrison and Bennett, 2009).

restrained eating An alternative term for dieting.

restraint theory A theory developed by Herman and Mack (1975), who explored the impact of imposing cognitive restraint on eating.

role play A learning activity in which participants assume a role in order to practise a variety of skills. Participants act out particular behavioural roles as a way of expanding their awareness of differing points of view and learning new skills to cope with different situations. Role playing therefore allows participants the freedom to learn and practise new skills without the fear of failure.

self-efficacy How confident a person is in their ability to perform a certain action and attain anticipated outcomes (Albery and Munafo, 2008).

self-empowerment approach A health promotion perspective that argues for the emphasis in activities to be on self-empowerment, derived by engagement and involvement with health-related activities at an individual or community-based level (Albery and Munafo, 2008).

Self-regulatory Model (SRM) This model is based on approaches to problem solving and suggests that illness and illness symptoms are dealt with by individuals in the same way as other problems (Ogden, 2007).

semi-structured interview A method of collecting data that involves the researcher asking a small number of open-ended questions that encourage the interviewee to talk at length about the topics of interest.

set-point theory A theory developed by Nisbett (1972) to explain how body weight is determined.

social cognitive approach An approach which emphasizes the way in which our thoughts and emotions are affected by the immediate social context (Albery and Munafo, 2008).

social context The positions and roles with which an individual participates or interacts.

social learning The process of observing other people's behaviour and the impact this has on our own behaviour.

social skills training Intervention designed to facilitate effective interaction and communication with others.

social support Generally defined as emotional, informational or practical support from others.

socioeconomic status (SES) A way of encapsulating a person's economic and social position using variables such as occupation, education and income, which has been shown to be linked to individuals' health and wellbeing.

Stages of Change Model A model which proposes five stages through which a person progresses as behaviour change is implemented.

stress Notoriously difficult to define, stress is described as the state that occurs following reaction to the stressor and stress–response.

stressor An event that a person interprets as endangering their physical or psychological wellbeing.

stress-response Refers to the reactions to the stressor.

subjective norm Beliefs we have about how other people we perceive as being important to us would like us to behave. From the Theory of Planned Behaviour (Albery and Munafo, 2008).

systematic desensitization A technique which draws on the discipline of classical conditioning. An individual is encouraged to identify a ranked list of behaviour they are anxious about; they are then encouraged to address the least frightening until they are no longer anxious. Once they have achieved mastery of this level, they progress to the next until they are facing the issue they were most afraid of.

target population The population about which information is required.

Theory of Planned Behaviour A model of health behaviour from social psychological theory which incorporates perceived control into the prediction of behaviour along with subjective norms and attitudes (Forshaw, 2002).

Theory of Reasoned Action A theory which proposes that the immediate antecedent of actual behaviour is behavioural intention. Behavioural intention is predicted by attitude and subjective norm (Albery and Munafo, 2008).

thrifty gene Thrifty genes are thought to explain our propensity to have large appetites, combined with the ability to take up energy quickly, because in our ancestors' times, this ability would have conferred an evolutionary advantage. Thrifty genes are those which enable individuals to efficiently collect and process food to deposit fat during periods of food abundance.

titration methodology A form of systematic desensitization which involves individuals moving forward with the task they are phobic of until anxiety is perceived, then going backwards until anxiety disappears and so on.

transactional model of stress A model proposed by Lazarus and Folkman (1984), which suggests that the interaction between the person and their environment (the 'transaction') is what results (or does not result) in stress.

Type A personality Type A behaviour includes impatience, intolerance, competitiveness, attempts to achieve too much in too little time, vigorous speech pattern and hostility.

Type B personality Type B behaviour is characterized by a relaxed, easy-going, cooperative style.

Type C personality Type C behaviour is characterized by cooperative, appeasing, passive, non-assertive, self-sacrificing behaviour, as well as inhibition of emotions.

Type D personality A person who experiences but inhibits the expression of negative emotions and, at the same time, actively avoids social interaction for fear of encountering feelings of disapproval is said to have a Type D personality.

unrealistic optimism The view that some people have that things will be better than they are statistically likely to be and that illnesses happen to 'other people' (Forshaw, 2002).

References

Abood, D.A., Black, D.R. and Coster, D.C. (2005). Loss-framed minimal intervention increases mammography use. *Women's Health Issues*, 15, 258–64.

Abraham, C., Conner, M., Jones, F. and O'Connor, D. (2008). *Health Psychology: Topics in Applied Psychology*. Hodder Education: London.

Abraham, C., Southby, L., Quandte, S. et al. (2007). What's in a leaflet? Identifying research-based persuasive messages in European alcohol-education leaflets. *Psychology and Health*, 22(1), 31–60.

Adam, T.C. and Epel, E.S (2007). Stress, eating and the reward system. *Physiological Behaviour*, 92, 449–58.

Adams, J., Rodham, K. and Gavin, J. (2005). Investigating the 'self' in deliberate self-harm. *Qualitative Health Research*, 15(10), 1293–309.

Aggleton, P. and Homans, H. (1987). *Educating about AIDS*. NHS Training Authority: Bristol.

Ajzen, I. (1991). The theory of planned behaviour. *Organizational Behavior and Human Decision Processes*, 50, 179–211.

Ajzen, I. and Fishbein, M. (1970). The prediction of behaviour from attitudinal and normative variables. *Journal of Experimental Social Psychology*, 6(4), 466–87.

Ajzen, I. and Fishbein, M. (1980). *Understanding Attitudes and Predicting Social Behaviour*. Prentice Hall: Englewood Cliffs, NJ.

Ala-Mursula, L., Batear, J., Linna, A. et al. (2005). Employee worktime control moderates the effects of job strain and effort reward imbalance on sickness absence: The 10-town study. *Journal of Epidemiology and Community Health*, 59(10), 851–7.

Albery, I.P. and Guppy, A. (1995). Drivers' differential perceptions of legal and safe driving consumption. *Addiction*, 90, 245–54.

Albery, I.P. and Munafo, M. (2008). *Key Concepts in Health Psychology*. Sage: London.

Alferi, S.M., Carver, C.S., Antoni, M.H. et al. (2001). An exploratory study of social support, distress and life disruption among low-income Hispanic women under treatment for early stage breast cancer. *Health Psychology*, 20, 41–6.

Amalraj, S., Starkweather, C., Nguyen, C. and Arash, C (2009). Health literacy, communication and decision-making in older cancer patients. *Oncology*, 23(4), 369–75.

American Medical Association (2003) *Assessment and Management of Adult Obesity: A Primer for Physicians*. American Medical Association: Atlanta, GA.

Antoni, M.H., Lechner, S., Diaz, A. et al. (2009). Cognitive behavioral stress management effects on psychosocial and physiological adaptation in women undergoing treatment for breast cancer. *Brain, Behavior and Immunity*, 23, 580–91.

Appel, L.J., Champagne, C.M., Marsha, D.W. et al. (2003). Effects of comprehensive lifestyle modification on blood pressure control: Main results of the PREMIER clinical trial. *Journal of the American Medical Association*, 289(16), 2083–93.

Ard, J.D. (2007). Unique perspective on the obesogenic environment. *Journal of General Internal Medicine*, 22(7): 1058–60.

Armitage, C. (2009). Is there utility in the transtheoretical model? *British Journal of Health Psychology*, 14, 195–210.

Armitage, C.J. and Connor, M. (2002). Reducing fat intake: Interviews based on the Theory of Planned Behaviour. In D. Rutter and L. Quine (eds) *Changing Health Behaviour*. Open University Press: Buckingham.

Armstrong, K., Schwartz, J.S., Fitzgerald, G. et al. (2002). Effect of framing as gain versus loss on understanding and hypothetical treatment choices: Survival and mortality curves. *Medical Decision Making*, 22(1), 76–83.

Ashton, W., Nanchahal, K. and Wood, D. (2001). Body mass index and metabolic risk factors for coronary heart disease in women. *European Heart Journal*, 22, 46–55.

Atkin, C. (2001). Theory and principles of media health campaigns, pp. 49–68. In R.E. Rice and C.K. Atkin (eds) *Public Communication Campaigns* (3rd edn). Sage: London.

Babyak, M., Blumenthal, J.A., Herman, S. et al. (2000). Exercise treatment for major depression: Maintenance of therapeutic benefit at 10 months. *Psychosomatic Medicine*, 62, 633–8.

Bäckström, A., Pirtilä-Backman, A.M. and Tuorila, H. (2004). Willingness to try new foods as predicted by social representation and attitude and trait scales. *Appetite*, 43, 75–83.

Baer, R. (2003). Mindfulness training as a clinical intervention: A conceptual and empirical review. *Clinical Psychology: Science and Practice*, 10(2), 125–43.

Baker, H. and Wardle, J. (2003). Sex differences in fruit and vegetable intake in older adults. *Appetite*, 40, 269–75.

Banks, J.K. and Gannon, L.R. (1988). The influence of hardiness on the relationships between stressors and psychosomatic symptomatology. *American Journal of Community Psychology*, 16, 25–37.

Bargh, J.A., McKenna, K.Y. and Fitzsimons, G.M. (2002). Can you see the real me? Activation and expression of the 'true self' on the Internet. *Journal of Social Issues*, 58(1), 33–48.

Becker, M.H. (1986). The tyranny of health promotion. *Public Health Reviews*, 14, 15–23.

Bekker, M.H., van de Meerendonk, C. and Molleras, J. (2004). Effects of negative mood induction and impulsivity on self-perceived emotional eating. *International Journal of Eating Disorders*, 36, 461–9.

Bennett, M.P. and Lengacher, C. (2009). Humor and laughter may influence health IV. Humor and immune function. *eCAM*, 6(2), 159–64.

Bennett, P. and Murphy, S. (1997). *Psychology and Health Promotion*. Open University Press: Buckingham.

Benson, J. and Britten, N. (2002). Patients' decisions about whether or not to take antihypertensive drugs: Qualitative study. *British Medical Journal*, 325, 873–77.

Berland, G.K., Elliott M.N., Morales, L.S. et al. (2001). Health information on the Internet: Accessibility, quality, and readability in English and Spanish. *Journal of the American Medical Association*, 285(20), 2612–21.

Bernardi, L., Porta, C. and Sleight, P. (2006). Cardiovascular, cerebrovascular, and respiratory changes induced by different types of music in musicians and non-musicians: The importance of silence. *Heart*, 92, 445–52.

Bertholet, N., Cheng, D.M., Palfai, T.P. et al. (2009). Does readiness to change predict subsequent alcohol consumption in medical inpatients with unhealthy alcohol use? *Addictive Behaviours*, 34, 636–40.

Biegel, G.M., Brown, K.W., Shapiro, S.L. and Schubert, C.M. (2009). Mindfulness-based stress reduction for the treatment of adolescent psychiatric outpatients: A randomised clinical trial. *Journal of Consulting and Clinical Psychology*, 77(5), 855–66.

Birch, L.L. and Marlin, D.W. (1982). 'I don't like it, I never tried it': Effects of exposure to food on two-year-old children's food preferences. *Appetite*, 3, 353–60.

Blair, Y., MacPherson, L., McCall, D. and McMahon, A. (2006). Dental health of 5-year-olds following community-based oral health promotion in Glasgow, UK. *International Journal of Paediatric Dentistry*, 16, 388–98.

Blaxter, M. (1995). *Health and Lifestyles*. Routledge: London.

Blundell, J.E. and Gillett, A. (2001). Control of food intake in the obese. *Obesity Research*, 9(Suppl 4), S263–70.

Booth-Butterfield, M., Anderson, R.H. and Booth-Butterfield, S. (2000). Adolescents' use of tobacco, health locus of control, and self-monitoring. *Health Communication*, 12(2), 137–48.

Boudreau, F. and Godin, G. (2009). Understanding physical activity intentions among French Canadians with type 2 diabetes: An extension of Ajzen's theory of planned behaviour. *International Journal of Behavioural Nutrition and Physical Activity*, 6, 35–45.

Brannon J. and Feist, J. (1997). *Health Psychology: An Introduction to Behaviour and Health*. Brooks/Cole: Pacific Grove, CA.

Brewer, H., Rodham, K., Mistral, W. and Stallard, P. (2006). Adolescent perception of risk and challenge. *Journal of Adolescence*, 29, 261–72.

British Broadcasting Corporation (BBC) (2006). Diet blog for Japanese ministers. http://news.bbc.co.uk/1/hi/world/asia-pacific/6205894. stm, accessed 12 December 2006.

Bulik, C.M., Sullivan, P.F. and Kendler, K.S. (1998). Heritability of binge eating and broadly defined bulimia nervosa. *Biological Psychiatry*, 44, 1201–18.

Burgoyne, R.W. and Saunders, D.S. (2000). Perceived support in newly registered HIV/AIDS clinic outpatients. *AIDS Care*, 12, 643–50.

Burke, V., Beilin, L.J., Cutt, H.E. et al. (2005). Effects of a lifestyle programme on ambulatory blood pressure and drug dosage in treated hypertensive patients: A randomized controlled trial. *Journal of Hypertension*, 23(6), 1241–9.

Burkhart, P.V. and Rayens, M.K. (2005). Self-concept and health locus of control: factors related to children's adherence to recommended asthma regimen. *Pediatric Nursing*, 31(5), 404–9.

Byrne, D. (2001). *Understanding the Urban*. Palgrave Macmillan: Basingstoke.

Caplan, P., Keane, A., Willets, A. and Williams, J. (1998). Concepts of healthy eating: Approaches from a social science perspective, pp. 168–82. In A. Murcott (ed.) *The Nation's Diet: The Social Science of Food Choice*. London: Longman.

Carter, J.C., McFarlane, T.L., Bewell, C. et al. (2009). Maintenance treatment for anorexia nervosa: A comparison of cognitive behaviour therapy and treatment as usual. *International Journal of Eating Disorders*, 42, 202–7.

Carver, C.S. and Scheier, M.F. (1994). Situational coping and coping dispositions in a stressful transaction. *Journal of Social and Personality Psychology*, 56, 267–83.

Carver, C.S., Pozo, C., Harris, S.D. et al. (1993). How coping mediates the effect of optimism on distress: A study of women with early stage breast cancer. *Journal of Personality and Social Psychology*, 65, 375–90.

Cavallo, D.A. and Pinto, A. (2001). Effects of mood induction on eating behavior and cigarette craving in dietary restrainers. *Eating Behaviors*, 2, 113–27.

Cepeda, M.S., Carr, D.B., Lau, J. and Alvarez, H. (2006). Music for pain relief. *Cochrane Database Systematic Review*, CD004843.

Chamberlain, K. (2004). Food and health: Expanding the agenda for health psychology. *Journal of Health Psychology*, 9(4), 467–81.

Chamove, A.S. (2007). Therapy toy for spider phobics. *International Journal for Clinical and Health Psychology*, 7(2), 533–6.

Chandon, P. and Wansink, B. (2007). The biasing health halos of fast-food restaurant health claims: Lower calorie estimates and higher side-dish consumption intentions. *Journal of Consumer Research*, 34, 301–14.

Charles, N. and Walters, V. (2008). 'Men are leavers alone and women are worriers': Gender differences in discourse of health. *Health, Risk and Society*, 10(2), 117–32.

Chartrand, T.L. and Bargh, J.A. (1999). The chameleon effect: The perception–behavior link and social interaction. *Journal of Personality and Social Psychology*, 76, 893–910.

Christensen, L. (2001). The effect of food intake on mood. *Clinical Nutrition*, 20(Suppl 1), 161–6.

Christensen, L. and Brooks, A. (2006). Changing food preference as a function of mood. *Journal of Psychology*, 140(4), 293–306.

Christensen, L. and Pettijohn, L. (2001). Mood and carbohydrate cravings. *Appetite*, 36, 137–45.

Cohen, S., Tyrell, D.A. and Smith, A.P. (1993) Life events, perceived stress, negative affect and susceptibility to the common cold. *Journal of Personality & Social Psychology*, 64, 131–40.

Connell, P., Wolfe, C. and McKevitt, K. (2007). Preventing stroke: A narrative review of community interventions for improving hypertension control in black adults. *Health and Social Care in the Community*, 16(2), 165–87.

Conner, M. and Norman, P. (2005). *Predicting Health Behaviour: Research and Practice with Social Cognition Models* (2nd edn). Open University Press: Maidenhead.

Connor, M. and Armitage, C. (1998). Extending the theory of planned behaviour: A review and avenues for further research. *Journal of Applied Social Psychology*, 28, 1430–64.

Cooke, R. and French, D.P. (2008). How well do the theory of reasoned action and theory of planned behaviour predict intentions and attendance at screening programmes? A meta-analysis. *Psychology and Health*, 23(7), 745–65.

Corcoran, N. (ed.) (2007). *Communicating Health: Strategies for Health Promotion*. Sage: London.

Corsica, J.A. and Spring, B.J. (2008). Carbohydrate craving: A double-blind, placebo-controlled test of the self-medication hypothesis. *Eating Behaviours*, 9, 447–54.

Courtenay, W. (2000). Constructions of masculinity and their influence on men's well-being: A theory of gender and health. *Social Science and Medicine*, 50, 1385–401.

Courtenay, W.H., McCreary, D.R. and Merighi, J.R. (2002). Gender and ethnic differences in health beliefs and behaviours. *Journal of Health Psychology*, 7(3), 219–31.

Crawshaw, P., Bunton, R. and Gillen, K. (2003). Health Action Zones and the problem of community. *Health and Social Care in the Community*, 11(1), 36–44.

Cullinan, P., Acquilla, S. and Ramana Dhara, V. (1997). Respiratory morbidity 10 years after the Union Carbide gas leak at Bhopal: A cross-sectional survey. *British Medical Journal*, 314(7077), 338–42.

Curtis, A.J. (2000). *Health Psychology*. Routledge: London.

Darker, C.D., Larkin, M. and French, D.P. (2007a). An exploration of walking behaviour: An interpretative phenomenological approach. *Social Science and Medicine*, 65, 2172–83.

Darker, C.D., French, D.P., Longdon, S. et al. (2007b). Are beliefs elicited biased by question order? A theory of planned behaviour belief elicitation study about walking in the UK general population. *British Journal of Health Psychology*, 12(1), 93–110.

Davidson, R.J., Kabat-Zinn, J., Schumacher, J. et al. (2003). Alterations in brain and immune function produced by mindfulness meditation. *Psychosomatic Medicine*, 65, 564–70.

De Vrient, T., Moreno, L.A. and De Henauw, S. (2009). Chronic stress and obesity in adolescents: Scientific evidence and methodological issues for epidemiological research. *Nutrition, Metabolism, and Cardiovascular Diseases*, 19, 511–19.

De Waal, F. (2001). *The Ape and the Sushi Master: Cultural Reflections of a Primatologist*. Basic Books: New York.

De Wit, J. and Stroebe, W. (2005). Social cognition models of health behaviour, pp. 52–83. In A. Kaptein and J. Weinman (eds) *Health Psychology*. Blackwell: London.

De Zwaan, M., Mitchell, J.E., Howell, L.M. et al. (2002). Two measures of health-related quality of life in morbid obesity. *Obesity Research*, 10, 1143–51.

DeLongis, A., Folkman, S. and Lazarus, R.S. (1988). Hassles, health and mood: Psychological and social resources as mediators. *Journal of Personality*, 54(3), 486–495.

Dembrowski, T.M., MacDougall, J.M., Costa, P.T. and Grandits, G.A. (1989). Components of hostility as predictors of sudden death and myocardial infarction in the Multiple Risk Factor Intervention Trial. *Psychosomatic Medicine*, 51, 514–22.

Denollet, J. (1998). Personality and coronary heart disease: The Type D scale 16 (DS16). *Annals of Behavioral Medicine*, 20, 209–15.

Department of Health (2004). *Health Survey for England 2003. The Risk Factors for Cardiovascular Disease*, vol. 2. TSO: London.

Diamond, J. (2003). The double puzzle of diabetes. *Nature*, 423, 599–602.

DiClemente, C.C., Prochaska, J.O., Fairhurst, S. et al. (1991). The process of smoking cessation: An analysis of precontemplation, contemplation and contemplation/action. *Journal of Consulting and Clinical Psychology*, 59, 295–304.

Dijkstra, K., Charness, N., Yordon, R. and Fox, M. (2009). Changes in physiological stress and self-reported mood in younger and older adults after exposure to a stressful task. *Ageing, Neuropsychology and Cognition*, 16, 338–56.

Dolan, C.A. and Adler, A.B. (2006). Military hardiness as a buffer of psychological health on return from deployment. *Military Medicine*, 171(2), 93–8.

Doucet, E., Imbeault, P., St Pierre, S. et al. (2000). Appetite after weight loss by energy restriction and a low-fat diet-exercise follow-up. *International Journal of Obesity and Related Metabolic Disorders*, 24, 906–14.

Doumas, D.M., Margolin, G. and John, R.S. (2003). The relationship between daily marital interaction, work, and health promoting behaviours in dual-earner couples: An extension of the work-family spillover model. *Journal of Family Issues*, 24, 3–20.

Drummond, M.J. (2002). Men, body image, and eating disorders. *International Journal of Men's Health*, 1, 89–103.

Druss, R.G. and Douglas, C.J. (1988). Adaptive responses to illness and disability: Healthy denial. *General Hospital Psychiatry*, 10, 163–8.

Edwards, I.R. and Hugman, B. (1997). The challenge of effectively communicating risk-benefit information, *Drug Safety*, 17, 216–27.

Eisler, I., Dare, C., Russell, G.F. et al. (1997). Family and individual therapy in AN: A 5-year follow-up. *Archives of General Psychiatry*, 54, 1025–30.

Engel, G.L. (1980). The clinical application of the biopsychosocial model. *American Journal of Psychiatry*, 137, 535–44.

Epstein, L. and Ogden, J. (2005). A qualitative study of GPs' views of treating obesity. *British Journal of General Practice*, 55, 750–4.

European Commission (1999). *A Pan-EU Survey of Consumer Attitudes to Physical Activity, Body Weight and Health*, DGV/F.3. EC: Luxembourg.

Ewles, L. and Simnet, I. (1995). *Promoting Health: A Practical Guide* (3rd edn). Scutari Press: London.

Fagerström, K.O. (1978). Measuring degrees of physical dependence to tobacco smoking with reference to individualization of treatment. *Addictive Behaviours*, 3, 235–41.

Fairburn, C.A. (1981). A cognitive behavioural approach to the treatment of bulimia. *Psychological Medicine*, 11, 707–11.

Fairburn, C.G. and Harrison, P.J. (2003). Eating disorders, *The Lancet*, 361, 407–16.

Fairburn, C.G., Marcus, M.D. and Wilson, G.T. (1993). Cognitive-behavioural therapy for binge eating and bulimia nervosa: A comprehensive treatment manual, pp. 361–404. In C.G. Fairburn and G.T. Wilson (eds) *Binge Eating: Nature, Assessment and Treatment*. Guilford Press: New York.

Fairburn, C.G., Shafran, R. and Cooper, Z.A. (1999). A cognitive-behavioural theory of anorexia nervosa. *Behavioural Research and Therapy*, 37, 1–13.

Farber, E.W., Schwartz, J.A., Schaper, P.E. et al. (2000). Resilience factors associated to adaptation to HIV disease. *Psychosomatics*, 41(2), 140–6.

Farrant, W. (1991). Addressing the contradictions: health promotion and community health action in the United Kingdom. *International Journal of Health Services*, 21(3), 423–39.

Fernstrom, J.D. and Wurtman, R.J. (1971). Brain serotonin content: Increase following ingestion of carbohydrate diet. *Science*, 174, 1023–5.

Fisher, J.O. and Birch, L.L. (2002). Eating in the absence of hunger and being overweight in girls from 5 to 7 years of age. *American Journal of Clinical Nutrition*, 76, 226–31.

Flight, I., Leppard, P. and Cox, D.N. (2003). Food neophobia and associations with cultural diversity and socio-economic status amongst rural and urban Australian adolescents. *Appetite*, 41, 51–9.

Folkman, S. and Moskowitz, J.T. (2004). Coping: Pitfalls and promise. *Annual Review of Psychology*, 55, 745–74.

Forshaw, M. (2002). *Essential Health Psychology*. Arnold: London.

Fox, C.R. and Irwin, J.R. (1998). The role of context in the communication of uncertain beliefs. *Basic and Applied Psychology*, 20(1), 57–70.

Friedman, M. and Rosenman, R.H. (1959). Association of specific overt behaviour pattern with blood and cardiovascular findings: blood cholesterol level, blood clotting time, incidence of arcus senilis and clinical coronary artery disease. *Journal of the American Medical Association*, 169, 1286–96.

Friedman, M. and Rosenman, R.H. (1974). *Type A Behaviour and your Heart*. New York: Knopf.

Garn, S.M., Bailey, S.M., Solomon, M.A. and Hopkins, P.J. (1981). Effects of remaining family members on fatness prediction. *American Journal of Clinical Nutrition*, 34, 148–53.

Gascon, J.J., Sanchez-Ortuno, M., Llor, B. et al. (2004). Treatment compliance in hypertension study group: Why hypertensive patients do not comply with the treatment: results from a qualitative study. *Family Practitioner*, 21(2), 125–30.

Gatward, N. (2007). Anorexia nervosa: An evolutionary puzzle. *European Eating Disorders Review*, 15, 1–12.

George, J.M., Scott, D.S., Turner, S.T. and Gregg, J.M. (1980). The effects of psychological factors and physical trauma on recovery from oral surgery. *Journal of Behavioural Medicine*, 3, 291–310.

Gerrard, M., Gibbons, F.X. and Bushman, B.J. (1996). The relation between perceived vulnerability to HIV and precautionary sexual behaviour. *Psychological Bulletin*, 119, 390–409.

Gerritsen, A.A. and Deville, W.L. (2009). Gender differences in health and health care utilisation in various ethnic groups in the Netherlands: A cross-sectional study. *BMC Public Health*, 9, 109, doi:10.1186/1471-2458-9-109.

Ghaemi, S.N. (2009). The rise and fall of the biopsychosocial model. *British Journal of Psychiatry*, 195, 3–4.

Gibson, L., Leavey, C., Viggiani, N. and Sands, R. (1995). Interviews: Professor Don Nutbeam. *Journal of Contemporary Health*, 2, 18–19.

Gidron, Y., McGrath, P.J. and Goodday, R. (1995). The physical and psychosocial predictors of adolescents' recovery from oral surgery. *Journal of Behavioural Medicine*, 18, 385–99.

Gilroy, L.J., Kirkby, K.C. and Daniels, B.A. (2003). Long term follow up of computer-aided vicarious exposure versus live graded exposure in the treatment of spider-phobia. *Behavior Therapy*, 34, 65–76.

Gorin, S.S. and Heck, J.E. (2005). Cancer screening among Latino subgroups in the United States. *Preventive Medicine*, 40, 515–26.

Gough, B. (2007). 'Real men don't diet': An analysis of contemporary newspaper representations of men, food and health. *Social Science and Medicine*, 64, 326–37.

Gowers, S.G. (2008). Management of eating disorders in children and adolescents. *Archives of Diseases of Childhood*, 93, 331–4.

Gredig, D., Nideroest, S. and Parpan-Blaser, A. (2006). HIV-protection through condom use: Testing the theory of planned behaviour in a community sample of heterosexual men in a high income country. *Psychology and Health*, 21(5), 541–55.

Green, L.W. and Kreuter, M.W. (1999). *Health Promotion Planning: An Educational Tool and Ecological Approach* (3rd edn). Mayfield: Mountain View, CA.

Greenhalgh, T., Helman, C. and Chowdury, A.M. (1998). Health beliefs and folk models of diabetes in British Bangladeshis: a qualitative study. *British Medical Journal*, 316, 978–83.

Greenough, A., Cole, G., Lewis, J. et al. (1998) Untangling the effects of hunger, anxiety and nausea on energy intake during intravenous cholecystokinin octapeptide (CCK-8) infusion. *Physiology and Behavior*, 65(2), 303–10.

Griva, K., Myers, L.B. and Newman, S. (2000). Illness perceptions and self-efficacy beliefs in adolescents and young adults with insulin dependent diabetes mellitus. *Psychology and Health*, 15, 733–50.

Gröpel, P. and Kuhl, J. (2009). Work-life balance and subjective well-being: The mediating role of need fulfillment. *British Journal of Psychology*, 100, 365–75.

Guisinger, S. (2003). Adapted to flee famine: Adding an evolutionary perspective on Anorexia Nervosa. *Psychological Review*, 110(4), 745–61.

Gurung, R.A. (2006). *Health Psychology: A Cultural Approach*. Thomson Wadsworth: Belmont, CA.

Habra, M.E., Linden, W., Anderson, J.C. and Weinberg, J. (2003). Type D personality is related to cardiovascular and neuroendocrine reactivity to acute distress. *Journal of Psychosomatic Research*, 55, 235–45.

Halpern, D.F., Blackman, S. and Salzman, B. (1989). Using statistical information to assess oral contraceptive safety. *Applied Cognitive Psychology*, 3, 251–60.

Han, M.K., Postma, D., Mannino, D.M. et al. (2007). Gender and chronic obstructive pulmonary disease: Why it matters. *American Journal of Respiratory and Critical Care Medicine*, 176(12), 1179–84.

Harris, S.M. (2004). The effect of health value and ethnicity on the relationship between hardiness and health behaviours. *Journal of Personality*, 72, 379–411.

Hart, K.E. and Chiovari, P. (1998). Inhibition of eating behaviour: Negative cognitive effects of dieting. *Journal of Clinical Psychology*, 54, 427–30.

Harvey-Berino, J. Pintauro, S.J. and Gold, E.C. (2002). The feasibility of using Internet support for the maintenance of weight loss. *Behaviour Modification*, 26(1), 103–16.

Hawton, K., Rodham, K. and Evans, E. (2006). *By Their Own Young Hand: Deliberate Self-harm and Suicidal Ideas in Adolescents*. Jessica Kingsley: London.

Health Education Authority (1997). *Health Update: Workplace Health*. HEA: London.

Health Promotion Agency (1998). *Campaigning for Health*. Health Promotion Agency: Northern Ireland.

Hempel, S. (2006). *The Medical Detective: John Snow, Cholera and the Mystery of the Broad Street Pump*. Granta: London.

Herman, C.P. and Polivy, J. (1984). A boundary model for the regulation of eating, pp. 141–56. In A.J. Stunkard and E. Stellar (eds) *Eating and its Disorders*. Raven Press: New York.

Herman, P. and Mack, D. (1975). Restrained and unrestrained eating. *Journal of Personality*, 43, 646–60.

Hermans, R.C., Engels, R.C., Larsen, J.K. and Herman, P.K. (2009). Modeling of palatable food intake. The influence of quality of social interaction. *Appetite*, 52, 801–4.

Hill, A.J., Weaver, C.F. and Blundell, J.E. (1991). Food craving, dietary restraint and mood. *Appetite*, 17, 187–97.

Hill, F.J. (2003). Complementary and alternative medicine: the next generation of health promotion? *Health Promotion International*, 18(3), 265–72.

Hill, J.O. and Peters, J.C. (1998). Environmental contributions to the obesity epidemic. *Science*, 280, 1371–4.

Hjelm, K.G., Bard, K., Nyberg, P. and Apelqvist, J. (2005). Beliefs about health and diabetes in men of different ethnic origin. *Issues and Innovations in Nursing Practice*, 50(1), 47–59.

Hoffner, C. and Ye, J. (2009). Young adults' responses to news about sunscreen and skin cancer: The role of framing and social comparison. *Health Communication*, 24, 189–98.

Holmes, T.H. and Rahe, R.H. (1967). The social readjustment rating scale. *Journal of Psychosomatic Research*, 11, 213–18.

Holmgren, K., Dahlin-Ivanoff, S., Björkelund, C. and Hensing, G. (2009). The prevalence of work-related stress, and its association with self-perceived health and sick-leave, in a population of employed Swedish women. *BMC Public Health*, 9 (73), doi:10.1186/1471-2458-9-73.

Holzwarth, H., Huber, D., Majkrzak, A. and Tareen, B. (2002). Outcome of gastric bypass patients. *Obesity Surgery*, 12(2), 262–4.

Horne, R., James, D., Petrie, K. et al. (2000). Patients' interpretation of symptoms as a cause of delay in reaching hospital during acute myocardial infarction. *Heart*, 83(4), 388–93.

Hsu, L.K., Chesler, B.E. and Santhouse, R. (1990). Bulimia nervosa in eleven sets of twins: a clinical report. *International Journal of Eating Disorders*, 9, 275–82.

Hursti, U.K. and Sjödén, P. (1997). Food and general neophobia and their relationship with self-reported food choice: Familial resemblance in Swedish families with children of ages 7–17 years. *Appetite*, 29, 89–103.

Ingham, R. (1993). Old bodies in older clothes, *Health Psychology Update*, 14, 31–6.

Ingledew, D.K., Hardy, L., Cooper, C.L. and Jemal, H. (1996). Health behaviours reported as coping strategies. *British Journal of Health Psychology*, 1, 263–81.

Jeffrey, R.W., Baxter, J., McGuire, M. and Linde, J. (2006). Are fast food restaurants an environmental risk factor for obesity? *International Journal of Behavioral Nutrition and Physical Activity*, 3, 2.

Jeffrey, R.W., Drewnosku, A., Epstein, L.H. et al. (2000). Long term maintenance of weight loss: Current status. *Health Psychology*, 19(1suppl), 5–16.

Jeffrey, R.W., Forster, J.L., Schmid, T. et al. (1990). Community attitudes towards public policies to control alcohol, tobacco and high fat food consumption. *American Journal of Preventive Medicine*, 6, 12–19.

Jerome, J.K. (1889, reprinted 1994). *Three Men in a Boat*. Penguin Books: London.

Jones, R.M. (1985) Smoking before surgery: The case for stopping. *British Medical Journal*, 290(6484), 1763–4.

Jull, G. and Sterling, M. (2009). Bring back the biopsychosocial model for neck pain disorders. *Manual Therapy*, 14, 117–18.

Kanner, A.D., Coyne, J.C., Schaeffer, C. and Lazarus, R.S. (1981). Comparison of two modes of stress measurement: Daily hassles and uplifts versus major life events. *Journal of Behavioural Medicine*, 4, 1–39.

Kaptchuk, T.J. (2000). *The Web that has no Weaver: Understanding Chinese Medicine*. Contemporary Books: Chicago.

Kaptein, A. and Weinman J. (eds) (2004). *Health Psychology*. BPS Blackwell: Oxford.

Kaye, W.H., Nagata, T., Weltzin, T.E. et al. (2001). Double-blind, placebo-controlled administration of fluoxetine in restricting- and restricting-purging type AN. *Biological Psychiatry*, 49, 644–52.

Ker, J.H. and Kuk, G. (2001). The effects of low and high intensity exercise on emotions, stress and effort. *Psychology of Sport and Exercise*, 2, 173–86.

Kiecolt-Glaser, J.K., Bane, C., Glaser, R. and Malarkey, W.B. (2003). Love, marriage and divorce: Newlyweds' stress hormones foreshadow relationship changes. *Journal of Consulting and Clinical Psychology*, 71, 176–88.

Kiecolt-Glaser, J.K., Marucha, P.T., Malarkey, W.B. et al. (1995). Slowing wound healing by psychosocial stress. *Lancet*, 4, 1194–6.

King, G., Willoughby, C., Specht, J.A. and Brown, E. (2006). Social support processes and the adaptation of individuals with chronic disabilities. *Qualitative Health Research*, 16(7), 902–25.

Kingston, K., Szmukler, G., Andrewes, D. et al. (1996). Neuropsychological and structural brain changes in anorexia nervosa before and after refeeding. *Psychological Medicine*, 26(1), 15–28.

Kipling, M.D. and Waldron, H.A. (1975). Percivall Pott and cancer scroti. *British Journal of Industrial Medicine*, 32, 244–50.

Kissane, D.W., Boloch, S., Smith, G.C. et al. (2003). Cognitive-existential group psychotherapy for women with primary breast-cancer: A randomised controlled trial. *Psychooncology*, 12, 532–46.

Klump, K.L., Miller, K.B., Keel, P.K. et al. (2001). Genetic and environmental influences on anorexia nervosa syndromes in a population-based twin sample. *Psychological Medicine*, 31, 737–40.

Kobasa, S.C., Maddi, S. and Kahn, S. (1982). Hardiness and health: A prospective study. *Journal of Personality and Social Psychology*, 42, 168–77.

Kohn, P.M., Hay, B.D. and Legere, J.L. (1994). Hassles, coping styles and negative well-being. *Personality and Individual Differences*, 17, 169–79.

Kopelman, P.G. and Grace, C. (2004). New thoughts on managing obesity. *Gut*, 53, 1044–53.

Kortegaard, L.S., Hoerder, K., Joergensen, J. et al. (2001). A preliminary population-based twin study of self-reported eating disorder. *Psychological Medicine*, 31, 361–5.

Kramer, M.S., Seguin, L., Lydon, J. and Goulet, L. (2000). Socioeconomic disparities in pregnancy outcome: Why do the poor fare so badly? *Paediatric and Perinatal Epidemiology*, 14(3), 194–210.

Krebs, J.R. (2009). The gourmet ape: Evolution and human food preferences. *American Journal of Clinical Nutrition*, 90(Suppl), S707–11.

Kreuter, M.W. and Wray, R.J. (2003). Tailored and targeted health communication: Strategies for enhancing information relevance. *American Journal of Health Behaviour*, 27(Suppl 3), S227–32.

Kumanyika, S., Jeffrey, R.W., Morabia, A. et al. (2002). Obesity prevention: The case for action. *International Journal of Obesity*, 26, 425–36.

Larson, R. (1995). Secrets in the bedroom: Adolescents private use of media. *Journal of Youth and Adolescence*, 24, 535–50.

Lau, J.T., Ho, S.P., Yang, X. et al. (2007). Prevalence of HIV and factors associated with risk behaviours among Chinese female sex workers in Hong Kong. *AIDS Care*, 19(6), 721–32.

Lazarus, R.S. and Folkman, S. (1984). *Stress, Appraisal and Coping.* Springer: New York.

Lazarus, R.S. and Launier, R. (1978). Stress related transactions between person and environment, pp. 287–327. In L.A. Pervin and M. Lewis (eds) *Perspectives in International Psychology.* Plenum: New York.

Lean, M.E., Han, T.S. and Morrison, C.E. (1995). Waist circumference as a measure for indicating need for weight management. *British Medical Journal*, 311, 158–61.

Lenard, N.R. and Berthoud, H.R. (2008). Central and peripheral regulation of food intake and physical activity: Pathways and genes. *Obesity*, 16(3), S11–22.

Lepore, S.J. and Greenberg, M.A. (2002). Mending broken hearts: Effects of expressive writing on mood, cognitive processing, social adjustment and health following a relationship breakup. *Psychology and Health*, 17, 547–60.

Lepore, S.J., Greenberg, M.A., Bruno, M. and Smyth, J.M. (2002). Expressive writing and health: Self-regulation of emotion-related experience, physiology, and behaviour, pp. 199–232. In S.J. Lepore and J. Smyth (eds) *The Writing Cure: How Expressive Writing Influences Health and Well-being.* American Psychological Association: Washington DC.

Leventhal, H., Meyer, D. and Nerenz, D. (1980). The commonsense representation of illness changes, pp. 7–30. In S. Rachman (ed.) *Contributions to Medical Psychology*. Pergamon: Oxford.

Levine, M.P. and Smolak, L. (2006). *The Prevention of Eating Problems and Eating Disorders*. Lawrence Erlbaum: Mahwah, NJ.

Levy, S.M. and Heiden, L.A. (1990). Personality and social factors in cancer outcome, pp. 254–279. In H.S. Friedman (ed.) *Personality and Disease*. John Wiley and Sons: New York.

Lichtenthal, W.G., Cruess, D.G., Schuchter, L.M. and Ming, M.E. (2003). Psychosocial factors related to the correspondence of recipient and provider perceptions of social support amongst patients diagnosed with, or at risk for malignant melanoma. *Journal of Health Psychology*, 8(6), 705–19.

Lidwall, U. and Marklund, S. (2006). What is healthy work for women and men? A case control study of gender and sector-specific effects of psychosocial working conditions on long term sickness absence. *Work*, 27(2), 153–63.

Lindeman, M. and Stark, K. (2001). Emotional eating and eating disorder psychopathology. *Eating Disorders*, 9, 251–9.

Loader, B.D., Muncer, S., Burrows, R. et al. (2002). Medicine on the line? Computer-mediated social support and advice for people with diabetes. *International Journal of Social Welfare*, 11(1), 53–65.

Lohaus, A., Klein-Hebling, J., Vogele, C. and Kuhn-Hennighausen, C. (2001) Psychophysiological effects of relaxation training in children. *Psychology and Health*, 6, 197–206.

Louis, W.R., Chan, M.K. and Greenbaum, S. (2009). Stress and the theory of planned behavior: Understanding healthy and unhealthy eating intentions. *Journal of Applied Social Psychology*, 39(2), 472–93.

Lowe, C.F., Dowey, A. and Horne, P. (1998). Changing what children eat, pp. 57–80. In A. Murcott (ed.) *The Nation's Diet: The Social Science of Food Choice*. Addison Wiley Longman: Harlow.

Luebbert, K., Dahme, B. and Hasenbring, M. (2001). The effectiveness of relaxation training in reducing treatment-related symptoms and improving emotional adjustment in acute non-surgical cancer treatment: A meta-analytical review. *Psychooncology*, 10, 490–502.

Lyman, B. (1989). *A Psychology of Food: More than a Matter of Taste*. Van Nostrand Reinhold: New York.

McCarthy, S.C., Lyons, A.C., Weinman, J. et al. (2003). Do expectations influence recovery from oral surgery? An illness representation approach. *Psychology and Health*, 18(1), 109–26.

McCormick, R.A., Dowd, E.T., Quirk, S. and Zegarra, J.H. (1998). The relationship of NEO-PI performance to coping styles, patterns of use and triggers for use amongst substance abusers. *Addictive Behaviors*, 23, 497–507.

McCrae, R.R. and Costa, P.T. (1987). Validation of the five-factor model of personality across instruments and observers. *Journal of Personality and Social Psychology*, 52, 81–90.

McCrory, M.A., Fuss, P.J., Hays, N.P. et al. (1999). Overeating in America: Association between restaurant food consumption and body fatness in healthy adult men and women ages 19–80. *Obesity Research*, 7, 564–71.

McEwen, A., Straus, L. and Croker, H. (2009). Dietary beliefs and behaviour of a UK Somali population. *Journal of Human Nutrition and Dietetics*, 22, 116–21.

McGuire, K.M., Greenberg, M.A. and Gevirtz, R. (2005). Autonomic effects of expressive writing in individuals with elevated blood pressure. *Journal of Health Psychology*, 10, 197–207.

Macintyre, S., Hunt, K. and Sweeting, H. (1996). Gender differences in health: Are things really as simple as they seem? *Social Science and Medicine*, 42(4), 617–24.

Macintyre, S., Reilly, J., Miller, D. and Eldridge, J. (1998). Food choice, food scares and health: The role of the media, pp. 228–49. In A. Murcott (ed.) *The Nation's Diet: The Social Science of Food Choice*. Addison Wiley Longman: Harlow.

MacKay, C., Cox, T., Burrows, G. and Lazzerini, T. (1978). An inventory for the measurement of self-reported stress and arousal. *British Journal of Social and Clinical Psychology*, 17(3), 283–4.

McLenahan, C., Shevlin, M., Adamson, G. et al. (2007). Testicular self-examination: A test of the health belief model and the theory of planned behaviour. *Health Education Research*, 22(2), 272–84.

Malkin, A.R., Wornian, K. and Chrisler, J.C. (1999). Women and weight: Gendered messages on magazine covers. *Sex Roles*, 40, 647–55.

Mankar, M., Joshi, R.S., Belsare, P.V. et al. (2008). Obesity as a perceived social signal. *Plosone*, 3(9), e3187 doi:10.1371/journal.pone.003187.

Mansoor, L.E. and Dowse, R. (2006). Medicines information and adherence in HIV/AIDS patients *Journal of Clinical Pharmacy and Therapeutics*, 31(1), 7–15.

Manzoni, G.M., Pagnini, F., Gorini, A. et al. (2009). Can relaxation training reduce emotional eating in women with obesity? An exploratory study with 3 months of follow-up. *Journal of the American Dietetic Association*, 109, 1427–32.

Marks, D.F., Murray, M., Evans, B. et al. (2005). *Health Psychology: Theory, Research and Practice*. Sage: London.

Marteau, T.M., Kinmouth, A.L., Pyke, S. and Thompson, S.G. (1995). Readiness for lifestyle advice: Self-assessments of coronary risk prior to screening in the British Family Heart study. *British Journal of General Practice*, 45, 5–8.

Martin, R. and Dobbin, J. (1988). Sense of humor, hassles and immunoglobulin A: Evidence for a stress-moderating effect of humor. *International Journal of Psychiatric Medicine*, 18, 93–105.

Mellin, G.W. and Katzenstein, M. (1962). The saga of thalidomide: Neuropathy to embryopathy, with case reports of congenital abnormalities. *New England Journal of Medicine*, 267, 1238–44.

Michie, S. and Abraham, C. (2008). Advancing the science of behaviour change: A plea for scientific reporting. *Addiction*, 103, 1409–10.

Mielewczyk, F. and Willig, C. (2007) Old clothes and an older look: The case for a radical makeover in health behaviour research. *Theory and Psychology*, 17(6), 811–37.

Milio, N. (1986). Promoting health promotion: Health or hype? *Community Health Studies*, winter, 490–6.

Miller, J.J., Fletcher, K. and Kabat-Zinn, J. (1995). Three-year follow-up and clinical implications of a mindfulness meditation-based stress reduction intervention in the treatment of anxiety disorders. *General Hospital Anxiety*, 17, 192–200.

Miller, T.Q., Smith, T.W., Turner, C.W. et al. (1996). A meta-analytic review of research on hostility and physical health. *Psychological Bulletin*, 119, 322–48.

Milliken, M.E. (1998). *Understanding Human Behaviour: A Guide for Health Care Providers* (6th edn). Delmar Learning: Clifton Park, NY.

Miranda, D. and Claes, M. (2009). Music listening, coping, peer affiliation and depression in adolescence. *Psychology of Music*, 37(2), 215–33.

Miró, J., Raichle, K.A., Carter, G.T. et al. (2009). Impact of biopsychosocial factors on chronic pain in persons with myotonic and facioscapulohumeral muscular dystrophy. *Rehabilitation Medicine and Palliative Care*, 26(4), 308–19.

Mitchell, J.E., Pomeroy, C. and Adson, D.E. (1997). Managing medical complications, pp. 383–93. In D.M. Garner and P.E. Garfinkel (eds) *Handbook of Treatment for Eating Disorders* (2nd edn) Guilford Press: London.

Mittman, R. and Cain, M. (1999). *The Future of the Internet in Health Care: Five Year Forecast*. Retrieved September 11, 2007, from http://www.chcf.org/documents/healthit/forecast.pdf.

Montoro, J., Mullol, J., Jáuregui, I. et al. (2009). Stress and allergy. *Journal of Investigational Allergology and Clinical Immunology*, 19(Suppl 1), 40–7.

Moodie, D.S. and Salcedo, D. (1983). Cardiac function in adolescents and young adults with anorexia nervosa. *Journal of Adolescent Health*, 4(1), 9–14.

Moore, H., Summerbell, C.D., Greenwood, D.C. et al. (2003). Improving management of obesity in primary care: cluster randomised trial. *British Medical Journal*, 327, 1085–8.

Morgen, C.S., Bjork, C., Andersen, P.K. et al. (2008). Socioeconomic position and the risk of pre-term birth: A study within the Danish national birth cohort. *International Journal of Epidemiology*, 37(5), 1109–20.

Morrison, V. and Bennett, P. (2009). *An Introduction to Health Psychology* (2nd edn). Pearson Prentice Hall: London.

Moss-Morris, R., Petrie, K.J. and Weinman, J. (1996). Functioning in chronic fatigue syndrome: Do illness perceptions play a regulatory role? *British Journal of Health Psychology*, 1, 15–25.

Munch-Hansen, T., Wieclaw, J., Agerbo, E. et al. (2009). Sickness absence and workplace levels of satisfaction with psychosocial work conditions at public service workplaces. *American Journal of Industrial Medicine*, 52, 153–61.

Munz, P., Hudea, I., Imad, J. and Smith, R.J. (2009). When Zombies attack!: Mathematical modelling of an outbreak of zombie infection, pp. 133–50. In J.M. Tchuenche and C. Chiyaka (eds) *Infectious Disease Modelling Research Progress*. Nova Science: Hauppauge, NY.

Mussell, M.P., Crosby, R.D., Crow, S.J. et al. (2000). Utilization of empirically supported psychotherapy treatments for individuals with eating disorders: A survey of psychologists. *International Journal of Eating Disorders*, 27, 230–7.

Naidoo, J. and Wills, J. (2003). *Health Promotion: Foundations for Practice* (2nd edn). Ballière Tindall/Royal College of Nursing: London.

National Eating Disorders Association (2002). Eating disorders and their precursors, http://www.nationaleatingdisorders.org/nedaDir/files/documents/handouts/stats.pdf, accessed 7 November 2009.

Neely, M.E., Schallert, D.L., Mohammed, S.S. et al. (2009). Self-kindness when facing stress: The role of self-compassion, goal regulation and support in college students' well being. *Motivation and Emotion*, 33, 88–97.

Neff, K.D. (2003). Self-compassion: An alternative conceptualisation of a healthy attitude toward oneself. *Self and Identity*, 2, 85–101.

Newman, S. (1984). Anxiety, hospitalisation and surgery, pp.132–53. In R. Fitzpatric, J. Hinton, S. Newman et al. (eds) *The Experience of Illness*. Tavistock: London.

Newman, S., Steed, L. and Mulligan, K. (2004). Self-management interventions for chronic illness. *The Lancet*, 364, 1523–37.

Newton, J.R., Freeman, C.P., Hannan, W.J. and Cowen, S. (1993). Osteoporosis and normal weight bulimia nervosa: Which patients are at risk? *Journal of Psychosomatic Research*, 37(3), 239–47.

NHS (2009). Type 2 diabetes. http://www.nhs.uk/planners/nhshealthcheck/pages/diabetes.aspx, accessed 3 September 2009.

Nieto, J., Abad, M.A., Esteban, M. and Tejerina, M. (2004). Estrés y enfermedad. Psiconeuroinmunologia. Cap 8. En: Psicologia para ciencias de la salud. Estudio del compartamiento humano ante la enfermedad. McGraw-Hill: Madrid.

Nilsson, U. (2008). The anxiety- and pain-reducing effects of music interventions: A systematic review. *AORN (Association of periOperative Registered Nurses) Journal*, 87, 780–807.

Nilsson, U. (2009). The effect of music intervention in stress response to cardiac surgery in a randomized clinical trial. *Heart and Lung*, 38(3), 201–7.

Nilsson, U., Unosson, M. and Ramal, N. (2005). Stress reduction and analgesia in patients exposed to calming music postoperatively: A randomized controlled trial. *European Journal of Anaesthiology*, 22, 96–102.

Nisbett, R.E. (1972). Hunger, obesity, and the ventromedial hypothalamus. *Psychological Review*, 79, 433–53.

Noar, S.M. (2006). A 10 year retrospective of research in health mass media campaigns: Where do we go from here? *Journal of Health Communication*, 11(1), 21–42.

Norman, P. and Brain, K. (2005). An application of the extended health belief model to the prediction of breast self-examination among women with a family history of breast cancer. *British Journal of Health Psychology*, 10, 1–16.

Nutrition Forum, UK (2003). *National Diet and Nutrition Survey of Adults*, Paper NF 05/03. Food Standards Agency, London.

Offer, A. (2001). Body, weight and self-control in the United States and Britain since the 1950s. *Social History of Medicine*, 14, 79–106.

Ogden, J. (1992). *Fat Chance: The Myth of Dieting Explained*. Routledge: London.

Ogden, J. (2007). *Health Psychology: A Textbook* (4th edn). Open University Press/McGraw-Hill: Maidenhead.

Ogden, J. and Flanagan, Z. (2008). Beliefs about the causes and solutions to obesity: A comparison of GPs and lay people. *Patient Education and Counselling*, 71, 72–8.

Ogden, J. and Hills, L. (2008). Understanding sustained behaviour change: the role of life crises and the process of reinvention. *Health: An Interdisciplinary Journal for the Social Study of Health*, 12(4), 419–37.

Ogden, J. and Jubb, A. (2008). How consistent are beliefs about cause and solutions to illness: An experimental study. *Psychology Health and Medicine*, 13(5), 505–15.

Ogden, J. and Mitandabiri, T. (1997). Examination stress and changes in mood and health-related behaviours. *Psychology and Health*, 12, 288–99.

Ogden, J., Clementi, C. and Aylwin, S. (2006). The impact of obesity surgery and the paradox of control: A qualitative study. *Psychology and Health*, 21(2), 273–93.

Ogden, J., Clementi, C., Aylwin, S. and Patel, A. (2005). Exploring the impact of obesity surgery on patients' health status: A quantitative and qualitative study. *Obesity Surgery*, 15, 266–72.

Ogden, J., Branson, R., Bryett, A. et al. (2003). What's in a name? Patient views of the impact and function of a diagnosis. *Family Practitioner*, 20, 248–53.

O'Hegarty, M., Pederson, L.L., Nelson, D.F. et al. (2006). Reactions of young adult smokers to warning labels on cigarette packages. *American Journal of Preventive Medicine*, 30(6), 467–73.

Olabi, A., Najm, N.E., Baghdadi, O.K and Morton, J.M. (2009). Food neophobia levels of Lebanese and American college students. *Food Quality and Preference*, 20, 353–62.

Ozolins, A.R. and Stenstrom, U. (2003). Validation of health locus of control patterns in Swedish adolescents. *Adolescence*, 38, 651–7.

Parducci, A. (1968). Contraceptive risk evaluation: The relativism of absolute judgements. *Scientific American*, 219(6), 84–90.

Peberdy, A. (1997). Evaluation design, Ch. 17. In J. Katz and A. Peberdy (eds) *Promoting Health: Knowledge and Practice*. Macmillan/Open University Press: Basingstoke.

Pengilly, J.W. and Dowd, E. (2000). Hardiness and social support as moderators of stress. *Journal of Clinical Psychology*, 56, 813–20.

Pennebaker, J.W. (1993). Putting stress into words: health linguistic and therapeutic implications. *Behavioral Research Therapy*, 31, 539–48.

Pennebaker, J.W. and Seagal, J.D. (1999). Forming a story: The health benefits of narrative. *Journal of Clinical Psychology*, 1243–54.

Pennebaker, J.W. and Skelton, J.A. (1978). Psychological parameters of physical symptoms. *Personality and Social Psychology Bulletin*, 4(4), 524–30.

Pennebaker, J.W., Zech, E. and Rimé, B. (2001). Disclosing and sharing emotion: psychological, social and health consequences, pp. 517–43. In M.S. Stroebe and H. Schut (eds) *Handbook of Bereavement Research: Consequences, Coping and Care*. American Psychological Association: Washington DC.

Perry, M. (2002). *Eating Disorders for the Primary Care Team*. Quay: Dinton.

Petrie, K.J., Booth, R.J., Pennebaker, J.W. et al. (1995). Disclosure of trauma and immune response to hepatitis B vaccination program. *Journal of Consulting and Clinical Psychology*, 63, 787–92.

Petrie, K.J., Cameron, L., Ellis, C.J. et al. (2002). Changing illness perceptions after myocardial infarction: An early intervention randomised controlled trial. *Psychosomatic Medicine*, 64, 580–6.

Pinel, J.P. (2003). *Biopsychosociology* (5th edn). Allyn & Bacon: Boston.

Pinel, J.P., Assanand, S. and Lehman, D.R. (2000). Hunger, eating and ill-health. *American Psychologist*, 55, 1105–16.

Pliner, P. and Hobden, K. (1992). Development of a scale to measure the trait of food neophobia in humans. *Appetite*, 19, 105–20.

Pliner, P., Pelchat, M. and Grabski, M. (1993). Reduction of neophobia in humans by exposure to novel foods. *Appetite*, 20, 111–23.

Pollard, T.M., Steptoe, A., Canaan, L. et al. (1995). Effects of academic examination stress on eating behaviour and blood lipid levels. *International Journal Behavioural Medicine*, 2, 299–320.

Porcelli, A.J. and Delgado, M.R. (2009). Acute stress modulates risk taking in financial decision making. *Psychological Science*, 20(3), 278–83.

Prentice, A.M. (2005) Early influences on human energy regulation: Thrifty genotypes and thrifty phenotypes. *Physiology and Behaviour*, 86, 640–5.

Prochaska, J.O. and DiClemente, C.C. (1983). Stages and processes of self-change in smoking: Toward an integrative model of change. *Journal of Consulting and Clinical Psychology*, 51, 390–5.

Prochaska, J.O., DiClemente, C.C. and Norcross, J.C. (1992). In search of how people change: Applications to addictive behaviours. *American Psychologist*, 47, 1102–14.

Provencher, V., Polivy, J. and Herman, C.P. (2009). Perceived healthiness of food. If it's healthy, you can eat more! *Appetite*, 52, 340–4.

Randolf, W. and Viswanath, K. (2004). Lessons learned from public health mass media campaigns: marketing health in a crowded media world. *Annual Review of Public Health*, 25(1), 419–37.

Raudenbush, B. and Frank, R.A. (1999). Assessing food neophobia: The role of stimulus familiarity. *Appetite*, 32, 261–71.

Ravussin, E. and Bogardus, C. (1989). Relationship of genetics, age and physical activity to daily energy expenditure and fuel utilisation. *American Journal of Clinical Nutrition*, 49, 968–75.

Reime, B., Ratner, P.A., Tomaselli-Reime, S.N. et al. (2006). The role of mediating factors in the association between social deprivation and low birth weight in Germany. *Social Science and Medicine*, 62, 1731–4.

Reiter, P.L., Brewer, N.T., Gottlieb, S.L. et al. (2009). Parents' health beliefs and HPV vaccination of their adolescent daughters. *Social Science and Medicine*, 69, 475–80.

Remick, A.K., Polivy, J. and Pliner, P. (2009). Internal and external moderators of the effect of variety on food intake. *Psychological Bulletin*, 135(3), 434–51.

Renz, A.N. and Newton, J.T. (2009). Changing the behaviour of patients with peridontitis. *Peridontology*, 51, 252–68.

Rigotti, N., Neer, R., Skates, S. et al. (1991). The clinical course of osteoporosis in anorexia nervosa. *Journal of the American Medical Association*, 265(9), 1138.

Rise, J., Kovac, V., Kraft, P. and Moan, I.S. (2008). Predicting the intention to quit smoking and quitting behaviour: Extending the theory of planned behaviour. *British Journal of Health Psychology*, 13, 291–310.

Risi, L., Bindman, J.P., Campbell, O.M. et al. (2004). Media interventions to increase cervical screening uptake in South Africa: An evaluation of effectiveness. *Health Education Research*, 19(4), 457–68.

Ritchley, P.N., Frank, R.A., Hursti, U.K. and Tuorilla, H. (2003). Validation and cross-national comparison of the food neophobia scale (FNS) using confirmatory factor analysis. *Appetite*, 40, 163–73.

Rodham, K., McCabe, C. and Blake, D. (2009). Seeking support: An interpretative phenomenological analysis of an internet message board for people with complex regional pain syndrome. *Psychology and Health*, 24(6), 619–34.

Rorty, M., Yager, J., Rossotto, E. and Buckwalter, G. (2000). Parental intrusiveness in adolescence recalled by women with a history of bulimia nervosa and comparison. *International Journal of Eating Disorders*, 28(2), 202–8.

Rotter, J.B. (1966). Generalised expectancies for internal vs external control of reinforcement. *Psychological Monographs*, 80, 1–28.

Rozin, P., Fischler, C., Imada, S. et al. (1999). Attitudes to food and the role of food in the life in the USA, Japan, Flemish Belgium and France: Possible implications for the diet-health debate. *Appetite*, 33, 163–80.

Rugulies, R., Aust, R. and Syme, S.L. (2004). Epidemiology of health and illness: a socio-psycho-physiological perspective, pp. 27–68. In S. Sutton, A. Baum and M. Johnston (eds) *The Sage Handbook of Health Psychology*. Sage: London.

Ruiter, R.A., Abraham, C.A. and Kok, G. (2001). Scary warnings and rational precautions: a review of the psychology of fear appeals. *Psychology and Health*, 16, 613–30.

Russell, G.F., Szmukler, G.I., Dare, C. and Eisler, I. (1987). An evaluation of family therapy in anorexia and bulimia nervosa. *Archives of General Psychiatry*, 44, 1047–56.

Ruston, A., Clayton, J. and Calnan, M. (1998). Patients' action during their cardiac event: qualitative study exploring differences and modifiable factors. *British Medical Journal*, 316, 1060–5.

Rutters, F., Nieuwenhuizen, A.G., Lemmens, S.G. et al. (2009). Acute stress-related changes in eating in the absence of hunger. *Obesity*, 17(1), 72–7.

Ryechetnik, L., Frommer, M., Hawe, P. and Shiell, A. (2002). Criteria for evaluating evidence on public health interventions. *Journal of Epidemiology and Community Health*, 56, 119–27.

Salbach-Andrae, H., Schneider, N., Seifert, K. et al. (2009). Short-term outcome of anorexia nervosa in adolescents after in-patient treatment: A prospective study. *European Child and Adolescent Psychiatry*, 18, 701–4.

Salmon, P. (2001). Effects of physical exercise on anxiety, depression, and sensitivity to stress: A unifying theory. *Clinical Psychology Review*, 21, 33–61.

Sapolsky, R. (1998). *Why Zebras Don't Get Ulcers: An Updated Guide to Stress, Stress-related Diseases, and Coping*. W.H. Freeman: New York.

Saunders, V., Attard, G., Cremona, M. and Gatt, R. (2009). A new proposal for reducing the risk of developing acute mountain sickness, http://www.basecamp.co.uk/weblog/en/?weblog_id=897, accessed 3 September 2009.

Sayegh, R., Schiff, I., Wurtman, J. et al. (1995). The effect of a carbohydrate-rich beverage on mood, appetite and cognitive function in women with premenstrual syndrome. *Obstetrics and Gynaecology*, 86, 522–8.

Scala, D., d'Avino, M., Cozzolino, S. et al. (2008). Promotion of behaviour change in people with hypertension: An intervention study. *Pharmacy World and Science*, 30, 834–9.

Schluter, G. and Lee, C. (1999). Changing good consumption patterns: Their effects on the US food system. *Food Review*, 22, 35–37.

Schofield, I., Kerr, S. and Tolson, D. (2007). An exploration of the smoking-related health beliefs of older people with chronic obstructive pulmonary disease. *Journal of Clinical Nursing*, 16, 1726–35.

Schüler, J., Job, V., Fröhlich, S.M. and Brandstätter, V. (2009). Dealing with a 'hidden stressor': emotional disclosure as a coping strategy to overcome the negative effects of motive incongruence on health. *Stress and Health*, 25, 221–33.

Schwartz, K.D. and Fouts, G.T. (2003). Music preferences, personality style, and developmental issues of adolescents. *Journal of Youth and Adolescence*, 32, 205–13.

Seale, H., Leask, J., Po, K. and MacIntyre, C.R. (2009). 'Will they just pack up and leave?': Attitudes and intended behaviour of hospital health care workers during an influenza pandemic. *BMC Health Services Research*, 9, 30.

Selye, H. (1956). *The Stress of Life*. McGraw-Hill: New York.

Semmer, N.K. (2006). Personality, stress and coping, pp. 73–113. In M.E. Vollarth (ed.) *Handbook of Personality and Health*. John Wiley and Sons: London.

Shaffer, J.W., Graves, P.L., Swank, R.T. and Pearson, T.A. (1987). Clustering of personality traits in youth and the subsequent development of cancer among physicians. *Journal of Behavioural Medicine*, 10, 441–7.

Shapiro, S.L., Carlson, L.E., Astin, J.A. and Freedman, B. (2006). Mechanisms of mindfulness. *Journal of Clinical Psychology*, 62, 373–86.

Sharifirad, G., Entezari, M.H., Kamran, A. and Azadbakht, L. (2009). The effectiveness of nutritional education on the knowledge of diabetic patients using the health belief model. *Journal of Research in Medical Sciences*, 14(1), 1–6.

Sharma, D. (2005). Bhopal: 20 years on. *The Lancet*, 365(9454), 111–12.

Sheeran, P. (2002). Intention-behaviour relations: a conceptual and empirical review, pp. 1–30. In W. Strobe and M. Hewstone (eds) *European Review of Social Psychology*, vol. 12. Wiley: Chichester.

Sheeran, P. and Abraham, C. (1996). The health belief model, pp. 23–61. In M. Connor and P. Norman (eds) *Predicting Health Behaviour*. Open University Press: Buckingham.

Sherman, D.K., Mann, T. and Updegraff, J.A. (2006). Approach/avoidance motivation, message framing and health behaviour: Understanding the congruency effect. *Motivation and Emotion*, 30(2), 165–9.

Sherman, P.W. and Billing, J. (1999). Darwinian gastronomy: Why we use spices. *Bioscience*, 49, 453–63.

Sherman, P.W. and Hash, G.A. (2001). Why vegetable recipes are not very spicy. *Evolution and Human Behaviour*, 22, 147–63.

Shisslak, C.M., McKeon, R.T. and Crago, M. (1990). Family dysfunction in normal weight bulimic and bulimic anorexic families. *Journal of Clinical Psychology*, 46(2), 185–9.

Shoebridge, P.J. and Gowers, S.G. (2000). Parental high concern and adolescent anorexia nervosa. *British Journal of Psychiatry*, 176, 132–7.

Siegel, P.Z., Brackbill, R.M. and Heath, G.W. (1995). The epidemiology of walking for exercise: Implications for promoting activity among sedentary groups. *American Journal of Public Health*, 85(5), 706–10.

Simpson, E.E., McConville, C., Rae, G. et al. (2009). Salivary cortisol, stress and mood in healthy older adults: The Zenith Study. *Biological Psychology*, 78, 1–9.

Siru, R., Hulse, G.K. and Tait, R.J. (2009). Assessing motivation to quit smoking in people with mental illness: a review. *Addiction*, 104, 719–33.

Sloan, D.M. and Marx, B.P. (2004). Taking pen to hand: Evaluating theories underlying the written disclosure paradigm. *Clinical Psychology: Science and Practice*, 11, 121–37.

Smith, B., Ferguson, C., McKenzie, J. et al. (2002). Impacts of repeated mass media campaigns to promote sun protection in Australia. *Health Promotion International*, 17, 51–60.

Smith, L.A. and Foxcroft, D.R. (2009) The effect of alcohol advertising, marketing and portrayal on drinking behaviour in young people: Systematic review of prospective cohort studies. *BMC Public Health*, 9: 51. doi: 10.1186/1471-2458-9-51.

Sniehotta, F. (2009). An experimental test of the theory of planned behaviour. *Applied Psychology: Health and Well-Being*, 1(2), 257–70.

Sniehotta, F., Scholz, U. and Schwarzer, R. (2005). Bridging the intention–behaviour gap: Planning self-efficacy, and action control in the adoption and maintenance of physical exercise. *Psychology and Health*, 20(2), 143–60.

Soban, C. (2006). What about the boys? Addressing issues of masculinity within male anorexia nervosa in a feminist therapeutic environment. *International Journal of Men's Health*, 5(3), 251–67.

Soderstrom, M., Dolbier, C., Leiferman, J. and Steinhardt, M. (2000). The relationship of hardiness, coping strategies, and perceived stress to symptoms of illness. *Journal of Behavioral Medicine*, 23, 311–28.

Solomon, M. (2001). Eating as both coping and stressor in overweight control. *Journal of Advanced Nursing*, 36, 563–73.

Spalding, K.L., Arner, E., Westermark, P.O. et al. (2008). Dynamics of fat cell turnover in humans. *Nature*, 453, 783–7.

Sriramachari, S. (2004). The Bhopal gas tragedy: An environmental disaster. *Current Science*, 86(7), 905–920.

Sriramachari, S. (2005). Bhopal gas tragedy: Scientific challenges and lessons for the future. *Journal of Loss Prevention in the Process Industries*, 18(4-6), 265–7.

Stansfield, S.A., Fuhrer, R., Shipley, M.J. and Marmot, M.G. (1999). Work characteristics predict psychiatric disorder: Prospective results from the Whitehall II Study. *Occupational and Environmental Medicine*, 56(5), 301–7.

Stearns, P. (1997). *Fat History*. New York University Press: New York.

Steed, L., Newman, S.P. and Hardman, S.M. (1999). An examination of the self-regulation model in atrial fibrillation. *British Journal of Health Psychology*, 4, 337–47.

Steinhausen, H.C. (2002). The outcome of anorexia nervosa in the 20th century. *American Journal of Psychiatry*, 159, 1284–93.

Stephens, R., Atkins, J. and Kingston, A. (2009) Swearing as a response to pain. *Neuroreport*, 20(12), 1056–60.

Steptoe, A. and Wardle, J. (2004). Health-related behaviour: Prevalence and links with disease. In A. Kaptein and J. Weinman (eds) *Health Psychology*. BPS Blackwell: Malden, MA.

Strahan, E.J., Wilson, A.E., Cressman, K.E. and Buote, V.M. (2006). Comparing to perfection: How cultural norms for appearance affect social comparisons and self-image. *Body Image*, 3, 211–27.

Strauss, R.S. and Pollack, H.A. (2001). Epidemic increase in childhood overweight, 1986–1998. *Journal of the American Medical Association*, 286, 2845–8.

Stroebe, W. (2008). *Dieting, Overweight, and Obesity: Self-regulation in a Food-rich Environment*. American Psychological Association: Washington DC.

Stroebe, W., Papies, E. and Aarts, H. (2008). From homeostatic to hedonic theories of eating: Self-regulatory failure in food-rich environments. *Applied Psychology: An International Review*, 57, 172–93.

Suls, J. and Martin, R. (2005). The daily life of the garden-variety neurotic: reactivity, stressors exposure, mood spillover, and maladaptive coping. *Journal of Personality*, 73, 1–25.

Sutton, S. (2002). Testing attitude-behaviour theories using non-experimental data: An examination of some hidden assumptions, *European Review of Social Psychology*, 13, 293–323.

Swinburn, B.A., Egger, G. and Raza, F. (1999). Dissecting obesogenic environments: the development and application of a framework for identifying and prioritising environmental interventions for obesity. *Preventive Medicine*, 29, 563–70.

Sykes, J.B. (ed.) (1989). *Oxford English Dictionary* (7th edn). Oxford University Press: Oxford.

Szarewski, A. and Mansour, D. (1999). The 'pill scare': The responses of authorities, doctors and patients using oral contraception. *Human Reproduction Update*, 5(6), 627–32.

Tailor, A. and Ogden, J. (2009). Avoiding the term 'obesity': An experimental study of the impact of doctors' language on patients' beliefs. *Patient Education and Counselling*, 76, 260–4.

Tannahil, A. (1985). What is health promotion? *Health Education Journal*, 44(4), 167–8.

Temoshok, L. (1985). Biopsychosocial studies on cutaneous malignant melanoma: Psychosocial factors associated with prognostic indicators, progression, psychophysiology and tumour-host response. *Social Science and Medicine*, 20, 833–40.

Temoshok, L. (1987). Personality, coping style, emotion and cancer: Towards an integrative model. *Social Sciences and Medicine*, 20, 833–40.

Temoshok, L.R., Waldstein, S.R., Wald, R.L. et al. (2008). Type C coping, alexithymia, and heart rate reactivity are associated independently and differentially with specific immune mechanisms linked to HIV progression. *Brain, Behavior and Immunity*, 22(5), 781–92.

Thompson, S.B. (1993). *Eating Disorders*. London: Chapman and Hall.

Throne, L.C., Bartholomew, J.B., Craig, J. and Farrar, R.P. (2000). Stress reactivity in fire fighters: An exercise intervention. *International Journal of Stress Management*, 7, 235–46.

Tilford, S., Delaney, F. and Vogels, M. (1997). Effectiveness of mental health promotion interventions: A review. *Health Promotion Effectiveness Reviews*, 4, HEA: London.

Tokuda, Y., Takahashi, O., Ohde, S. et al. (2007). Health locus of control and use of conventional and alternative care: A cohort study. *British Journal of General Practice*, 57, 643–9.

Tones, K. and Green, J. (2004). *Health Promotion: Planning and Strategy*. Sage: London.

Torgerson, J.S. and Sjostrom, L. (2001). The Swedish Obese Subjects (SOS) study: Rationale and results. *International Journal of Obesity*, 25(Suppl 1), S2–4.

Townsend, P. and Davidson, N. (1982). *Inequalities in Health: The Black Report*. Penguin: London.

Trask, P.C., Paterson, A.G., Griffith, K. et al. (2003). Cognitive-behavioral intervention for distress in patients with melanoma. *Cancer*, 98, 854–64.

Trento, M., Tomelini, M., Basile, M. et al. (2008). The locus of control in patients with type 1 and type 2 diabetes managed by individual and group care. *Diabetic Medicine*, 25, 86–90.

Tung, W.C., Farmer, S., Ding, K. et al. (2009). Stages of condom use and decisional balance among college students. *International Nursing Review*, 56, 346–53.

Tuorila, H., Lähteenmäki, L., Pohjalainen, L. and Lotti, L. (2001). Food neophobia among the Finns and related responses to familiar and unfamiliar foods. *Food Quality and Preference*, 12, 29–37.

Turner, J., Batik, M., Palmer, L.J. et al. (2000). Detection and importance of laxative use in adolescents with anorexia nervosa. *Journal of the American Academy of Child and Adolescent Psychiatry*, 39(3), 378–85.

Ulijaszek, S.J. (2002). Human eating behaviour in an evolutionary ecological context. *Proceedings of the Nutrition Society*, 61(4), 517–26.

Ulijaszek, S.J. (2007). Obesity: A disorder of convenience. *Obesity Reviews*, 8(Suppl 1), 183–7.

Van Cleemput, P., Parry, G., Thomas, K. et al. (2007). Health-related beliefs and experiences of Gypsies and Travellers: A qualitative study. *Journal of Epidemiology and Community Health*, 61, 205–10.

Van de Putte, E.M., Engelbert, R.H., Kuis, W. et al. (2005). Chronic fatigue syndrome and health control in adolescents and parents. *Archives of Disease in Childhood*, 90, 1020–4.

Vingård, E., Lindberg, P., Josephson, M. et al. (2005). Long term sick listing among women in the public sector and its associations with age, social situation, lifestyle, and work factors: a three year follow-up study. *Scandinavian Journal of Public Health*, 33(5), 370–5.

Voland, E. and Voland, R. (1989). Evolutionary biology and psychiatry: The case of anorexia nervosa. *Ethology and Sociobiology*, 10, 223–240.

Vos, M.S., Putter, H., van Houwelingen, H.C. and de Haes, H.C. (2009). Denial and physical outcomes in lung cancer patients: A longitudinal study. *Lung Cancer*, DOI: 10.1016/j.lungcan.2009.04.003.

Wadden, T.A., Butryn, M.L., Sarwer, D.B. et al. (2006). Comparison of psychosocial status in treatment seeking women with class III vs class I-II obesity. *Obesity*, 14, S90–8.

Wallack, L., Dorfman, L., Jernigan, D. and Themba, M. (1993). *Media Advocacy and Public Health: Power for Prevention.* Sage: Newbury Park, CA.

Walsh, B.T., Kaplan, A.S., Attia, E. et al. (2006). Fluoxetine after weight restoration in AN: A randomised controlled trial. *Journal of the American Medical Association*, 295, 2605–12.

Wansink, B. (2007). *Mindless Eating: Why we Eat more than we Think.* Bantam Books: New York.

Wansink, B., Painter, J.E. and North, J. (2005). Bottomless bowls: Why visual cues of portion size may influence intake. *Obesity Research*, 13(1), 93–100.

Wansink, B., Payne, C.R. and Chandon, R. (2007). Internal and external cues of meal cessation: The French paradox redux? *Obesity*, 15(12), 2920–4.

Ward, S.E., Leventhal, H. and Love, R. (1988). Repression revisited: tactics used in coping with a severe health threat. *Personality and Social Psychology Bulletin*, 14, 735–46.

Wardle, J., Steptoe, A., Oliver, G. and Lipsey, Z. (2000). Stress, dietary restraint and food intake. *Journal of Psychosomatic Research*, 48, 195–202.

Watson, D., Clark, L.A. and Tellegen, A. (1988). Development and validation of brief measures of positive and negative affect: The PANAS scales. *Journal of Personality and Social Psychology*, 54, 1063–70.

Weinstein, N.D. (1987). Unrealistic optimism about susceptibility to health problems: Conclusions from a community-wide sample. *Journal of Behavioural Medicine*, 10, 480–99.

Weisman, A.D. and Hackett, T.P. (1961). Predilection to death: Death and dying as a psychiatric problem. *Psychosomatic Medicine*, 23, 232–56.

Wenzel, L., Glanz, K. and Lerman, C. (2002). Stress, coping and health behaviour, pp. 210–39. In K. Glanz, B.K. Rimer and F.M. Lewis (eds) *Health Behavior and Health Education: Theory, Research and Practice.* Jossey-Bass: San Francisco.

Whitehead, D. (1999). The relationship between health promotion and complementary therapies. *Complementary Therapies in Nursing and Midwifery*, 5, 171–5.

Whitelaw, S. and Watson, J. (2005). Whither health promotion events? A judicial approach to evidence. *Health Education Research: Theory and Practice*, 20(2), 214–25.

Whittle, G., Patently, D. and Wilson, M. (1994). A dental health promotion campaign in a shopping centre. *Health Education Research: Theory and Practice*, 9, 261–5.

Williams, L., O'Caroll, R.E. and O'Connor, R.C. (2009). Type D personality and cardiac output in response to stress. *Psychology and Health*, 24(5), 489–500.

Winefield. H. (2006). Support provision and emotional work in an internet support group for cancer patients. *Patient Education and Counselling*, 62(2), 193–7.

Wong, C.L. and Mullen, B.A. (2009). Predicting breakfast consumption: An application of the theory of planned behaviour and the investigation of past behaviour and executive function. *British Journal of Health Psychology*, 14, 489–504.

Woodruff, S.I., Edwards, C.C., Conway, T.L. and Elliott, S.P. (2001). Pilot test of an Internet virtual world chat room for rural teen smokers. *Journal of Adolescent Health*, 29(4), 239–43.

World Health Organization (1946). Preamble to the Constitution of the World Health Organization, as adopted by the International Health Conference, New York, 19–22 June, 1946.

World Health Organization (1981). *Health Programme Evaluation: Guiding Principles*, WHO: Geneva.

World Health Organization (1984). *Health Promotion: A Discussion Document on Concepts and Principles*. WHO: Geneva.

World Health Organization (1986). *Ottawa Charter for Health Promotion*, 17–21 November, Ottawa. Available at www.who.int/hpr/NPH/docs/ottawa_charter_hp.pdf, accessed 31 Aug 2009.

Wringe, A., Roura, M., Urassa, M. et al. (2009). Doubts, denial and divine intervention: Understanding delayed attendance and poor retention rates at a HIV treatment programme in rural Tanzania. *AIDS Care*, 21(5), 632–7.

Wurtman, J. (1990). Carbohydrate craving: Relationship between mood and disorders of carbohydrate intake. *Drugs*, 39(Suppl 3), 49–52.

Wurtman, R.J. and Wurtman, J.J. (1995). Brain serotonin, carbohydrate-craving, obesity and depression. *Obesity Research*, 3, 477–80.

Wyer, S.J., Earl, L., Joseph, S. et al. (2001). Increasing attendance at a cardiac rehabilitation programme: an intervention study using the theory of planned behaviour. *Coronary Health Care* 5(3), 154–9.

Yaskowich, K.M. and Stam, H.J. (2003). Cancer narratives and the cancer support group. *Journal of Health Psychology*, 8(6), 720–37.

Yoo, S., Butler, J., Elias, T.I. and Goodman, R.M. (2009). The 6-step model for community empowerment: Revisited in public housing communities for low-income senior citizens. *Health Promotion Practice*, 10(2), 262–75.

Yoo, S., Weed, N.E., Lempa, M.L. et al. (2004). Collaborative community empowerment: An illustration of a six-step process. *Health Promotion Practice*, 5(3), 256–65.

Young, L.R. and Nestle, M. (2002). The contribution of expanding portion sizes to the US obesity epidemic. *American Journal of Public Health*, 92, 246–49.

Young, S. and Oppenheimer, D.M. (2009). Effect of communication strategy on personal risk perception and treatment adherence intentions. *Psychology, Health and Medicine*, 14(4), 430–42.

Yzer, M., Sierra, F. and Bunk, B. (2000). can public campaigns effectively change psychological determinants of safer sex? An evaluation of three Dutch campaigns, *Health Education Research: Theory and Practice*, 15, 339–52.

Zola, I.K. (1966). Culture and symptoms: An analysis of patients' presenting complaints. *American Sociological Review*, 31, 615–30.

Index

Reading guide

This table identifies where in the book you'll find relevant information for those of you studying or teaching A-level. You should also, of course, refer to the Index and the Glossary, but navigating a book for a particular set of items can be awkward and we found this table a useful tool when editing the book and so include it here for your convenience.

Topic	AQA(A)	AQA(B)	OCR	Page
Attitudes to food and eating: culture	x			133, 137, 147
Attitudes to food and eating: health concerns	x			128
Attitudes to food and eating: mood	x			135
Autonomic nervous system and stress		x		93–4
Behavioural methods of measuring stress		x	x	100
Biological explanations of anorexia nervosa	x			148–50
Biological explanations of bulimia nervosa	x			150
Biological explanations of obesity	x			154
Causes of stress: hassles and life events			x	101–3
Causes of stress: lack of control			x	23
Causes of stress: work			x	99
Defence mechanisms: denial		x		114–15
Defence mechanisms: rationalization		x		114–15
Defence mechanisms: regression		x		114–15
Defence mechanisms: repression		x		114–15
Dieting: explanations for failure	x			142
Dieting: explanations for success	x			143
Emotion-focused strategies		x		112–14

Topic	AQA(A)	AQA(B)	OCR	Page
Endocrine system and stress		x		93–5
Evaluating public health interventions	x			70–88
Evolutionary explanations of food preference	x			133
Fear arousal			x	73
HBM			x	34
Media campaigns			x	62–8
Mediating stress: hardiness		x		20
Mediating stress: locus of control		x	x	23
Mediating stress: personality types		x		18–19, 113
Neural mechanisms in eating and satiation	x			132
Physiological methods of measuring stress		x	x	100
Problem-focused strategies		x		112–14
Psychological explanations of anorexia nervosa	x			148
Psychological explanations of bulimea nervosa	x			148
Psychological explanations of obesity	x			156–7
Public health interventions	x		x	51–69
Self-efficacy			x	37, 44
Self-report methods of measuring stress		x	x	100
Social support		x	x	116
Stress management: biofeedback		x	x	118–19
Stress management: cognitive therapy		x	x	121–2
Stress management: systematic desensitization		x	x	118–19